PF
HEAR.

From the viewpoint of one who has experienced the very journey that Carly so eloquently records, I would highly recommend this book to anyone who has or is dealing with a loved one with dementia and now finds themselves in the role of caregiver. This intimate and sometimes raw journal of their experience will take the reader from tears to rage in a narrative that will certainly resonate in the hearts of those who have lived through it. Lewis Thomas, in his book The Problem with Dementia wrote, "It is the worst of all diseases, not just for what it does to the patient, but for it's devastating effects on families and friends." Carly "Bennett" Stenmark has, with great emotion and clarity, documented this truth for all who will open the pages of this wonderful book.
    G. Mardsen Blanch, Chairman, Lynden Legacy Foundation

Carly writes of her personal experiences from the heart. This heartfelt and honest story sheds light on the challenges faced by families wanting to do the best they can to support their loved one with a dementia diagnosis. Carly's willingness to share her story can help others as they navigate the caregiver journey. As a former caregiver and a mental health professional, I would suggest this as a recommended reading.
    Ellen Silver, Executive Director, Jewish Family Service

Carly tells her story in a beautiful heartfelt way and shares education and advice along the way. Carly was able to capture the heart and soul of the caregiving journey, the highs and lows, the joys and pains. I could not put it down.
    Rosemary Quatrale, Older Adult Care Manager,
    Jewish Family Service

Carly brilliantly captures the complexity of grief that comes with an Alzheimer's diagnosis, highlighting the emotional toll on both caregivers and their loved ones. She also offers hope, showing that love and connection can still thrive despite the challenges. I highly recommend this book to anyone affected by a dementia diagnosis.
Katie Young, CSW, Older Adult Services Supervisor,
Jewish Family Service

Carly beautifully tells her journey as a caregiver of a spouse with Alzheimer's. Not only does she share the ups and downs of living with the disease, she gives great first hand advice on how she learned to communicate, redirect, and find humor in the most difficult situations. From the beginning to the end you can feel the love, pain, and resilience that one faces with the disease. This is a fabulous book for anyone who thinks their loved one might have dementia or has been diagnosed with dementia. She touches on the grieving process of dementia, as it begins and your loved one's memory fades. Her stories and the struggles are real and will bring great comfort and humor to any caregiver!
Debbie Morton, Past Alzheimer's Caregiver, Volunteer
Alzheimer's Association

This book is destined to become a cornerstone resource for Lynden Legacy and all Alzheimer and dementia related caregivers. No caregiver is an island, and no one should have to navigate this journey alone. Thank you for sharing your incredible story with such vulnerability and honesty. Your writing is a beautiful and inspiring as the life you've poured into it.
Katie Blanch, Lynden Legacy Foundation Director

HEART GET READY

To the Grimme Family ~
Please remember to hold
your loved ones close &

Carly Bennett Stewart
"2025"

Heart Get Ready

MY HUSBAND'S RAPID DESCENT INTO THE CRUEL WORLD OF ALZHEIMER'S DISEASE

CARLY BENNETT STENMARK

Surrogate Press®

Copyright ©2025 Carly Bennett Stenmark

All rights reserved.

No part of this publication may be reproduced, stored in a retrieval system, or transmitted in any form or by any means, electronic, mechanical, photocopying, recording, or otherwise, without written permission of the author.

Published in the United States by Surrogate Press®

an imprint of Faceted Press®

Surrogate Press, LLC

Park City, Utah

SurrogatePress.com

ISBN: 978-1-964245-14-0

Library of Congress Control Number: 2024927049

Book cover design by Michelle Rayner, Cosmic Design LLC

Interior design by: Katie Mullaly, Surrogate Press®

Photo credit: Debra Macfarlane

Table of Contents

Chapter 1: Where Do I Sign? 1
Chapter 2: You Can Never Outrun Love 7
Chapter 3: Of All These Things I Am Sure 15
Chapter 4: The Only Place to Start 18
Chapter 5: Still Amazing Me 24
Chapter 6: Attitude 30
Chapter 7: Hearts Against the Wall 35
Chapter 8: Strangers to Lovers to Strangers 41
Chapter 9: 25-Hour Day 49
Chapter 10: Whenever I Fall 54
Chapter 11: Lover to Lover 59
Chapter 12: True Love 63
Chapter 13: Where I'm At 76
Chapter 14: "Roamance" 81
Chapter 15: Due Time 90
Chapter 16: Good Memory Gone Bad 98
Chapter 17: HeartBent 104
Chapter 18: Lucky for Me 110
Chapter 19: Warm Place to Hide 116
Chapter 20: Cheating Was Part of the Game 123
Chapter 21: Never Blue 130
Chapter 22: Loving You is the Only Place to Start 137
Chapter 23: No Me Without You 143
Chapter 24: Old Lovers 148

Chapter 25: Anywhere But There 154
Chapter 26: Is There Enough 160
Chapter 27: Rebels & Outlaws 165
Chapter 28: Long Time Lonely 171
Chapter 29: Read Between the Lies 178
Chapter 30: Love is Talking 185
Chapter 31: Am I Losing My Place 198
Chapter 32: Now and Forever 207
Chapter 33: Nobody Else 213
Chapter 34: It's You 218
Chapter 35: Meeting of Hearts 222
Chapter 36: Keep Me in Your Heart 228
Chapter 37: Til' 233
Chapter 38: Walls of My Own Invention 239
Chapter 39: Lovin' Mood 244
Chapter 40: Love Looks Like You 250
Chapter 41: I'll Never Find Another You 257
Chapter 42: Two Hearts Coming Home 272
Chapter 43: Love Knows the Difference 278
Chapter 44: Don't Apologize 283
Chapter 45: How Do We Carry On? 293
Acknowledgments 299
About the Author 302

Dedicated to Ken Stenmark,
my rock and beloved husband,
whose life was unexpectedly transformed
when Alzheimer's disease stepped into the
drivers seat, taking the wheel
and forever changing both our lives .

Carly and her husband, Stenmark, 2015.

Ken Stenmark, 2016.

CHAPTER 1
Where Do I Sign?

My husband, Stenmark, and I loved to golf nine holes early Sunday mornings, then sit on the cafe deck overlooking the golf course as we ate breakfast together. It was a ritual for us close to eighteen years. So, when the alarm awakened us to *our* song, "Amazed" by Lonestar, we would jump up after a good morning kiss and an eight second hug. We always hugged for at least eight seconds, which I read was a necessity years ago in a happy love life manual. Being the hopeless romantic that I am, I was fortunate enough to find someone who was as well, and we both treasured every second of being together as a loving, passionate couple.

It was a gorgeous June day in 2019 in beautiful Park City, Utah, as we loaded our golf bags onto our walking carts and headed for the number ten tee box. I turned Pandora on my iPhone and connected it to an external speaker, which hung off my golf bag. We listened to the Eric Clapton channel and began to play "our game," as we playfully named it. I always played better when I was out with my music man. It didn't hurt that he was also a golf pro.

Of course, Stenmark always played lights out and I so enjoyed watching him master this difficult game so effortlessly.

The golf season was just beginning, in fact there were traces of snow on the course that morning, but the sun was shining bright, and we felt blessed to be out and enjoying our life together. We finished in record time and sat on the deck as we ordered breakfast. "Ladies first," Stenmark said, as he smiled and winked at me. I have always loved his smile, and that cute wink coupled with it melted my smitten heart.

I smiled back, "I'd like a fruit plate and an oat bran muffin with black coffee."

The efficient waitress turned to Stenmark, "I'll take a side of sausage, hash browns, cinnamon roll and a Diet Pepsi." I smiled and shook my head slightly. Stenmark asked me what was wrong.

I giggled lightheartedly and replied, "Not a thing my love."

♡♡♡♡♡

I'd given up many years ago trying to persuade him to eat healthier. He was a carnivore, a Diet Pepsi and Rockstar freak. He used to tell me, "I'm easy... no fish, no eggs, no cheese." I found that funny in an interesting way since he was Swedish, but just went with it. After all, he worked out daily and did not have a weight problem, standing six foot three and weighing one hundred ninety-five pounds, broad shoulders and excellent posture. I wasn't just along for the ride; I was his biggest fan.

So, what did I have to complain about? Nothing, truly nothing.

The next morning, we woke up early. Stenmark had to open the golf course at six-thirty, so he left about six a.m. "You should come over later and hit balls, maybe putt a little," he said as he kissed me goodbye.

"Okay, honey, but I have to go to Salt Lake today, so I might not have time." I answered. "A little practice wouldn't hurt you, Babe," he said with a smile.

I smiled back. "I know, honey, I know" I said as I got out of bed. Those who know me, know I do not like to practice. In fact, Stenmark used to say he was surprised I was as good as

I was at golf, since I never practiced and only played once or twice a week. But I love working out at the gym and it usually took priority.

This day, I went to the gym before heading to Salt Lake City for my Monday errands. I reflected on the day before and how much I loved this man of mine. *We have such an amazing life filled with kindness, mutual respect, and oh so much love*, I thought. I truly didn't know where I would be without him in my life.

I finished up my errands in the city and stopped by Meier's Chicken on my way home. Stenmark loved that place and I wanted to surprise him with one of his favorite dinners. He worked in the pro shop until noon, then had golf lessons until four o'clock. I knew the timing would be just perfect.

Stenmark called, as he always did to tell me he was on his way home.

I sat the table, lit a candle, and poured the chilled Chardonnay. I heard the garage door open, as I ran to the bottom of the stairs to greet him. He opened the door, and I threw my arms around his neck as I kissed him all over his face. Another ritual of mine.

He even wrote a song about it, envisioning Allison Krauss singing it.

He hugged me tight and said, "Okay, okay, okay, dear heart."

I laughed as I knew that was just his sweet way.

♡♡♡♡♡

Stenmark changed out of his golf clothes making his way to the dining room table. He stopped for a hug as he passed by and told me he missed me.

"Wow, Meier's Chicken. Did you get me potato salad without eggs?" he asked.

"Did you want it without eggs," I asked teasing him, but pretending to be dead serious. I knew he despised eggs.

"Bennett," he said drawing out my name, "You know better, don't be a smart ass." I laughed as I put the eggless potato salad on his plate. "Yes dear, I did, of course I did."

Then he shook his head. I think by now he knew my dry humor.

We each talked about our day, then he told me from now on he was only going to do golf lessons. He was no longer going to work behind the desk in the golf shop. He never liked that part of the job so it made sense to me.

He went on, "I spoke to Vaughn (his close friend, head professional and just an all-around great guy at Park City Golf Course) about it and told him how much I disliked being behind the desk. I would rather be teaching golf." We had discussed this over the years and I knew he loved the people, but truly despised standing there and handling the money.

"I've never liked that part and counting it at the end of the day has always bugged me. It's not my money and if I make a mistake, it's on me."

"Okay, honey, I get it, whatever makes you happy is fine with me. I'm right there with you and you know that." I said being supportive of his decision. He forever counseled me and supported me, not to mention cheered me on, in whatever made me happy.

Why should I be any different with his life choices?

Stenmark added, "Don't worry about me losing income. I will be able to give golf lessons all day long and that will make up for me not working inside."

"I'm not worried at all," I said confidently. And I wasn't.

I'd been with Stenmark since 1999, and I knew he would do whatever it took, just like he always did. He once told me that he could live in a cardboard box, if he was with me. However,

I made it clear that I couldn't, so he never did put that to the test. I would tease him that his leather chair wouldn't fit unless it was an extremely large cardboard box.

Stenmark always worked hard at everything, and he excelled in all of it. That always amazed me. He was so good at whatever he decided to do. There truly wasn't anything he couldn't do once he put his mind to it.

We both agreed we really liked the comforts of our home, and I knew how much he loved his leather chair. Plus, it fit the two of us comfortably; at least it was comfortable for me, as I always hopped on his lap. Maybe his legs went numb, but he never complained or asked me to sit elsewhere.

Wherever we sat, I was either on his lap in his leather chair or we would lay side by side on the couch. We just fit so comfortably together.

Stenmark was the perfect man for me. He was always happy and in a good mood. I loved his sweet ways and his captivating charm. I knew I wanted to be by his side for all eternity and then some. I used to tease him in the beginning, jumping on his lap and reciting the words in a *sing songy* kind of way, from the Sandra Bullock movie, Miss Congeniality. *"You think I'm gorgeous, you think I'm scrumptious, you want to kiss me, you want to hug me, you want to love me, you want to date me, you want to marry me."*

The first time I added the last line about marriage, he replied in a very serious tone, "Where do I sign?" Then he wrote a song for me with that exact title.

My sweet hubby always thought I resembled Sandra Bullock especially after we watched *Miss Congeniality*. I didn't see the resemblance, but he certainly did, and I considered it a huge compliment. That was Stenmark. He was always full of compliments and there wasn't much he ever complained about...except when I drove through Parleys Canyon. He worried so much about me when I had to go to Salt Lake City.

The fact that I have macular degeneration, an age-related eye disease, was paramount in his mind, but so far so good with my eyes. My eyesight still allows me to drive and has stayed the same for almost fourteen years, and I am so grateful for that.

Thank you, Lord... and big thanks to my Retina Specialist for having the skill, knowledge and expertise to give me injections in both eyes every month, so my vision still allows me to drive...anywhere.

But mostly thank you God for not giving up on me and answering my prayers. *I know I am blessed.*

CHAPTER 2
You Can Never Outrun Love

The work week was upon me, and I was off to the salon early the next morning. I have a very successful manicurist business in a salon located in Park City, Utah. Doing nails has always been a passion for me.

I have been at Silver Shears Salon for twenty-two years and working at my profession for close to forty-five years. I am also a published author.

A few years ago, I wrote a book about my life as a nail technician and a single mother of four coming to Park City without knowing a soul and starting over.

I was doing a lot of book signings, holiday and street fares, and even speaking at beauty colleges and schools to students in the cosmetology field.

I really wanted to inspire young people, especially women.

The goal was to help them realize that you can get there from where you are now with determination and hard work. I really enjoyed doing this and it quickly became another passion of mine. I always ended my talk with one of my favorite Dr. Seuss quotes, *"Today you are exactly where you are supposed to be, but tomorrow is entirely up to you."* Isn't that the truth?

My cute husband used to tell people that the best part of my book was the last couple of chapters. Which were all about when I met him…and he was so right. Being a single mother while trying to make a living and trying to create some semblance of a stable life for all of us was tough, to say the least. Starting over isn't easy but often it's necessary to survive, learn and grow. I've always believed that it's never too late for a new beginning.

Sometimes things collapse to make room for better things. That certainly was the case for me. Life before Stenmark was an emotional struggle. My children were grown by then and raising families of their own, but I was a mess with another failed marriage and two other significant relationships that ended badly. Even when you are the one who ends a relationship, you still grieve and have to heal to move on. And that can be difficult.

One of the hardest battles I ever fought was between knowing what was best in my head and what I felt deep down in my heart and soul.

Then I met the man of my dreams, and I knew that this was a once in a lifetime love. We were made for each other. It was as if the angels looked down upon us, conspired, and then looked at each other and said…perfect! We had so much in common, we discovered we both had a bigger than life love for music, we were both family oriented, and enjoyed a lot of similar interests, and passions. Plus, we had the same political beliefs, which was huge for me.

But most of all, we had fun! Stenmark made me laugh with his incredible sense of humor. I once had a friend, more of an acquaintance, really, who asked me how I knew when it was time to let go and move on in a relationship? *She knew I'd been through it once or twice.*

I answered her by saying, "When they stop making me laugh."

She looked at me with her big, beautiful brown eyes, and I noticed a real sadness as she said, "What if they never did?"

Yikes… I had no good answer, because a sense of humor is vital for me when it comes to a life partner.

Fortunately, with Stenmark, I'd fallen for a man who did make me laugh. And for the first time, my head and heart were in sync, and I knew, *he was the one*. I'd met him by fate, and it was an instant connection, as if our souls recognized each other. The chemistry we shared was way above what my head could fully comprehend, coupled with his terrific sense of humor.

I knew life would never be dull or boring with Stenmark by my side.

After all, I'm a Gemini, and I do get bored very easily.

I met this brilliant husband of mine, twenty-four years ago, after a few "practice marriages," it sounds so much better than "failed marriages," at least to me. Just as I like to say he was "tangled up" rather than "married" when we met.

But the truth was, I'd waited my whole life for a man like Stenmark. We met and we fell in love. I've always believed in love at first sight and eventually I got to experience it firsthand. Fortunately, Stenmark felt the same way. He understood me like no other and loved me in a way I'd never been loved. He was the man in the songs.

Unfortunately, when we first met, he *was* tangled up, so a romantic relationship was off limits. Somewhere in our minds we thought we could just be friends in the beginning. It must've been the hopeless romantic in both of us. I thought I could just be his golf student, and he could just be my golf teacher. But we were soulmates and deep down we both knew it, but didn't act on it.

For over six months, we tried to deny this deep, passionate and beautiful love we felt for each other. We met as friends, and both of us tried to keep it that way, even calling each other by our last names, 'Stenmark and Bennett,' a practice that stuck for the rest of our time together. I was always Bennett, and he was always Stenmark. Maybe it was something in our psyches trying to help us keep our distance. I don't know.

But it didn't work. There was no denying our attraction and love for each other.

You can never outrun love.

I've always believed that true love will always win, and in our case, we crossed that finish line early on. I think one of the most difficult things for me was having a 'boyfriend' at the age of forty-four. It sounded so juvenile to introduce him as such, so I began to find other adjectives to describe this awesome love I'd found.

I started with "my friend," but that was weird, as much as he was my best friend, that just didn't cut it. Then I went with "my pal" and found that was just as bad, and so was "my buddy."

Then I decided to try out, "my Kenny," but that sounded childish to me. So, I went on to try others such as, "my date," "my escort," "my beau," "my partner," "my mate," and "my male friend." Nothing even came close for me, and I laugh thinking back on it. It was a good thing we were a popular couple in Park City, because everyone else figured out our relationship status, just by looking at us!

But still, I continued to find other ways to introduce the love of my life at all the functions we were invited to. Then one evening, I tried what I thought was the perfect description of Stenmark. I went up to a group of friends and clients with my man, and after we got all of the greeting-hugs out of the way, I stepped back, pointed to Stenmark, and said, "This is 'my lover,' Ken Stenmark."

I thought Ken was going to faint. Everyone was somewhat speechless, as they stared wide-eyed, some with slight smiles, some stifling a laugh, some turning around so they could pretend their laugh was a cough. *Pause for effect.*

On the drive home Stenmark looked at me and asked, "What was wrong with just... *this is Ken*?"

He had a point and we joked about it over the years, but I know he secretly found it endearing. I could tell by the smile on his handsome face when I continued to introduce him as "*my lover.*" From then on, it stuck.

Some people believe that when a relationship begins dishonestly, there isn't a chance in hell that it will last. But ours lasted for over twenty-four years.

Looking back, I admit I was embarrassed and ashamed about the way our relationship began. Stenmark was a married man, even if only on paper. The bottom line was, he was still married to someone else. My feelings about that would bubble up more often than not. I felt extreme guilt for not having more respect for myself as a woman. But yet, I continued to stifle these feelings as they arose, rationalizing them with the love I felt in my heart for Stenmark, even though I knew it wasn't right. I just couldn't stop. I pushed those feelings down over and over again. I won't go into details, but suffice it to say, Ken was still legally married when we finally evolved from friends to lovers. But even so, I could not deny the gravitational pull I felt towards this beautiful man. It overrode all commonsense and any feelings of guilt I felt.

I think I rationalized our relationship by knowing he had other "lovers" before me, while he was still married.

So, thank you for indulging me even if you don't agree.

But the truth is, we met and straight away fell in love, as much as we tried to deny it, it was too strong and beyond what either of us could do to stop it. Believe me, we tried. I never once gave him an ultimatum or asked him to leave. Stenmark would have had to come to that entirely on his own. It had to be his choice, what *he* wanted.

The cold hard truth was Stenmark left a long time ago, but this time he closed the door. During those six months, we shared so much with each other. I told him about all my other loves and he told me about the fact that he had always been an "alley cat," which was how he described himself as a *person who missteps*. Before he was a golf pro, he was a musician on the road, and I think "misstep" sounded better to him.

But truly it can happen to anyone, not just musicians or men. Trust me, as a nail technician forty years in the business, I've heard from many of my female clients, from all walks of life, about their occasional indiscretions.

But for Stenmark and me, I made it clear that I wouldn't put up with that.

"You wouldn't give me another chance?" he asked.

"No. Absolutely not." And I meant it.

"But you gave those other guys in your life a second chance," he said with his bottom lip sticking out.

Damn...why did I share so much with him?! But I had a good answer, and it was the absolute truth. "Back then I needed those guys. I had young kids, and I was a single mother. But now, I don't *need* a man in my life at this point. My kids are grown and out on their own, and I easily support myself. So there will be no second chances. Period." And then I held my breath, hoping he'd get it.

Fortunately, his answer was just what I needed to hear. "Bennett, I can't imagine ever cheating on you. You're so sweet, I just couldn't do that to you. You're what I've looked for my entire life and there is no way I would fuck that up."

Good answer, Stenmark.

We both have said numerous times over the years, we should have done it differently and spared others the pain and heartache we put them through. Too bad life doesn't have a rewind button.

Nevertheless, I know the heart wants what the heart wants, and ours were no different. We both realized we had done it the wrong way up to this point.

One of the many things I loved about Stenmark was his deep love for his son, McLane. When I divorced from my childrens' fathers, those men not only dropped out of my life, but their childrens' lives as well. But not Stenmark, he called his son every night until he went to college. When he wasn't working, he drove down to Salt Lake City to spend time with his son as often as possible. For the first couple of years after he moved in with me, he got up at four in the morning every Tuesday and Thursday to make the drive to Salt Lake City to get his son up and off to school.

His mother, Retta, had early morning shifts at the hospital in those days and Stenmark never once complained. Those early Christmas mornings he drove to Salt Lake from Park City, often in a huge snowstorm, making first tracks down I-80, before his son woke up to see what Santa had brought. He was always there for his son, and I was so proud of his dedication. We had McLane every other weekend without fail, and had a blast taking him skiing, golfing, working out at the gym, movies, or whatever else he wanted to do, we did it.

I found out McLane's favorite foods and made sure we included them in our meals. We also had fun making cookies, cakes, and other treats together. So much so, that he fell in love with a very cool spatula I had and always wanted to use it. So, guess what he got in his Easter basket that year? Yep, one just like it, and he loved it. We did everything we could to ensure McLane's happiness when he was with us.

I even sold my condo in Park City to move down to Holladay, Utah, so Stenmark could be closer to his son, after McLane turned twelve. It was Stenmark's desire to live physically closer to his son. I knew from raising my own four children, how pivotal this time in a young boy's life can be. McLane's upcoming teenage years could be challenging, so when Stenmark and I talked about, I was prepared and all in. I could see that being near his son made Stenmark very happy, and that was important to me as well. We agreed that a move would be in the best interest of everyone.

We bought our first property together in Holladay, Utah.

After that we were able to see McLane more often. Sometimes I would ask Stenmark if he would like to golf or ski, just the two of them. I felt time alone was important for his sons' emotional growth, healing and this huge adjustment of his new reality. Stenmark only did it a few times, saying he wanted his son to get to know me, as I was going to be in his life forever.

Then he'd kiss my forehead so lovingly. I've always loved forehead kisses and I didn't even have to tell him. *He just knew.*

CHAPTER 3
Of All These Things I Am Sure

I always said I was ready for anything and everything life threw my way. I was a survivor, a strong independent woman. I believed with my whole heart that things would always work out, no matter how tough the situation. I was a huge believer in the manifestation of getting what you want in life. I tell my children and grandchildren constantly that we attract what we put out into the Universe and thinking positively is paramount. That is my core belief system, and prayers don't hurt either. But that very belief system came into question big time during the beginning of fall 2019, and Stenmark was just sixty-eight years old. A very young sixty-eight.

I was at a street fair in Salt Lake City, promoting my first book with Utah Women Writers when my husband called me and told me he lost his wallet and iPhone. He was wondering if I'd seen them. He was heading off to work at the golf course and was frantic he couldn't find them.

I suggested several places for him to look and offered to hunt for them when I arrived at home. I'd carpooled with Bonnie, a friend and fellow writer, so I was stuck there for a few more hours. Stenmark couldn't wrap his head around driving without his wallet to the golf course. He was a staunch believer when it came to obeying the law and especially the rules of the road. By then, we were living on the side of a mountain just outside of Park City in a beautiful condo with our two cats, so the ride into the golf course was only a short eight minutes.

Heart Get Ready

I convinced him it would be okay, and I knew he would obey the speed limit! I told him if by chance he got pulled over, he could explain the situation. The officer could look him up and confirm he had a valid Utah Driver's license. He finally agreed and made it to work and back home without incident. The next day, we retraced his steps. Stenmark was an expert with Mac computers and all things electronic but couldn't remember how to track his iPhone.

I honestly thought he was just frazzled because he, unlike me, was a huge worrier like his mom.

The computer showed his phone was at the Park Meadows Golf Course, so we jumped in my car, and I drove to the course. As we were headed in the direction of the course, Stenmark asked me where it was because he was trying to find it yesterday and he couldn't. *GULP!* I told him I knew the way, but I found his comment upsetting.

When we got to the golf course, the young guy in the pro shop was so helpful when I asked about my husband's phone. He looked, but it wasn't in the drawer. He asked if he could see my phone to see where it was pinging. He then pointed out that it was at the MARC, a gym in Park City in the same area. He showed me how to pinpoint the exact location instead of just the general area.

As we drove to the gym, Stenmark said with *conviction* he knew it wasn't there. "Let's just check anyway," I answered.

He began telling me that, after he left the gym, he went to the Park City Market to get a Rockstar. He told a story about some kids on skateboards in the parking lot. They must have taken his wallet and phone when he was in the store. Stenmark was so sure of all these things, adamant in fact that it was the kids.

My head started to spin. I felt confused as I asked him if he called the police. He had not, so I suggested we drive to the gym first. Thank goodness we did, because his phone was in the desk at the gym, but no wallet so far. All the way home, he was convinced "those kids" took his wallet out of his truck. I calmly told him we would find it and not to worry. I drove back to our townhome, silently freaking out while trying my best to remain calm.

While I made dinner, Stenmark proceeded to look for his wallet when the doorbell rang. I opened it to find a Wasatch police officer standing there with my husband's wallet. Stenmark came to the door and was so relieved, he was in tears. He thanked him repeatedly. The kind officer told us that a man found it on the road near our house. Thankfully he was an honest soul and turned it into the police station with everything in it. My best guess is that Stenmark had set it on top of his truck and drove off, but who knows? We were both very grateful, and I breathed a huge sigh of relief.

This was just the beginning of his missing wallet and phone, and unfortunately the list of his missing things began to grow rapidly. We spent so much time searching for his things, it got to the point that I oversaw his belongings. Time to get a bigger purse, *darn it...*

Those of you who know me know I am a purse freak. Of course, I really didn't mind holding his things for him. *We are both getting older, and I sometimes misplace my own things, too*, I told myself.

Little did I know, I'd been thrown smack dab into my first day in an upside-down world. *"Heart Get Ready."*

CHAPTER 4
THE ONLY PLACE TO START

My husband was always very frugal. We had nice things, but he was very careful in his purchases. He researched everything to the max, finding the best possible deal, and making sure we really needed that purchase, and both of us agreeing that it was a must. Because we met later in life, we each already had our own vehicles, credit cards, bank accounts, etc.... Stenmark insisted on a savings account that we both contributed to monthly. No excuses. He also had a life insurance policy he paid monthly. He was so financially together, but I didn't have any of those things.

But at least my credit was excellent, and I owned my own place.

Stenmark was a very organized guy particularly when it came to his finances. He never carried a balance on his credit cards and taught me to do the same. I admit that was foreign to me, as I usually struggled to make ends meet when I was a single mother of four.

But now I was solvent and on my own and I was in great shape financially.

Stenmark paid his bills online with the payments automatically taken out of his checking account, and he taught me to do the same. That was so much easier!

I took care of my own bills and Stenmark took care of his. It was all online, except when I wrote him a check for my half of our mortgage payment and house expenses each month. He was responsible for those, and he did such a great job on things like that. I never worried, as I knew he would make sure those things were taken care of, it was just his responsible way of living.

We had a timeshare in Mesquite, Nevada, that we used on more than a regular basis. Mesquite is a golf mecca pretty much all year round. We didn't just go yearly; we went all the time. It was our fun romantic getaway, our time to be with and enjoy each other with no distractions. It was something we looked forward to with great anticipation. We had friends down there and usually went five or six times a year. We decided we needed a bit of a break from the snow in January of 2020, so we went down for a weekend.

We'd been making plans to retire in Mesquite, so we contacted a real estate agent. She lined up several properties for us to see and we narrowed it down to three places. We had a townhome to sell first, so we listed it as soon as we got back to Park City. We were both excited to start a new and different life, both of us ready to move, and Mesquite, Nevada was the place.

I admit I was a bit apprehensive about being so far away from family and friends, but I was also excited to be able to retire and golf more than twice a week. *I may even have time to practice, I thought.* Mesquite was a very special place for us, so that outweighed my apprehension. The fact that we did know quite a few people down there was a plus and it truly wasn't that far for our kids to come and visit. Stenmark was very excited about it and that made me even more happy to make the move.

We both agreed that retirement was in our very near future. Besides, how long can I sit hunched over my table doing nails ten hours a day? I'm not getting any younger, either.

Stenmark was tired of me working so hard and reminded me of this on a regular basis. He would spread his arms wide out to the side saying, "Bennett, we don't have this much time anymore." Then he would bring his hands about a foot apart, and say, "we only have *this* much time, *if* we're lucky."

I completely agreed. It was time for us to live out the time we had left with each other. My kids were grown and now busy with their own children. His son was still living with his mother, but busy with work and his own friends. They all had their own lives going on and we had become secondary, which is the way it supposed to be.

I know our Park City friends thought we were crazy to even *entertain* the idea of moving to Mesquite, and they let us know. But none of them had spent the time in Mesquite that we had for the last twenty years. We loved it, and the more we thought about moving, the more excited we became. It felt like the only place to start our new venture.

We laughed about how we would probably see our children more down there! It was time to make a move, time to start enjoying what we had left of our wonderful life together.

Stenmark spent his time on his laptop looking endlessly at the three properties we had our eye on. We compared the pros and cons of each for close to two weeks until we narrowed it down. We called our real estate agent and put in an offer contingent on our place selling with an agreement of the down payment at that time. Our agent specified a refundable amount, and we signed the papers via the internet.

Our condo was listed with Angela, a realtor friend of ours, and she worked hard to get it sold. It took a while, but during that time, I noticed some things about my sweet husband that were just not right. He seemed to be getting more forgetful and continued to misplace things on a regular basis.

It was no longer an occasional misplaced item because *we-are-getting-older* type of thing. I became more concerned and wondered if perhaps I was doing some of the same things. I didn't think so, but how often do we notice these things in ourselves? But I knew for a fact it was becoming more frequent in my sweet music man. Something was happening, but I didn't know what it was.

I began to keep track of these things on my phone and the list was growing rapidly day by day. Stenmark was still driving at this point but had started to complain more than usual about other drivers. I had a new hybrid car that he couldn't figure out how to start. I'd remind him to step on the brake and hold it as he pushed the start button, but his memory never retained it. This frustrated him and he began to lose patience.

On my days off we would go to the gym together, and one day, we were there for close to two hours. When we walked out, he ran into a friend of his. They were chatting and he introduced me to Joe. I politely shook his hand and told Stenmark, "I will be in the car, honey." He handed me the key and I walked to my car. I smiled at Joe and told him it was nice to meet him. As I walked over to the car, my legs were so tired from an hour on the track, I worried they might give out before I got there.

As I approached my car, I pushed the *open* button on the key fab and noticed a red light flashing and a beeping sound coming from inside the vehicle. Puzzled, I opened the door only to find I didn't need the key at all. My car was still running and had been since we walked into the gym, almost two hours ago.

Stenmark had forgotten to turn off the car.

Damn! I hadn't even noticed, and that was on me. But in his defense and mine, these new hybrids are so quiet, it's like a panther sneaking upon you. Not to mention, Park City is a "no idle town." I'm surprised it wasn't towed or at least had a ticket under the wiper blade. I turned off the car but remained in the driver's seat. I stared straight ahead with a million thoughts running through my brain. *I think I should probably drive home today.*

I realized in that moment, my car was just too complicated for him to drive, and he was no longer able to learn a new way. He could still drive his twenty-two-year-old Toyota Tundra. It was familiar and easy for him. Stenmark continued talking with his friend, so I started the car once again, and drove over to him. That was another thing I found different about him; I was always the chatty social one. He was usually quiet and spoke very low and soft. But now he was being more talkative, except the feathery tone of his voice remained the same.

So much so, that our friends referred to him as the 'low talker' from a Seinfeld episode. Over the years, I guess I'd become accustomed to it. From the beginning, Stenmark spoke in such a soft, angelic way, I trusted everything he had to say partly because of it.

I honestly felt he was heaven sent.

But now, these incidents were becoming more frequent, and I was starting to pay much closer attention.

As I pulled up to him, I rolled down the window and said, "C'mon Babe, you better let Joe get to his workout now." They shook hands and said their goodbyes, as Joe smiled and gave a quick wave. Stenmark walked over to the passenger side and jumped in.

There was not even a question of me being in the driver's seat. Stenmark reached for the seatbelt.

"Honey, *we* left the car running while we were working out."

Stenmark answered with a confused look, "Did we really?"

I nodded my head yes, and at that point I decided it was best to let it go. The last thing I wanted to do was make him feel stupid or confused. I knew in my heart the day was drawing near when I must approach him about my worst fears.

But first, I had to throw down the flag on moving to Mesquite. *Dammit!*

As soon as we arrived at our condo, we went inside, and I emailed the real estate agent in Mesquite, and asked her to cancel our contract. I told her there was something serious going on with my husband, something *very serious*. I wasn't sure what, but I had my suspicions and shared them with her. She'd had her own heartbreak with memory issues. Her mother had lost her battle with dementia the year before. I never discussed it with Stenmark, and he never mentioned moving to Mesquite again.

I did catch him a few times looking at the Mesquite listings on his laptop, and he would even ask my opinion on places, but we never had a real conversation again about moving to Mesquite.

At this point, the pandemic was looming, but we had not yet really heard much about it… I picked up my phone. My mind was spiraling as I re-read my notes. I decided to look up the signs of Alzheimer's disease and there it was in black and white staring me right in the face:

1. Difficulty with everyday tasks
2. Repetition
3. Communication problems
4. Getting lost
5. Personality changes
6. Confusion about time and place
7. Misplacing things
8. Loss of Interest
9. Troubling behavior
10. Forgetting memories

CHAPTER 5
STILL AMAZING ME

I couldn't believe my eyes. My husband had seven out of ten of these *early indicators*, as they were called. I was in shock. I had so many thoughts swirling through my head, I worried it might explode. I looked over at the love of my life in disbelief. Stenmark was sitting in his leather chair watching the Minnesota Vikings play football but kept messing with his phone and changing the channel. That was extremely unusual and not like him at all.

Oh, no. Now it was eight out of ten, because it was clear I had to add "loss of interest" to his early indicators list. This struck me to the core. He loved watching football, particularly The Vikings, and he never missed a game. He even played Fantasy Football with his friends online for years. He would always set the television and record it if he was busy, so this was indeed very strange to me. It was completely out of character, there is no way he is not interested in "his guys," which was our way of referring to The Vikings.

I watched him with tears streaming down my face for a good fifteen minutes and my heart sank. Stenmark never even noticed my tears. I think it was at that point I knew my worst fears were about to become my new reality and I wondered how I was going to deal with this. I had no experience with Alzheimer's disease. My parents died young, but they were both sharp as tacks, their neglected bodies just gave out. More reasons to stay as active as possible as we age.

Silently, and deep down, I tried to convince myself this wasn't that. No it can't possibly be, he's so young, so active, so happy and so intelligent. I got up and walked to the kitchen to start dinner.

I was in a fog and eating was the last thing on my mind.

I made him his other favorite dinner, four 'White Castle' hamburgers from the frozen section at Smiths. (When we first met, I ordered a dozen of them for his birthday from White Castle in Minnesota. Imagine my surprise, a week later when I saw them in the freezer section at Smiths grocery store!)

Oh well. We live and learn, don't we? *At least that's the goal…*

This was an easy, one minute in the microwave dinner and tonight I needed that. After that one-minute beep, I would take the tops off and write with mustard an 'X and O' on the buns then I would make a heart on the patties of meat. They were served open faced, and he loved it, and I loved doing it.

It made him so happy and that was my top priority.

I recall one day I was in a hurry and skipped my usual decorations on the White Castle buns and meat patties. I quickly handed the plate to him, covered in a napkin and rushed to feed our kitties that were impatiently waiting at the bottom of the stairs.

Next thing I knew he was at the top of the stairs asking me, "What? No kisses, hugs, or hearts on my dinner tonight? I guess the love is gone," as he stuck out his bottom lip.

"Oh, Babe, I'm sorry. I will fix it for you, my love." Then I laughed as I ran up the stairs to complete the usual finishing touches on his White Castle hamburgers.

But later that night, I did anything but laugh. I made myself a cup of Chamomile tea to try to relax. I needed to calm the anxiety that was quickly building in me, making my hands shake and my heart race without warning. I never eat when

I'm upset or feeling down. *It's a fault, I know.* I watched my sweet husband eat his favorite meal as I sipped the hot tea, expecting some kind of comfort that never came. This can't be happening to him, to us. We have the rest of our life together; we have made plans and this isn't part of those plans. My mind went to another place, a safe place of self-preservation to keep me from going insane. I needed to protect myself from spinning out of control. I closed my weepy eyes as I did my breathing exercises, trying to focus while my oblivious husband just sat there.

This too was completely out of character for him. Stenmark always asked me what was wrong if I seemed out of sorts. He held me when I cried, asked what he could do, offered solutions and comforted me endlessly. After all, he had various degrees in psychology, communication skills, and was a licensed mediator. What do I do now? I always felt so understood, loved and protected by him. Stenmark was my safety net once he was divorced, and we were officially a couple. As independent as I was, I relied and counted on him endlessly.

But this evening as I looked over at my wonderful, loving and caring husband, I never felt so lost, afraid and alone. I wiped my tears and opened my phone once again. This time I looked up the *stages* of Alzheimer's Disease.

I read all seven stages and then the guilt began to set in. If only I would have put it together with the memory loss symptoms maybe I would have been able to help my sweet husband sooner.

I'd read there is no cure for Alzheimer's disease, and that was enough to push me over the edge. But if I would have paid closer attention, maybe I could have slowed down the progression of it. This was killing me. Why hadn't I noticed? Why didn't I pay closer attention to it? Why didn't I notice this serious disease coming on sooner? I racked my brain for answers.

I know I am not oblivious to what is going on around me. I am smarter than that, and pride myself on being so intuitive. What happened to me?

I am and always have been so detail-oriented. Stenmark would often stop me mid-sentence, while I was telling him a story to say, "Bennett, I don't need to know the details," as he winked at me.

Lord, how I miss those *not-a-care-in-the-world* days. Back then it only took the three of us...Stenmark, me and time. He was the man who amazed me in so many ways. I was in awe of this beautiful man of mine. But now this?

The next day, I woke up groggy from lack of sleep but prepared to face the day the best way I knew how. There were things I needed to do. I made coffee, put on a happy face and grabbed the reins, so to speak. I sat down and made my list for the day. I was surprised to see Stenmark walk out of our bedroom at six in the morning. He was a musician and if there was one thing I knew about inside and out, it was musicians! And like most musicians, Stenmark was a full-on night owl, sleeping in until ten or later when he didn't have to be at work. At the time, he was in between seasons of teaching golf and skiing, and here he was, wide awake. "You're up early," I said cheerfully.

Stenmark answered, "I wanted to see my woman." *There he is,* I thought to myself as I jumped up and threw my arms around his neck kissing him all over his handsome face. Suddenly, I found myself going to my happy place; the place where I wasn't sure if he was sick or not. I think that's called self-preservation or is it called denial? Probably a little of both.

There must be a logical explanation for this new and strange behavior. *He can't be sick; he just can't be. Please say it isn't so.* As much as I tried to think positively about my new situation, I was failing miserably. Probably due to the numerous things that occurred every day, all of which pointed to memory loss. I've always been one to think on the bright side, but my optimism began to fade. As hard as I tried, the brightness of our life together was turning very dim, very quickly. My mother used to say, "Tell the truth to yourself first, and the rest will fall neatly in place."

But will it really?

I know we attract what we put out there. I've always tried to live by this. *Carly, make sure you're thinking in the most positive way possible.* I found giving myself a pep talk now and then had become a necessity at this juncture. *But I won't jump to any conclusions just yet.*

I believed whole heartedly that things would work out. But now I was questioning my whole belief system. I needed a shift in my thinking, especially now. I must remain steadfast and get back to believing not only for my own peace of mind, but for Stenmark. I wish I knew what he was feeling and thinking. I closed my eyes and put on my thinking cap.

I thought for a few minutes, threw in a prayer or two, and remembered that Stenmark hit his head hard, real hard at the golf course last June. He was sitting on a rolling chair that slipped out from under him and had to go to the Park City InstaCare Clinic. Looking back, that time frame seemed to be the moment I started to notice these troubling things.

Could this be the reason? I thought with hope in my heart.

It was an aha moment for me, *That's it!* I thought, with a huge sense of relief. I wanted desperately to believe this was the reason.

Time to shift your thoughts and practice what you preach, Carly!

I've never been a negative thinker and have always surrounded myself with positive uplifting souls. I cannot stand being around negativity.

Still Amazing Me

I started the next morning with a completely different gratitude list and my affirmations to myself that things were going to work out. Who knows? Mesquite may still be on the table. I smiled as I contained my thoughts in a more-than-usual upbeat, positive manner. *You can do this, Carly. Manifest what you want your life with Stenmark to be like and it will be.* I *can* do this. I have practiced this my entire life, and it usually turns out just the way I've envisioned it. I smiled as I turned over my new bright green leaf and promised myself I would do better, especially with my amazing *lover*.

CHAPTER 6
Attitude

I was getting ready for work when Stenmark walked into our bedroom, saying he had his physical with Dr. Smith that morning. "I have to be there at one o'clock," he said.

My thoughts quickly turned to changing my afternoon appointments. *I need to be there with him and speak to his trusted family doctor.* "I want to go with you, if that's okay?"

He answered quickly with a smile, "I would love that, Bennett." Then he kissed me on the top of the head, as I told him I'd be home at noon.

I needed to go over my list of things I noticed before asking Dr. Smith about them. The last thing I wanted to do was blindside Stenmark in front of his family physician, former neighbor and trusted friend.

I went into work and changed my afternoon appointments so I could accompany him to this important appointment. *I will ask Dr. Smith for two referrals, one for a CT scan and one for a neurologist.* This was my sole purpose of going. Then we will find out if his memory loss was something related to his fall, and if they could correct it. I was so excited and happy that I remembered about that fall. I couldn't wait to get to Dr. Smith's office and get the referrals I needed. I was positive that was it. My excitement grew so much, as I continued to reassure myself this was in fact the problem. And that it was probably something that could be fixed. I was beyond hopeful.

Attitude

Stenmark's driving at this point was still stellar like always, so we took his truck. I thought to myself, *we will run errands together while we are down in Salt Lake City.* The drive also gave me the opportunity to go over my notes with Stenmark before we arrived at Dr. Smith's office.

This was in February of 2020, and I'd never met Dr. Smith before, although he had been Stenmark's physician for close to thirty years. He walked in, sat down and looked at Stenmark's chart, while Stenmark introduced me to Dr. Smith and his nurse, who happened to be the doctor's wife. She was cold and very matter of fact. *Chilly!* I knew they were neighbors with Stenmark when he was with his first wife, so undoubtedly this was the reason for her attitude, but it didn't matter. I knew in my heart exactly what I had to do, and I was on a mission to do just that. *I'm not here to make friends.*

The doctor said, "Well, this is the visit where I ask you to recall the three words, draw a clock, and yada yada…" Yet, he didn't even mention the three words, he only mumbled something about the government, as he rolled his eyes. There was no drawing of a clock or anything else even resembling a cognitive test. Dr. Smith then asked Stenmark about refilling his statin medication, and if he needed anything else. Stenmark asked for a refill on his Viagra. Of course, Dr. Smith agreed to refill that in a hot second as I sat there feeling invisible. He also asked Stenmark "Are you teaching skiing again this year?"

"No, not yet. I will as soon as the season gets going this year."

As soon as the season gets going! What? It's mid-February!

Finally, at this point, I felt the need to jump in, and I did with both feet. I was here for a reason, two reasons, and I wasn't leaving without them, so I made my intent for joining in on this appointment crystal clear. I told Dr. Smith about Stenmark hitting his head at work, and how I now noticed a few out-of-the-ordinary things happen since then. I listed them calmly, clearly and in order. "I'd like a referral for a CT scan and another one for a neurologist, please," I politely requested.

Dr. Smith looked at me like I had two heads and continued examining my husband without so much as an acknowledgment of my request.

After a couple of minutes, without even looking in my direction, Dr. Smith sat back down and added something to the computer. He was solely focused on his patient, as he checked Stenmark's reaction time with the little rubber hammer. Then he instructed him to walk to the door on his tip toes, turn around, then walk backwards on his heels. Then motioned for him to have a seat and without looking even close in my direction he said, "I just gave you a quick neurological exam and you're fine," as he patted my husband's leg.

I sat there stunned. *Wait...what...that's it?*

Before I could ask him if he was out of his fucking mind, Dr. Smith turned to me and explained, "I have two types of patients," he spread his arms out to his side, shoulder width apart. He nodded to his left hand, "One is over here, and when I tell him he needs to see a specialist, because it might be cancer, he tells me if it isn't better by his next physical, he'll think about it." Then his nod went to his right hand. "The other type of patient is the guy who wants a referral if he doesn't have a bowel movement by seven a.m. And that second type is Ken."

I was stunned and amazed at how this guy's ego thought he could shut me down with a comment like that. Fortunately, I was able to quickly pull myself out of the stupor he'd put me in, and managed to say, "With all due respect, Dr. Smith, I realize you have known Stenmark for many years, but I live with him, and I'm telling you something is not right." *What's up with the attitude, Dr. Smith?* My voice quivered and began to break, as I pulled out my phone and read him the twenty-five plus things I had noticed. It included everything from Wells Fargo stealing all his money to him forgetting how to prep for a colonoscopy and getting upset with me for not letting him eat and making him drink that "bad juice," as Stenmark called it. "And let's not forget, my husband has been getting colonoscopies due to family history for over twenty years now."

At that point, Stenmark looked at me, his eyes were questioning, and he said as if hearing those things for the first time, "What are you talking about, Bennett?"

I answered him saying, "Babe this is the list I read to you while you were driving here today." I shot a look of *"see what I mean"* at Dr. Smith.

He looked at Stenmark and asked, "Ken, did you get angry when you drove here today?

Stenmark answered "no" as I nodded my head "yes."

Is that his only criteria when examining someone who may or may not be losing his memory. What the hell, doc? I didn't give him a chance to shut me down and I quickly I went on to say, "I didn't take off a day of work for no reason. There's something wrong, and I'd like those referrals, please," I said fighting back tears. Dr. Smith looked at me briefly and then he sighed saying to Stenmark, "Well, I'm sure you're fine, but let's give her the referrals, it'll keep her happy."

Yes, let's keep the little lady happy. Are you kidding me right now? I was beyond furious, but I needed those referrals, so I calmly thanked him. I might need him in the future, I thought, so I kept my cool. Dr. Smith printed off the referrals and reluctantly handed them to me. *Whew! I got what I came here for, but what a condescending asshole!*

I made the appointment on the drive home for the CT scan and it was scheduled for Monday. I thought it couldn't possibly be anything but that, and they would take care of it. I found getting into a neurologist would be much more difficult. They had a wait of four, yes, four months much to my surprise and sorrow. I took the first appointment available, June 15, 2020, the day after my birthday. But I called every single Monday morning at eight a.m. sharp to see if there were any cancelations. Not one in a four-month period, but then who would cancel an appointment this important. I know I wouldn't.

Two days after the CT scan, we received the results, and there was good and bad news. *The good news was his brain was not injured due to the fall at the golf course. The bad news was his brain was not injured due to the fall at the golf course.* There was no injury present to indicate a serious blow to the head, yet he still was experiencing memory loss issues daily.

CHAPTER 7
Hearts Against the Wall

By now it was still early 2020, and even though the pandemic was now in full swing, the country had not shut down yet. Still the occurrences pointing to Stenmark's memory loss issues were mounting. I tried to keep my cool, but I was spinning in a million directions, not knowing which way to turn.

I decided to have a heart-to-heart conversation with Stenmark. You know those times that it just feels like a good time to talk? Well, it was one of those times after a glass of well-chilled Chardonnay, so I seized the moment as I took my first sip. Then another bigger sip. Got to love that liquid courage, especially during times like these.

"So, honey," I began cautiously, "I'd like to talk to you about your memory and the results of your CT scan. I was hoping it was something to do with the injury to your head at the golf course, but since it isn't, I think we better talk about some memory issues I've noticed. Is that okay with you?"

Stenmark looked at me and asked flatly, "What memory issues?"

I picked up my phone and opened my notes, once again. I decided not to remind him this would be the third time he heard me read my list. I needed to protect his feelings at all costs. I carefully said, "I've been keeping track of a few things that I've noticed since last fall. Then I began reading as he just quietly stared at me. I continued to read these troubling things and adding kindness as I did so. But man, this was so hard. The look on his face was so sad, it brought tears to my already red eyes. *I wondered if he had been noticing these things as well. He is bright, does he know that something is off?*

Before continuing with these seemingly unending occurrences, I stopped to ask him how he was doing. "Are you okay, Babe."

Then he said in a not-so-calm voice, "Do you really think I'm losing my fucking mind, Bennett?"

I was so caught off guard, I didn't know what to say. This was my hero speaking. I was so shaken by his comment, I actually wondered if I was mistaken. Maybe the sadness I thought I noticed was not sadness at all. Stenmark was upset with me, and that was something I was not accustomed to.

I took in a deep breath before responding and calmly said to him, "I don't know Babe. Let's wait until we see the neurologist. We will know more then."

For the first time in almost twenty-five years, Stenmark raised his voice, ever so slightly, but sternly, saying, "I'm fine, Bennett. Dr. Smith said so and I trust him more than some random doctor who doesn't even know me."

Thanks for that, Dr. Smith.

I tried to compose myself and said, "Please don't be mad at me, sweetie. I love you so much and it's my job to take care of you, especially if I notice troubling things happening. We said it in our marriage vows, and I know without a single doubt, you would do it for me if the roles were reversed, wouldn't you, Babe?"

Stenmark put his arms around me and whispered softly as he kissed my neck, "Of course I would, Bennett." Stenmark had a paradigm shift. Despite his disease, I knew he still cared.

I decided not to continue the conversation until after his appointment with the neurologist. My heart just couldn't take it.

In the meantime, the list continued to grow, as my attitude turned from positivity to complete fear. I was scared to death. But still I prayed and prayed for this to not be the outcome. It's hard for me to even comprehend that this could be our new existence. But the "infamous list was now over forty observations long. I felt I had no choice but to turn it over completely and solely into God's hands.

I'm not really a religious person, and sometimes I swear when I feel like I need to get my point across. But I am a spiritual soul, and I try to be a good person and follow the Golden Rule, even when my heart is against the wall. I knew without a doubt now, this was completely out of my control. I couldn't fix this, and neither could my loving husband.

I will admit I do pray on a regular basis and thank God for the things he has helped me through during my life. But these last few years, my prayers had been more about asking for forgiveness than anything else. There was life before Stenmark. It was probably my Mormon upbringing coming into play. But this evening as I kissed Stenmark goodnight and went into our bedroom. I knelt by my bedside, but this time not to pray and ask for forgiveness. No, this time I prayed for strength.

The next morning, I woke up once again with puffed-up eyes and a heavy heart. Stenmark woke up a few minutes later after giving me a hug and kiss. I noticed all was forgotten from the night before. I put on the coffee and poured his orange juice. After my much needed first cup of coffee and he finished his juice, he announced he was going to take a shower.

I followed him into his bathroom asking if I could use his laptop.

"Well, of course, Bennett."

I poured myself another cup of the strong brew and sat on our leather loveseat. I opened his Mac laptop and couldn't believe my eyes. Stenmark had not closed his last window or cleared his history, and there it was big as life, "Signs of Dementia."

I just stared at the words in disbelief.

The tears clouded my already stinging eyes, and I wept like a baby.

My husband knew something wasn't right and had searched his computer, as far back as *five months ago*, without even mentioning it to me!

My poor sweet hubby, how scared and fearful he must be.

I didn't mention my findings to him. I really don't know why. Maybe I felt like it was snooping. Maybe he wouldn't remember even looking it up. Maybe I was in denial myself. Maybe I was too exhausted to deal with it, or maybe, *just maybe,* I couldn't face the reality of the situation.

Reality bites *hard*. For whatever reason I decided to wait, but for what I didn't have a clue.

All I knew was I just had to get through this and wait patiently for the appointment with the neurologist. *It seemed to be taking forever.* Instead of thinking about the rewind button, all I could think about was the fast-forward button. As much as I wanted so badly to go back to the beginning, I was anxiously awaiting a clear diagnosis now.

At this point, I decided snooping became a necessity. I had to make sure things were being taken care of. I opened his phone and found our mortgage company. I was in shock when I found out we were two months behind.

I opened his email. There were several notices about other debts.

I heard the shower stop as I scrolled down.

Stenmark had not been paying any of his part of the bills, our mortgage, HOA fees or his credit cards. I had to address this with him. This was serious and I needed answers now. He came out dressed for the day and he looked so handsome. I approached him and asked what happened and why he was delinquent.

His response was, "It isn't my fault. Wells Fargo stole all of my money, the bastards."

I told myself it was the disease, and I answered him with a kind response. "Okay Babe." I had no idea what else to do but knew I couldn't go *there*. Not now and maybe not ever.

I didn't have the energy to go any further with this. I now know for certain it's all up to me from here on out. I suggested we go in and talk to the bank. We made numerous trips to his bank and the results were always the same. Stenmark kept wanting to return and find out where his money was, and I knew better than to tell him no. At this point I really didn't know what his reaction would be. But I had read enough to know it could be bad. I felt so sorry for the people at the bank trying to explain to him.

It was really a lost cause. Dementia had wrangled his precious brain.

We were both very good at math, but now it was only me who remembered how to add and subtract. I added and re-added with the same result, of course. There was no money in his checking or our savings accounts. Stenmark had spent all his money, and his checking account was in the red. He even owed Wells Fargo for checks they paid. *What?* Even his credit card charges were legit. It all added up correctly. I was sick to my stomach. This was not my frugal husband. This was a stranger; someone I didn't recognize in oh so many ways.

Stenmark asked if he could use the restroom. The young lady that was helping us pointed it out to him, and as he walked towards it, I knew this was my chance.

I said to the Wells Fargo woman, "I am so sorry, but I think my husband is losing his memory," and I started to blink back tears. She stood up from her desk, and sympathetically rubbed my shoulder as she walked over to a large man.

I noticed Stenmark coming back and I wiped my tears in a hurry. He still looked like my big strong husband but he was different, clearly.

The next thing I knew they both walked over to us, and the man handed my husband an envelope. Then he said, "Kenneth, I am the branch manager here at Wells Fargo. You have been with us for over forty years, and you have never had a single problem, so I am reimbursing your late charges."

♡ ♡ ♡ ♡ ♡

Ken opened the white envelope and looked inside. His face lit up and he hugged the branch manager, thanking him profusely as if he were Santa Claus. You would have thought he had given him his almost thirty thousand dollars back. He was just like a little kid with those three hundred dollars in cash.

I thanked the branch manager and asked if it would be better if we closed that account, and he agreed it would be best. Of course that was the plan all along. I asked Stenmark if that was okay with him and he happily agreed while still staring at the money in the bank envelope. I took it as a plus with memory issues.

All the disdain for Wells Fargo was suddenly gone, at least for now.

But our condo needed to sell – like yesterday.

Lots more prayers, Carly, you still have a big mess to clean up. As kind as the branch manager was, the three hundred wouldn't cover his (and now quickly becoming *my*) deficit. He was in the red on so many other things and I needed to fix them as I now understood Stenmark couldn't.

CHAPTER 8
Strangers to Lovers to Strangers

I had a close friend and client who paid me yearly and had done so for about thirty years. I sent her a text asking if she could please possibly pay me early. We were a couple of months away from our yearly marker, but I had to fix this and fast. She texted me back asking if everything was okay, and that she could drop off a check in about an hour. I thanked her and told her I would explain when she came in.

There was a very prominent business owner in town, named Gary Cole, who had been diagnosed with memory loss a few years before my husband. We both knew Gary well. Sadly, dementia ran in his family, so his wife had told us they knew what it was when his memory began to fade. She was such a lovely woman with a kind heart that was now broken, and my heart was getting ready to do the same.

When my friend arrived with check in hand, I told her my worst fear, "I'm worried Ken is having issues like Gary Cole had."

Zena immediately threw her arms around me. Then I told her about the bank and the unpaid bills. "I have to get us caught up."

She nodded her head and said, "Of course you do. Is this enough?" she said, referring to her check.

I said it was, along with the money I had.

Zena hugged me again and said, "I'm sorry Car, but you can do *this*, if *this* is what it is."

My eyes welled up with tears and I told her how grateful I was for her help. Zena is the epitome of spirituality and positivity, which is probably the reason for our more than forty-year friendship.

With Zena's help, my positive mind went back to the task at hand. I thought about how happy I was that it was my job to take care of the utilities, or we would probably be sitting in the dark with no water, no heat, or phone service. *Thank you, Zena.*

It was at this point; I began checking his texts and emails, and that was so hard for me to deal with. I trusted my sweet husband with my whole heart, but I had no choice now. That's how his golf students reached out to him for lessons. He needed to make money and I needed to help him. I realized I'd become his secretary and his caretaker, with no formal training whatsoever. When I wrote my first book, he taught me to type and of course I had children, so being a caretaker was now built in, sort of.

After all, teaching was his only source of income until I was able to convince him to start drawing on his Social Security. Prior to these things happening, he always said he was waiting until he turned seventy. But that was not going to happen now. I helped him file the very next day and he never said a word about waiting.

This condo needed to sell and fast, and I continued to pray.

A few weeks passed and we finally received a low offer on our condo. We countered with an offer in between their low offer and our asking price.

They accepted it but of course they had "conditions," like really picky conditions. The only valid one was the hot tub needed to be fixed, but the rest were just nitpicking. I decided with my current situation and the pandemic in full swing, I would just go with it. We needed this house to sell and felt fortunate that we got the offer, so I began to work on the list.

We finally closed on the condo and I started packing up, which was a huge job.

We had stuff, so much stuff. I was still working as the pandemic closures had not happened yet, so I left notes for Stenmark to pack up his music room, closet and his huge dresser. I would arrive home, and it would not be done.

The boxes I put in the rooms for him to fill with his things had one shoe, a pair of jeans or a tee shirt in them...maybe. I don't know why I was expecting anything different. Yes, I do. It was that four-letter word...*hope*.

♡♡♡♡♡

I continued to pack everything else with nothing from my husband. I can't even express the way I felt, so many emotions that I didn't know what to do with. I was losing my husband more every day. He was becoming more and more of a stranger. I thought for sure he would at least pack up his music room, which was filled with hundreds of thousands of dollars of top-of-the-line music and recording equipment, and he was so protective of it all. It was all insured for a million dollars that he religiously paid yearly, or at least he used to. At this point I prayed for a small flood, just in that room.

I am kidding...sort of.

On that Saturday morning, the movers along with my children, grandchildren and friends came to help me with the move. Stenmark sat on the sofa sleeper watching television on his laptop. Not an offer to help, but if anyone asked him to help move something, he would say, "sure" and jump up to help the best he could. He was still a big strong man but his ability to know what to do was now gone. That ship had sailed, but I didn't know it until I was already treading water. We had rented three storage units in Salt Lake City, so the drive was about forty minutes from our townhome.

Then it all had to be unloaded into the units. It was a ton of work for everyone, but especially the guys. They did all the heavy lifting. It took us all day and into the night and I will be forever grateful to the friends and family who stepped in and really got the job done for us.

Without all their help, I don't know what I would have done. I looked around the house and noticed just a few smaller things (as there usually is) when a big move is made. You know all those little annoying things we need before we close the front door for the last time. But it was nothing we couldn't handle with Stenmark's big Toyota Tundra truck.

I brought dinner home that night again from Meier's Chicken, as the fridge and freezer were emptied out by the kids at my request. All that remained were bottles of water, Diet Pepsi, and two bottles of Clos Du Bois Chardonnay. Stenmark already had one opened and I quickly grabbed a paper cup. Normally, we drink wine out of our good glasses, but guess what? It was all packed and in storage down in the valley.

After dinner, we snuggled into the couch bed to watch some television. I must have fallen asleep so fast because I don't remember anything we decided to watch. I was beyond exhausted.

Moving is so stressful and physically hard anyway but coupled with the added emotional stress I was feeling, I wondered if I would even wake up.

Plus, I was anxiously waiting for the neurology appointment in two more days. And then oh yeah, tomorrow is my birthday. *Oh, yay.*

The next morning, I got up early and started on those small annoying little things left. They seem to take so much time. I went downstairs to start there, and I walked into his music room to find all the big stuff was moved, but there were cords and plugs everywhere. Stenmark was still upstairs, so I started unplugging cords and rolling them up, securing them with the heavy-duty zip ties. I was sitting on the floor winding them up as I thought about turning sixty-six that day. *Well, hell, Happy Birthday to me.*

Stenmark came down the stairs and walked into his music room, which of course was literally empty. He looked at me sitting on the floor and asked, "Why did those people come and take all of our things yesterday?"

I just looked at him, sadly realizing he didn't have his usual, fun, playful sense of humor. He was dead serious and wanted me to answer.

I took a deep breath and explained to him that it was because we had sold the townhome and we had to be out by Thursday.

He obviously didn't understand as he just stared at me for a minute, turned and walked back up the stairs as he answered softly OK. How confused he must be...

I watched him walk slowly and carefully up the stairs and I started sobbing uncontrollably, once again silently praying for God to help me through this unbearable part of my life. My husband had become a stranger and there wasn't anything I could to do about it.

I worked on the remaining packing while Stenmark watched television. It was Sunday and my birthday. I had never felt so broken hearted in my entire life. I went upstairs and decided I would tell my sweet hubby what today was. I thought he might remember it days later, and I didn't want to make him feel bad. He made such a big deal about my birthday every year even throwing me surprise parties on the big birthdays.

I worried it might hit him hard if he realized he'd completely forgotten. "Stenmark, guess what?"

He looked at me and answered with his own surprised, "What?"

I took a deep breath and said as cheerfully as I could, "I'm going to take a shower and we are going out for dinner, because today is my birthday." No use being sad and wallowing in my own self-pity. *Bull by the horns, Carly.*

My sweet husband came right over to me and gave me a big hug and kiss as he wished me a Happy Birthday. I thanked him and hugged him back as tight as I could. Oh, did I ever love this man of mine, I thought as I went into the shower. The hot water streamed down my head and body, as I stood there taking it all in. The feeling was so heavenly that I didn't want to get out.

As I shampooed my hair, my mind reflected to last year at this time. A sadness came over me as I thought about how perfect our life was. We had so many good times.

Sure, we had our stresses and dustups as any healthy relationship does. We both knew those rare times were healthy. We felt it was important to have passion, and what is more passionate than "fighting," for lack of a better word. There were no knock down drag outs, of course, but we did disagree now and then, and it was good for us. *After all, he was my lover.* But fighting is never as good as making up, not even close. We had a cute joke between just the two of us. When we were just relaxing at home at night, or on the weekends, one of us would look over at the other and say, "We're not fighting, but let's go kiss and make-up anyway." After all, who doesn't like makeup sex?

Must be all that pent up passion...

I got out of the shower and began getting ready for my birthday dinner with the man who stole my heart all those years ago. I quickly applied a little makeup, which I had not been doing for a few days due to the uncontrollable tears. I got dressed in a nice outfit and walked out of the master bedroom. No Stenmark.

I went down to the music room where I had left his favorite guitar out, the beautiful blue Washburn, thinking maybe he was down there.

I approached the door but heard nothing. As I opened it, I realized he was not in there. I panicked and ran up the stairs as fast as I could.

Maybe he's in the hot tub, I thought.

No, it was broken and drained.

Then I thought, Stenmark must be sitting outside with his laptop, in the sun. Yes, I'm sure that's where he must me. *I knew he absolutely loved doing that.*

Just as I was turning the doorknob, I heard the garage door open. I ran back into the living room just as he was coming up the stairs. "Honey, you scared me," I said, "I didn't know you left, where were you?" I was so alarmed and shook as I spoke.

Stenmark still drove his truck but not without me. And so far, he was still a good driver. But not long ago, he knew how to fix things around the house too, so that wasn't a very good comparison.

By the time he reached the top of the stairs, I noticed that Stenmark had a TJ Maxx bag in one hand, and flowers with a card in the other hand. He held out the gift, flowers, and the birthday card with no envelope.

My sweet husband excitedly said, "Happy Birthday, Bennett," and kissed my forehead.

Awe, my lover was back momentarily, but I will take it. I thanked him and told him how sweet it was. My wonderful husband was like a little boy when he told me to hurry and open my gift. I did as he asked and inside the bag were six pair of workout leggings, three purple, three navy blue. The sizes were half XL and the other half XS, no mediums at all.

Now, I'm tall and sort of slim, but I am not extra-small or not extra-large.

Stenmark tried, and I was grateful for that, bless his heart. I jumped up and down acting surprised, which I was, but in a different way. But I would never intentionally hurt his feelings. He meant way too much to me.

I thanked him as he handed me the beautiful flowers and the card sans envelope. I've always loved his cards, even more than his gifts.

Don't get me wrong, his gifts were always mind-blowing, but I am a *words* girl. Stenmark, a songwriter, had such a way with words that I looked forward to them in every little moment we celebrated. I opened the card, and although it was a 'happy birthday card for my loving wife,' and it said all the right things, it was unsigned, no name or his handwritten touching and loving sentiments. But it counted, and I loved it. As I read the pre-written sentiment inside, my eyes filled with tears and I gave my sweet husband a more than eight-second hug and thanked him.

It is so difficult when your hero becomes a stranger in your own life and you suddenly realize that you've gone from strangers to lovers and then back to strangers again in such a short time.

CHAPTER 9
25-Hour Day

The day was *finally* here for the neurology appointment. Why are these days dragging on? Did the government add an extra hour in each day and I didn't notice because I'm in my memory issue bubble? Everyday felt longer than the next. I'd waited not-so-patiently, for four long months and even though I was scared, I was also happy to know for sure what was going on in that big, bright brain of his. The appointment was later in the afternoon and I thought, could this day be any longer? My stomach was in knots as I waited.

I drove to the Salt Lake Clinic, where the neurologist was. Her name was Dr. Denise Skuster (rhymes with Rooster), but I wasn't sure about her. She was very matter of fact and professionally dressed. She was slightly stand-offish, not warm and fuzzy at all.

Dammit, doesn't she know this is the man I love and how scared I am?

I decided to not be so quick to judge, I'm usually so non-judgmental, and unassuming, but I was also protecting Stenmark, especially after our experience with Dr. Smith. She sees this all the time, maybe she's numb to it all, maybe it's the face masks (by now the quarantine and mandatory face masks had kicked in), I don't know. I calmed down and let her begin doing her job with Stenmark. She introduced herself and I think she did smile, but the damn masks are so prohibitive. It was hard to tell of course, but no handshakes due to the pandemic.

She got straight to business, beginning with the Montreal Cognitive Assessment, better known as the MOCA test. Dr. Skuster pulled a chair up right in front of Stenmark as I stayed seated to the right of him.

First, it was the clock test. Those of us who are sixty-five and over know all about that one. In horror, I looked at the clock he drew. It was a scrambled bunch of numbers outside of an oblong, broken and incomplete circle. Only the numbers 1, 6 and 12 were written inside the circle, which wasn't a circle at all. *Oh, this is not good.*

She continued with questions for Stenmark. He thought the year was 1951 (his birth year), she even gave him several hints that it was 2020, such as "the year we all wanted to forget," or "the year of the masks." It didn't help at all. Instead Stenmark kept repeating 1951.

Phone a friend?

He couldn't name two of the three pictures of animals. And forget about drawing a circle inside of a rectangle or connecting the numbers to the alphabet letters. I was barely holding myself together at this point. I reached for the Kleenex as the tears slid down my cheeks.

Then she asked him if he knew who the President was. His brow furrowed as he said, "Of course I do, it's that asshole, Trump." Well, that's something and it did give both of us a bit of a stifled chuckle. Dr. Skuster went on to say she wanted him to see a Neuroscientist, Dr. Samantha Allison, and gave him a referral for an MRI as soon as possible. I felt my heart racing, I was trying to hold back the tears, but my efforts were futile. The tears ran out of my eyes and onto the mask as I tried to get hold of my emotions.

Dr. Skuster went on to prescribe Donepezil, a cholinesterase inhibitor that is supposed to slow down the progression of Alzheimer's disease.

I was so upset, and I wanted so badly to control myself and be strong, but I just couldn't do it. This time, I reached for the entire box of tissues sitting on her desk as I sobbed.

My usually protective husband paid no attention to my overflowing sea of emotion. Instead, Stenmark was being his usual comedic self.

Dr. Skuster added that his score on the MOCA test was 13/30. None of this was even beginning to register in that brilliant brain of his. He just continued making jokes.

Dr. Skuster, was just as I presumed, not comforting to me, with not even a slight smile at his attempt at humor. Her Covid mask was on, but her eyes said it all.

I quickly asked her about him continuing to drive. Dr. Skuster replied looking straight at Stenmark she said, "No driving whatsoever. Let your wife drive from now on until we figure this all out."

I was beginning to like her more. Stenmark and I both nodded our heads in agreement with her instructions.

But once we got to the car, Stenmark still claimed he could drive. I told him we had to wait for his next appointment and see what the doctor said.

His mellow personality went along with that, although he did make it clear he didn't want to go back to *"Skuster School."*

I laughed, because to him it probably felt like school. I drove home and our conversation was pleasant. Stenmark was his usual funny and amusing self. Stenmark joked again and again about the Skuster School and we both laughed all the way up the canyon.

Once we arrived home, I scheduled his MRI. I loved the fact we now had a hospital in Park City. It was close by, and

Heart Get Ready

we could get in for the tests we needed so quickly. I set it up for my only weekday off, Monday.

Stenmark was confused. He didn't understand why he needed the MRI.

I tried to explain, as gently as possible, about his brain, and the tests he did at Skuster School, trying to add some levity to this delicate situation.

I explained that Dr. Skuster wanted to look at his brain and see what was causing his memory issue. I reminded him that in a week's time, he had lost his wallet and his cell phone eight times. I reminded him that the police even brought his wallet to our house and how an honest soul had found it on the highway and took it to the police station. I added, "Plus Babe the sooner we do all of these tests, the sooner you can drive again."

Stenmark looked at me like I was speaking in tongues. He had absolutely no recollection of those events whatsoever. He just stared at me.

I let it go. I needed this twenty-five-hour day to be over.

Even without the MRI, I was convinced his driving, along with his perfect top notch driving record were now things of the past *along with our hopes and dreams for the future. This was beyond crazy.*

P.S. we had to be completely out of our condo in two days.

I took Stenmark down the next morning to his son, who still resided with his mom in Holladay, Utah, so I could finish up the condo and garage by five.

Stenmark had no idea how to finish the move so my son, Sean, came up to help me. This was all so foreign to me. I was so accustomed to Stenmark helping me with everything and then more.

Still to this day, I don't know how I made it through this part of our life. The days felt so long and the nights even longer. It was only possible to put one foot in front of the other with the support of our amazingly good friends and our wonderful family. It still seems surreal, but in thinking about all of it I do know how I came through it. Simply put, I had to. I had no choice.

Back in 2002, our closest friends in Park City, Kacy and Dusty, hosted us the week after the Olympics, while the secret service rented my condo. Kacy also helped Stenmark throw me a surprise fiftieth birthday party that year, and later they hosted our wedding in their beautifully decorated home, catered by Kacy, a talented, and fabulous gourmet cook! Their generosity was endless. Most of our friends still talk about how it was the most beautiful wedding they ever attended...and oh the food!

When we sold our condo, I didn't have time to find a new home. So once again, Kacy and Dusty offered to have us stay with them until we found a new place to live. Our two cats went to the vet for boarding. Never in a million years would we have asked someone to take our two cats along with us for who knows how long. I was hoping it would only be a short time, a couple of weeks at most. Being the kind and loving people Kacy and Dusty are, they told us not to worry about it. Being the kind of person I am, of course, I worried.

When I wasn't working, I looked, full time, at property with our realtor, Angela. And when I was working, Angela and other close friends in and out of the real estate business were also looking for us, narrowing it down until I was able to find the perfect place to rent...or so I thought.

Little did I know, there were unforeseen things that eventually would spell disaster.

CHAPTER 10
Whenever I Fall

We needed our own place, even Stenmark realized that. After being at Dusty and Kacy's house for about a week, he told me we couldn't keep imposing on them. And I agreed completely. So I quickly signed a six-month lease.

We moved into a completely empty three-bedroom condo. I found it interesting that the bathrooms, closets and the kitchen were all fully stocked. Pots and pans, brooms, mops and everything else right down to the dishes. It had an amazing view and the deck overlooked The Preserve, a beautiful place in Park City. There were plenty of hiking and biking trails, and a beautiful, large and winding creek paralleled our place. It was so peaceful out there and it was only the beginning of summer.

Stenmark loved sitting outside enjoying a glass of wine and so did I.

But it had a couple of huge drawbacks. They all looked alike and ours was on the bottom floor, which is good if you don't have a family with seven children living directly above you. Since it was during the day when we looked at it, everyone was working and at school so we had no idea.

First off, because all the units looked the same, it was very confusing for Stenmark (part of the disease) to find our apartment. and the noise, coupled with young children running around above us, almost drove him insane (also, part of the disease). People with Alzheimer's do not like noise or confusion. He began to threaten to call the police, complain to the management, call the owners (whom we didn't even know), and worst of all, go upstairs and tell them to be quiet.

I understood and tried to explain to Stenmark that they were young kids that would, of course, occasionally run wild. That's what they do at that age.

The final straw was on July 4, 2020. We were sitting outside, watching the amazing fireworks from Glenwild, a very exclusive gated community located directly across from our deck and The Preserve. Stenmark loved fireworks and looked forward to them with great anticipation.

Usually, we were invited to a friend's house in Glenwild to watch Fourth of July fireworks. Julie lived on the golf course and she threw the best Fourth of July parties, but not this year due to the global pandemic.

By now, we were in the middle of the Covid19 lockdown, so of course we spent Fourth of July at home. We sat on the deck, waiting for darkness to come, enjoying a glass of Chardonnay. Meanwhile, our upstairs neighbors were also out on their own deck and the kids were so excited for the fireworks that they weren't quiet. They were just being kids, but Stenmark got extremely irritated.

He didn't understand, because his mind wouldn't let him. His dying brain didn't understand and he quickly became extremely agitated. The cherry on the sundae was when the fireworks started. We had a front row seat, a bird's eye view, if you will. Normal Stenmark would have seen that as a plus and loved it, but things were different now.

I'd lost track of the amount of wine he was freely pouring himself that evening, but it was clear to me, it was a lot. And that truly elevated his anger.

I told him to come inside, and he did so willingly. I closed the sliding door. America's birthday would not be celebrated this year in The Stenmark household.

Heart Get Ready

As I helped him dress for bed, he wanted to call the police, as we could still hear and see the fireworks from our bedroom sliding glass door. "Don't they know people are trying to sleep?" he said furiously.

I knew better than to argue with him-not wanting to start a mild battle. I tucked him into bed, and he fell fast asleep as I cried myself to sleep. I said a prayer and thanked God for the wine and prayed for his deep sleep, and peaceful slumber...as well as mine.

I woke up extra early the next morning to get Stenmark ready. These days it took longer than it used to, another interesting *factoid*.

While he showered, I thought about the previous night. Suddenly, my hands began to shake uncontrollably and I began to sob. I was unable to pull myself out of this place I'd landed, and I became extremely frightened. I've never felt like this before and I was starting to panic. What was happening to me? I grabbed my cell phone and quickly ran outside. I searched my contacts for my primary care physician. I'd only seen her once since my previous doctor had left last year, but she recommended her highly, and I really trusted my previous doctor's judgement.

My new doctor's receptionist politely answered and I was a mess. I couldn't stop crying when I desperately told her I needed to see Dr. Mary as soon as possible. I was in a panic, and she could tell as I was gasping for air between my words.

She asked if she could put me on a brief hold and I managed to answer a softly hurried yes. Please, please, please have availability.

"Carly, can you come in today at eleven o'clock?" the receptionist asked when she came back on the line.

I told her I could as I looked at my watch. It was nine-thirty in the morning and I was free falling into what felt like oblivion.

I showered, told Stenmark I had my wellness appointment, and then left.

I arrived ten minutes early all masked up. As I waited, I was still feeling like I had no control over my emotions, feelings or my life for that matter. I found the restroom, pulled down my covid mask and splashed my face with cold water. As I dried my face with the rough paper towel, I wondered if I would ever be able to face the ongoing chaos which now ruled my life. Would I ever get to a place of calm, still moments and be able to see past the wreckage? In this time and place, I felt so broken and lost. I wandered back to the waiting area just as the nurse came out and called my name. I followed her back for the dreaded weigh-in, but today I was surprised. I'd lost close to ten pounds without even trying. *Stress, for sure.*

Okay, something for the plus column.

The doctor came in. She was a very tall and slim brunette with an unassuming friendly smile, but she wasn't my doctor even though she introduced herself as "Mary."

It didn't matter. I was just happy to be there. As I began to talk, I was once again sobbing between words. Dr. Mary slid her rolling chair over to the counter and grabbed a box of Kleenex.

I took a few tissues from the box and wiped my eyes. As I apologized for my distressed state, I looked up to see she was blinking back her own tears.

Oh no, not sympathy. I always want it, but when I get it, I fall further into my own agony. It always makes the tears worse and uncontrollable, but I do appreciate it.

I looked down at my unkempt toes and crossed one of my feet over the other to hide them. "I need a pedicure. My toes look awful," I said which caused her to automatically look at my toes!

Heart Get Ready

Dr. Mary smiled and said, "I am hiding mine today for that very reason." She was so kind, which quickly put me at ease. I took a deep breath and spilled out my entire story, as I continued to cry.

She slid her chair up close to me and let me cry and talk as long as I needed to.

Almost an hour later, I left with a prescription for Lexapro, an anti-depressant.

I'd been on one mood elevator once in my life and only for a few months. I'd always been able to control my situational depression by exercising, particularly running, but this was beyond my control. Dr. Mary knew it and so did I. I drove straight to the nearest pharmacy, paid for my prescription and a bottle of water. I jumped into my car and immediately took my first anti-depressant in over thirty years.

When I arrived home, Stenmark asked me how my physical went. At this point, he was able to be left alone watching television with the sleeping cats on his lap, but I was still nervous and would never leave him for long periods of time. I told him I had a new doctor and it was a good appointment. I knew even though I had gone to the wrong Mary, I had found the right doctor who would catch me *whenever I fall*.

That had always been Stenmark's job. But no more.

CHAPTER 11
Lover to Lover

Finally, the day of Stenmark's MRI, another box I could check off. We walked into the Park City Hospital, and I was instructed to wait in the lobby, due to the Covid19 restrictions. I did as I was told, and after quite some time he finally came out.

Stenmark complained all the way home. "I don't understand why they don't let you know what's happening with all those sounds," he criticized.

This was not his first MRI, but this was his first one with his dying brain.

Stenmark was very upset, and it took the rest of the day and evening to calm him down. I'd read that some people with Alzheimer's disease can get fixated on certain things, so there was something else to watch for and try to learn how to deal with. It certainly was piling on these days. I kept my cool as I listened to him complain over and over. My thoughts went to what the poor medical technicians had to go through with him not being able to understand why he had to lie completely still. Not to mention the noises driving his mind to a place he couldn't even begin to comprehend. Oh, my poor husband. My heart ached for my sweet lover.

Looking back, I think this may have been when I learned to redirect him. *Squirrel!* I know it isn't funny but I had to use some humor, or I'd go crazy. I couldn't have made it through this without a sense of humor-no matter how dark.

Thankfully, humor was an easy thing that I allowed myself to experience. Easy things were few and far between those days. I considered them to be *tender mercies.*

Now we had to wait for the results from his MRI.

Stenmark had his appointment the next day to see the neuroscientist and I was told this would be a four-to-five-hour appointment and to plan accordingly, which I did. We walked in together the following Monday and met Dr. Samantha Allison.

We both liked her instantly. She was a friendly, bubbly, adorable younger woman, face mask and all. She went through the process of evaluating Stenmark and asked that I come back in four hours. They would call if they finished early. So off I went to run errands. It was a beautiful day, and the sun was shining…at least there was that, but my stomach was in knots as I went through the motions.

I went back to Dr. Allison's office after the four hours were up and found I still had another hour to wait. Finally, Dr. Allison came through the large double doors to greet me. We went into her office as the doors locked behind us. I thought about the series we watched and how the jailhouse doors locked behind the sentenced prisoners. *Jail would have been easier.* I sat down on the chair across from her desk as she began to give me her thoughts on my husband.

"I am ruling out Lewy Body Dementia," she said right off the bat. I breathed a sigh of relief and thanked God. Lewy Body Dementia, or LBD is the accumulation of alpha-synuclein protein in the brain, known as Lewy bodies. These accumulations alter brain chemistry affecting thought process, physical movement, behavior and emotional state. LBD is also common in people with Parkinson's disease. I have a close friend who lost her husband to that horrible disease. I was so grateful that would not be my journey, even though I was sorry it was hers. Life just isn't fair.

Dr. Allison continued, "However, I gave him several tests and scenarios and have concluded that he has less than one percent in his frontal lobe."

I had no idea what that meant, but I was about to find out.

She explained that being over sixty, I probably have seventy to eighty percent of my frontal lobe brain function, whereas someone in their teens or twenties, probably has close to one hundred percent.

Apparently, the brain lessens as we age. *Oh, joy more good news along the fun path of aging. That's the problem with old age; it always comes at such a bad time.*

Dr. Allison explained further, "What this means is he basically has no executive functioning. The CEO has left the building. Your husband has no judgement, insight, empathy, logic or reasoning."

My eyes once again filled with tears as she spoke. I was shocked as she continued to speak. It wasn't a complete surprise, but hearing the words felt like a gut punch. I now knew, even without the MRI results, I had a clear diagnosis. I didn't even need to hear the words from Dr. Skuster.

I wondered if I should talk to Stenmark about these results, you know lover to lover, in my own loving way. I didn't know what to do.

This is not our life, Carly. It can't possibly be.

She finished with, "You absolutely cannot leave him alone."

I shook my head as thoughts of me quitting my job and us being penniless swirled around. Stenmark can no longer work. What will we do? *I can't quit my job. But I can do it from home right now in secrecy.*

When we weren't in a quarantine from a pandemic, I worked as a nail technician and manicurist. The salon where I worked was closed, like everything else, but fortunately I was set up to work in our third bedroom. I followed all safety and sanitation protocol and gave my clients the choice to come to my home if they masked up.

I did have almost everyone come to the house and it worked out beautifully. I could still be home with my husband and support us with my income. When I shared the bad news with the golf course manager, Vaughn, he happily let him still do lessons with his previous clients, who I did give the choice to remain with him or choose one of the other qualified pros. His golf students all told me they loved him for who and what he was and wanted to be supportive, so they stayed with him.

A couple had already left before I became my husband's secretary and had bonded with their new instructor, and I totally get that. I just had to continue with my secretarial duties and, of course, drive him.

It's funny, when I shared the news with Vaughn, he wasn't surprised at all. He told me how he'd noticed last year when Stenmark could no longer work on the computer. Vaughn went on to say, "And he was the one that taught me how to use a computer years ago! I'm so sorry Carly, I should have said something to you back then."

At first, I wished he would have, but then how do you tell someone something that serious on only suspicion? You never know what their reaction is going to be. I didn't believe it myself. But I was so grateful to Vaughn for being so supportive and for loving and caring about his friend for over twenty-five years.

He is truly one of a kind.

CHAPTER 12
TRUE LOVE

Stenmark awoke fresh as can be with a cheery attitude the following morning. The previous day was forgotten. Of course, it was. That is just the way it goes with his *suspected* disease. That's a saving grace for me.

"What are we doing today," he asked with an innocence I hadn't seen before.

I took a deep breath, "Well, let's have breakfast first and then we can talk about it." I was trying my best to put on a happy face and match his sunny disposition.

Stenmark has never been much of a breakfast eater. He absolutely hates eggs and only would ever eat bacon, sausage, hash browns and fruit for his morning meal. Although he preferred an apple fritter or chocolate glazed donut! When we first met, he told me "No fish, no eggs, no cheese. I'm easy, I'm just a meat and potatoes kind of guy."

♡♡♡♡♡

I soon realized that the list of foods he didn't like. It had grown to include a lot of vegetables, including cucumbers, brussels sprout, carrots, and celery. I am a huge veggie eater and I eat very little sugar, chips or treats, for that matter.

In fact, when he moved in with me, he lost eight pounds in the first month. Then it was off to Costco to get some of the things *he* loved.

Stenmark also despised coffee and never had a cup in his life. He couldn't even stand the smell of it, saying his first wife "stunk" up the house with it every morning. *Hmmm...is this going to be a deal breaker?* I wondered back then.

Lucky for me, it wasn't. I'm a huge coffee lover, and he knew it. Although, he never once complained about me brewing my coffee first thing in the morning. That's true love, right there. However, I did have to brush my teeth before he would kiss me after drinking it.

Stenmark was hooked and I mean hooked on Diet Pepsi, drinking several cans a day. Oh well, I'm hooked on my morning coffee! But his "morning coffee" was a Rock Star. I tried for years to get him off that chemical laden stuff. After about ten years, he did cut down on his intake of Diet Pepsi, and eventually stopped. But then he started drinking more Rock Stars. I often wonder if that precipitated his memory issues.

I once heard that fake sugar could contribute to memory loss, but unfortunately the damage was probably done now. It wasn't worth the fight that could ensue if I tried to get him to stop, or even cut down. I had my vices, too. *Find what you love and let it kill you, I guess.*

Although we had not received a clear diagnosis and the results were not in yet from his MRI, my guess was I would not be surprised when we finally did. I had to educate myself. I read everything I could get my hands on concerning Alzheimer's disease. I knew no one who had this cruel and insidious disease.

Now, the person I love most in the world had it. I was beyond motivated to learn everything about it so I could deal with my sweet and wonderful husband in the most kind and loving way possible.

I believe one of the most important things I learned was to never disagree or argue with him. I needed to remember that.

Stenmark had basically no logic, reasoning, insight, empathy or judgement. That part of him was essentially gone and it wasn't going to suddenly return, no matter how hard I hoped, wished, and prayed. *Dammit.*

My incredibly talented, bright and devoted husband, best friend and partner no longer lived in my reality. I now had to learn to go into his because he couldn't come back into mine. It was rapidly becoming apparent; this would be my new reality. The world as I knew it no longer existed and I knew my heart would remain forever broken.

I still had high hopes of waking up from this nightmare, but now they were starting to wane. I bowed my head and silently prayed to God to help us both through this.

That evening, we walked out our back door and into the beautiful acreage along the creek behind the rented condo. This is what sold us on this place. It was a breathtaking view, and we were both excited to go for a long walk. Stenmark always loved our walks. We would hold hands and talk about our day, but now this too was different.

He began to complain, asking over and over how much longer. He was just like a bored little kid on a long road trip. He could no longer see the beauty. I would tell him just a few more minutes and he would be satisfied with my answer for about another twenty or so feet, then he would ask again and again.

Finally, he wore me down and we turned around, heading back after a grand total of four *long* minutes.

I found myself losing patience with his incessant whining. So much so that I began to pick up my pace. After a couple more minutes, I stopped, turned and looked back at him. My precious love was walking very slowly, looking down and he looked like a lost little boy. I had the worst feeling come over me, as my eyes filled with tears. *What in the hell is the matter with you, Carly*? I ran back to him, throwing my arms around his neck and began kissing him all over his face.

"What's all this about now," he asked.

I answered with a sweet smile, "I just love you so much, that's all."

Stenmark replied with one of his cute sayings that I always loved; "So you say," he smirked.

"I do say," I retorted as I grabbed his hand, and we walked home together.

After that, I did my best to be as patient as I possibly could. I'm not going to lie, it was hard and I didn't always succeed, but I was doing my best. I was blindsided by his disease. Our plan to grow old together didn't include dealing with Alzheimer's disease. It was never even discussed, because it never entered our minds that this would happen, and why would it? No family history for either of us, at least that we were aware of. Our road maps in life aren't always straight and smooth. I know this, but shit… Alzheimer's Disease?

When we arrived home, we went in through the front door and I noticed a worn-out pair of pink sparkly tennis shoes. They looked like they belonged to a small child. I was puzzled. "Where did these come from," I asked Stenmark.

"I found them, they're yours," was his answer.

"Show me where you found them," I said, still puzzled.

We walked back out our front door and he pointed to the condo next to us, just a few yards away. "You left them outside. Your good *tennies*, Bennett."

I quickly ran up to the door and sat them against it.

Stenmark was perplexed, asking over and over why I no longer wanted my cute shoes.

I finally said they were too small for me now and I wanted to give them to the little girl that lived there.

"How nice of you!" he said, and we left it at that.

My heart hurt so much; I wanted to scream out in pain. *C'mon Lexapro kick in, dammit!*

I just lied to my husband for the first time in our life, and on purpose. I had to. I was worried that due to all the condos looking the same, he had wandered in the wrong one, got distracted by the shoes and brought them home thinking they belonged to me. After all, he had tried to go in that condo on several occasions, but I caught him before he got too far.

I sat down with my iPad and wrote an email to Dr. Smith, telling him in detail about Stenmark wandering into other condos here and asked if he would write me a letter stating that we needed to move somewhere else. I was happy I did not burn that bridge with Dr. Smith, even though I really wanted to give him a piece of my mind. Honestly, if I were to run into him out enjoying his retirement, I don't think I could stop myself from telling him what I really thought of him.

But there was the six-month lease, and I was hoping a doctor's letter would help get me get out of it.

Dr. Smith did write the letter, and it did get me out of our lease, but we had to find a replacement renter, someone to take over our remaining four months.

Once again, Angela, to the rescue.

Angela found a couple from Harrisburg, Pennsylvania, who wanted to relocate in a couple of weeks, just like everybody else during the pandemic! I was so grateful.

Stenmark and I were sitting on the couch in the condo when Dr. Skuster's office called. The results from the MRI were in and we needed to set up a Zoom appointment to discuss them. Please don't tell me we have to wait months again.

We didn't. We were able to schedule for the following week.

In looking back, the signs of this disease began to show truly in December of 2017. Dr. Allison, the neuroscientist asked me to look back on some significant things I first started noticing but brushed off as normal signs of both of us aging. After all, I forget things too. So, I racked my brain and thought very, very hard. The first thing I noticed was his inability to fix things; three things immediately came to mind; a broken spring on the dishwasher, the malfunctioning ignitor to our gas barbeque grill, and our sticky Lazy Susan. I'd ordered the two parts for the dishwasher and grill, but he said all the directions were in a different language, and I needed to return them to Amazon, so I did without question.

I didn't realize that on the other side were the directions in English, until the new ones arrived. I thought it was strange, but honestly, I really didn't pay too much attention because I was so used to my husband taking care of things like that.

But he still had not fixed the spring on the dishwasher, or the Lazy Susan.

Then one day as I was headed out to work, I asked him to please fix the dishwasher, but to leave the Lazy Susan alone until I returned. I'd figured out there was a lid stuck under it and knew his hands were too big to reach underneath. I have always had small hands with long skinny fingers, so I knew my hands could easily grab it when I returned home.

Stenmark said, "Okay."

A close friend of his passed away, so I asked him to please give my condolences to his wife at the memorial. When I walked into the house after work, he was sitting on the kitchen floor, the Lazy Susan was all over the floor torn apart next to him.

I asked, "How was Julio's memorial?"

"Oh, shit I forgot. I'll have to call his wife or send her a text."

I told him to please do that, and he promised he would after he put the Lazy Susan back together.

I went along as I still had no clue about what was going on in his head. Weeks went by and still the parts were sitting all over the counter. I asked annoyed, "when will this mess be cleaned up."

Finally in desperation, I called a repair man, who charged us over a hundred dollars to put it back together. Twice.

Normal Stenmark would have done it right the first time, like he always did in the past.

I began to think harder. I racked my brain repeatedly and recalled another strange happening with him in 2017.

I was going to an annual golf girls Christmas party with a few girlfriends. It was a snowy December evening, so Stenmark volunteered to drive me. He dropped me off, and I told him someone could bring me home, or I would call an Uber. Either way I would let him know, so he wouldn't worry. I kissed him goodbye, and he drove off.

The party was so much fun, as it was every year with my wild and crazy golfing buddies. Great food and drink is always a treat, but let's not forget the infamous pirate gift exchange. The one where you can steal someone's gift instead of picking another one. Stealing a gift was something I could never bring myself to do. I always just picked another gift, and I got teased mercilessly about that every year.

I texted my husband to let him know the party had ended and I would be getting a ride home with a couple of friends in about an hour. No response, but it was after ten o'clock and I figured he was asleep, as he usually was when I returned home from this Christmas party. *I should be home by eleven*, I texted him.

When we said our goodbyes and walked outside, my friend's car had over a foot of snow on it. We marched back into the house to get a broom, as the car was a rental from Arizona, with no snow scraper. We used the broom, a scraper from someone else, our arms, and anything else we could find to clear off the snow-covered rental car.

Ah, winter in the mountains. You gotta love it. And we did.

I texted Stenmark several times to let him know I was on my way, but he didn't answer. I really didn't expect him to as I thought he was more than likely asleep.

It was slow going on this snowy night, and we all determined it might be safer to take the frontage road rather than the freeway. I text him again letting him know that we were on our way but could only travel at ten miles an hour due to the heavy snowfall.

Finally, we arrived at our condo in Black Rock Ridge. Barbara pulled into our driveway, and I thanked her, as I hopped out of the rented SUV. I ran up to the garage door and put in the code. My caring friends waited for the door to open, and I could get inside safely. You got to love thoughtful girlfriends.

The garage door opened effortlessly, but to my surprise my car was gone. Stenmark's big, huge Toyota Tundra truck was there. I stared at the empty place next to his truck and was beyond confused.

Barbara rolled down her window and asked what was wrong.

"My car is not here. Stenmark must have taken it out. That's weird. I wonder why he isn't in his truck on such a bad night. Then added, "I'm sure he will be here soon. You guys better get going, I'm sure he'll show up." I waved and they pulled away. I closed the garage door, looking at his big truck and went inside.

Maybe he got stuck with my car in the snow, after he dropped me off.

I looked in every room in the condo, including downstairs in his music room. He was not there. I wasn't thinking straight, obviously he was in my car somewhere. Why was I checking all the rooms in the house? I picked up my cell phone and called him. No answer. I text him, no answer. I called and text numerous times, still no answer. My confusion turned to worry. What if something happened to him and he needed help. I gave him one hour and then I would call the police, give them a description of my car and the license plate number.

I looked at my watch, it was now one o'clock in the morning. I frantically called again and again, leaving him tearful messages about how worried I was. Nothing. *I must call the police*, I thought.

Just then I heard the garage door open. I looked at my watch and it was half past one in the morning. Then I heard the garage door close and the basement door open. I ran down the stairs and he met me.

I said, "Honey, where have you been, I've been calling and texting you for over two hours.

He answered and it was clear he was angry, which was strange for my calm, cool sweet husband. In the eighteen years, we had been together at that time, he had never raised his voice at me, *ever*, not like this.

"Where the fuck have *you* been," he shouted. I looked at him in complete shock.

I was speechless! This wasn't the Stenmark I knew. He was never careless with his tongue. His charm, yes, but never his tongue.

Then he asked, "Did you have fun out with your new boyfriend, *the UBER driver?*"

What the hell? I asked him what he was talking about, I didn't understand a word he said. Puzzled, I responded. "I was at Beth's house for the golf girls Christmas party, honey." With his voice still raised he said, "You were not at Beth's. I went over there."

She said you left over an hour ago."

"I've been home for close to two hours waiting for you. Do you have your cell phone?" I asked.

Stenmark felt around his coat and in his pockets searching for his cell phone. He pulled it out of his coat pocket and tried to hand it to me.

"Look at it," I said, "I've called and texted you at least twenty times, I was worried about *you*." *Where is all of this coming from?* I thought.

Stenmark looked at his phone, and then walked over to the large sliding glass door and just stared out at the falling snow. He had no words whatsoever.

Okay, well now I'm a bit pissed. Actually I am MORE than a bit pissed!

I walked over to him and said in a sharp tone, "I was concerned about your safety and if you ever speak to me and accuse me of something like this again, I will divorce your ass, and I mean it! I will not be spoken to or treated this way, especially when I did nothing wrong." I waited for him to respond, but when he remained silent, I continued. "Look Stenmark, I love you, but this is bad on your part. And I am not kidding, I've divorced men for less, believe me."

He never apologized, offered an explanation, or uttered another word about it.

I told him quietly that I was going to bed, and I'd see him in the morning.

Still nothing from him. He just stared at the falling snow and the ensuing blizzard.

I thought, how weird! Maybe he'd had a few too many glasses of wine? As of late, he had been drinking more than usual, but I tried not to say anything about it to him. After all, he never overindulged.

After that, we never spoke of that night again.

Another time that makes more sense to me now than it did then, I recall from early in the summer of 2018. It was a warm evening in July and Stenmark was closing at the golf course that night. I heard the garage door open and as usual I ran down the stairs to greet him. As I kissed him all over his handsome face, I smelled alcohol. This was a first. My husband was so careful about drinking and driving that I was a little taken aback.

"Stenmark, have you been drinking," I asked.

"No, why?" he answered. I asked him to open his mouth and he became defensive. "Open my mouth for what? What's the matter with you, Bennett?"

"Babe, I think I can smell alcohol on your breath and it concerns me," I replied.

"Okay, I stopped at the Top Stop and bought a beer for the ride home. It was so busy today, I just wanted to unwind on the drive."

"Okay honey, no worries, but do you think that's wise? Park City cops aren't like they were back in the day. No one's going to let you go and just follow you home." I reminded him of just how much times had changed.

It isn't worth the risk.

Stenmark agreed and went in to change out of his work clothes. I thought about how much I loved seeing my big, tall, strong handsome man dressed in his golf attire, looking the part.

I poured the Chardonnay into the chilled glasses from the freezer as I sat down on the loveseat. I was waiting when he called out, "Bennett, come here. I got you a present." Now, this was not unusual, often he would buy me a shirt, shoes or a cool golf purse that came into the pro shop. I jumped up and went into the guest room. Stenmark had his hands behind his back. "What is it," I asked excitedly. "It's a surprise, Bennett."

He had very good taste, so I could count on it being something I would really love.

"You know the drill, close your eyes and put out your hands."

I giggled because I loved this little ritual. I closed my eyes and did as I was told.

Stenmark put something in my opened palms. I could tell it wasn't shoes, a purse or a golf shirt. What was this oddly feeling *surprise* that feels like cold metal. I opened my eyes to see I was holding two stainless steel forks.

I was puzzled and asked, "What's this for?"

Stenmark said, "Do you like your surprise, Babe?"

"Uh - yeah, I guess," I said tentatively. I was waiting for him to laugh and tell me he was teasing me and give me my *real* surprise present. I could tell he wasn't pleased with my reaction.

In fact, he was displeased, which I could also tell by his reaction.

"Bennett...those are nice forks I got for you."

I was still staring at him in dismay, "Where did you get them, Babe?"

Stenmark went on to tell me when he was cleaning up, he went out to the patio to make sure everything was picked up out there. Ruth Chris' Restaurant was adjacent to the golf course. He continued, "They were just sitting on the table and everyone had gone home, so I wanted to surprise you with them. They are nice, Bennett, and you don't even like them!"

I thought he was joking, and I was waiting for a laugh or smart-ass comment that never came. I just looked at him confused. He was truly bothered by my reaction, so I answered saying, "Yes, I do. I love them, honey, they are very cool. Thank you, Stenmark."

I hugged him and kissed him. I looked at his gorgeous face and I *knew* he was dead serious. *Fork me!*

I was making myself crazy, so I stopped trying to second guess what was happening. I never fully realized it at that time; but I know now he was beginning his deep decent into this cruel disease. It's often described as rapidly shrinking brain, as the person's brain slowly dies. They begin to change physically and mentally often forgetting who their loved ones are.

This is a horrific way to live out the end of one's nearly perfect life. I wouldn't wish Alzheimer's disease on my worst enemy, if I had one. I have been lucky in my life not to have made many enemies. The worst pain I have ever felt didn't come from an enemy, but from people who were *supposed* to love me. At this point in my life, I just didn't have the patience for bullshit anymore.

I had bigger fish to fry.

CHAPTER 13
Where I'm At

Our Zoom appointment was here for the MRI results. I had so many emotions running through my own brain. Stenmark was watching his favorite television program, *Heartland*. I reminded him of our appointment with Dr. Skuster, and all he said was he was happy he didn't have to go to "Skuster School." That brought a smile to my worried face.

The clock was fast approaching two o'clock and I was anticipating a confirmation of what I already knew. There had been way too many signs, way too many affirmations that pointed smack dab in the dreaded Alzheimer's direction.

I stared at my cell phone, not really speaking. My head was on his shoulder as I fought back the tears. I knew deep down without Dr. Skuster even telling me, but I was still silently praying and hoping it wasn't true. Was I in denial? Of course, I was. We're not talking about the flu here.

I'd read that diagnosis was rarely a surprise and the most common responses from loved ones are guilt and denial. I felt guilty for waiting so long when the signs were obviously there and of course I was in denial. I didn't want this for us. Nobody in their right mind would. This is a cruel way to end a life, especially a good and happy life.

I had a sense he was feeling the same way. But here is the problem; people usually know when there's something wrong with their brain. I'd often wondered if that was the case with Stenmark, even before I found he'd been searching for signs of dementia on his laptop. Did he notice he was losing things left and right?

I wondered if places looked strange to him, like these condos. I worried about how frightening that must be for him. Did my sweet husband know he was losing his memory but didn't want to worry me? Stenmark always wanted me to feel safe and secure. He'd ask me numerous times if I felt protected by him.

I looked at Stenmark. He was jumpy and nervous. After all, he was no dummy. In fact, he was extremely intelligent, a Mensa member, with a master's in psychology. He was also a licensed mediator and accountability trainer. Not to mention, an active singer/songwriter, professional ski instructor (one of three supervisors at the ski school for Park City Mountain Resort), and a PGA golf professional.

I could go on and on with his many accomplishments, but you get the idea.

But this wonderful man of mine was so much more than his achievements. He was truly the love of my life, my soulmate, my partner, the man of my dreams and the man in the songs! Have you ever listened to music and noticed the lyrics of just about every love song? Well, they all describe my husband to a tee, pun intended.

My iPhone rang right on time, two o'clock on the dot and there was Dr. Skuster smiling as I answered. Like all of us, she looked different without her facemask. Dr. Skuster looked kinder, perhaps softer. She had a nice smile that neither of us had seen before. She pulled up the MRI of Stenmark's brain as she started to explain just exactly what we were looking at.

My heart was pounding out of my chest, but my sweet husband remained calm and collected. Maybe his brain wasn't letting him be worried.

I've always loved his fun and upbeat personality along with his peaceful demeanor. Before his symptoms crept in, I had never heard him say anything bad about anyone. That is such a wonderful trait and speaks volumes about his character. He was always positive and kind towards others and would never put anyone down. He always said you should never completely cut anyone to the core; you should always leave them with something of value. He would never annihilate anyone, even if they deserved it.

Dr. Skuster went on to explain that on the right side of his brain, in the hippocampus and temporal lobe there were scattered T-2 abnormalities, also known as bright spots on the brain. There was also heavy plaque buildup, severe atrophy, and the presence of amyloid plaques and neurofibrillary tangles, all linked to Alzheimer's disease.

I sat in utter silence, unable to move, trying my best to hold it together. My eyes filled with tears, although his diagnosis was not a surprise, hearing the words completely wrecked me. It was at that moment I knew exactly, without question, where we were and where we were headed. Stenmark had received not only a life sentence, but a death sentence. This was where we were now, but how beat up and badly bruised we would be upon final arrival was anyone's guess.

As I said, we'd been in her office two weeks prior as she gave him the MOCA test, and he scored 13/30. Now here we are staring at pictures of his brain, his diseased, dying brain a month later. I was barely holding on. I wanted so badly to control myself and be strong, but I just couldn't do it and the tears began to flow. I put my hand over my mouth and began to sob.

Stenmark, still calm and collected, asked," Could this have been the result of playing football all through school?"

Dr. Skuster shook her head in a very sympathetic manner and said, "No, in looking at your brain, this began fifteen to twenty years ago, but there is no sign of this stemming from an injury." She pointed to the right side of his diseased brain and said, "This buildup also shows us that you are in stage five of the disease."

I'd read and researched, and I knew there were only seven stages of Alzheimer's disease. I was so destroyed; I couldn't utter a single word. This couldn't possibly be happening, yet it was. This wasn't what either of us had planned, even if he was unable to realize it. We had a beautiful life together. We made plans for our future. We were going to grow old together. We had a bucket list and Alzheimer's wasn't on it.

Dr. Skuster asked if there could be any family history? Parents?

Stenmark answered no and told her his parents were deceased.

"How old were you when they died," she asked. I watched as he struggled searching for an answer. I could see the wheels turning somewhere in there. He was trying *so* hard. That alone broke my already broken heart.

Finally, he answered, "I was twelve or thirteen."

I sadly shook my head no and mouthed the words, "In his twenties."

There was that sympathetic look again.

I needed to make sure, so I called his favorite nephew, who was only a few years younger than Stenmark. The answer was the same. Stenmark's parents died young, so who really knows. Maybe it was coming on slowly in their brains as well. I don't know and what does it really matter now. My precious husband was going to leave me, first mentally and then physically. That's what the dementia research means when it says you "lose" them twice. It had all begun and there was nothing either of us could do about it.

We thanked Dr. Skuster, said our goodbyes, ended the Zoom call, and then sat quietly together on the borrowed loveseat. As I began to cry softly, I looked at Stenmark and I asked him if he was scared? He wiped my tears, shook his head and said, "no." Then he stood up without saying a word, and calmly walked into the makeshift music room I'd put together for him in our rented condo. Stenmark picked up his guitar and began to play and sing one of *our* songs, "To make you feel my love," and I wept uncontrollably because I knew he knew.

CHAPTER 14
"ROAMANCE"

Finding somewhere to live in Park City proved to be more difficult than I had thought it would be. We went from place to place, staying a week to ten days each time while our dear friend and realtor, Angela, frantically looked for something we could afford. One day she called and said she found the perfect place for us.

"It's a home run," Angela said excitedly. We went the next morning to see this condo in Redstone, an area of Park City that has just about anything and everything you would want or need well within walking distance.

She was so confident this was the place, that she arrived papers in hand, with a full price cash offer, ready for our signatures.

They accepted and we were thrilled. Well, I was thrilled. Honestly, it really didn't matter to Stenmark. He just happily went along with whatever I said.

The funny thing about that is when this area was first developed, I said to him while driving by, "I love this area. If I was single, I'd live here in a hot second."

He looked at me in disbelief, "Yuck! I would never live in that crowded mess."

That was his reply back in the day, back before life threw us this curve ball. Now, it no longer mattered to him.

It was not smooth sailing getting into this place. We were ready to go, but the owners had troubles, lots of troubles.

First, it was her husband's knee surgery that delayed the closing, which I get. But after his healing, it was delay after delay. In the meantime, I was frantically looking once again for places to rent temporarily, and so was Angela.

Our cats were boarded, we had three storage units in Salt Lake City, plus my husband had Stage 5 Alzheimer's. Everything just piled on. Change is also very difficult for those with this disease, not to mention the prices of renting a place in Park City for a week or two at a time were astronomical. I got a call and our closing was once again delayed, the boarding facility called and said we needed to get the cats due to other reservations coming in. They had been there since July, and it was now almost September. We visited them a couple of times a week, but still…

I began to freak out, I was so upset. I cried, worried about our situation with my husband having to adapt to yet another change. Plus finding a place to take two cats is next to impossible. I called Angela and she was upset as well. Finally, she told me to go get my cats and move in with her. She had a small downstairs apartment that was very nice. It had a separate entrance and her renter had just moved out a few weeks prior.

She was going to delay finding another renter until we got into our place. Did I happen to mention she was a saint? I can't even begin to list everything Saint Angela did for us during this incredibly difficult time.

Stenmark and I were both close to her and felt at home. I went back to the salon and began working again, and Angela took him with her to run errands. She entertained him until I got off work. Lucky for us, she worked from home. I had coffee with her most mornings before work and those were precious times. We would talk about everything, and we would laugh and cry together. She loved my sweet husband, and they had fun together. But this disease also broke her heart. She truly is one of the most loving and kind souls I've ever known, truly heaven sent.

With that said, I couldn't just live there for free. It's just not in *my* DNA. When I told her I had to pay her something, she said no, but I did it anyway. I'm sure she could have rented it for more than the thousand dollars I paid her each month, after all this is Park City, but she never said a word.

She continued to be her warm, loving self and that is most definitely is in *her* DNA!

Then about a week later, I was at work when I received an email from Ruth (the wife of the couple from which we purchased our new home but had not moved into) telling me they couldn't find a new place they could qualify for (again this is *expensive* Park City). I continued to read, and the next line had me in utter disbelief. It stated they were going to "just move back in." All their belongings were in a rental truck parked outside, except a mattress on the floor of the condo and a few plants. The email went on to say she would send over a sale cancellation form to us.

Wait, what? I responded in four words... *not so fast, Ruth.*

My next client happened to be Ann MacQuoid, who was a close friend of mine and one of, if not *the* top realtor in Park City. She sold me my first house in Park City over thirty years ago, and it was her first sale as a realtor. I'd worked for Ann at the time in Park City's first high end salon and spa, Vie Retreat. She is an exceptional woman and friend, so I knew I could count on her to give me good advice and that's exactly what she did. She picked up her cell phone and called a real estate attorney while she was sitting there.

Ann's attorney told me he would write an email to Ruth and would send it to me prior to sending it out to Ruth. I agreed. He wanted all the facts, and he knew Angela so he called her to get the particulars of our contract.

HEART GET READY

I told the attorney, "Look, I don't want to sue anyone, but I want her to think I will."

Less than two hours later, I read a stern email from Ann's attorney that scared the hell out of me. It was so brutal that I got a sick feeling in my stomach—I was shaking, even though it was for *my* benefit!

The attorney gave Ruth one week to actively look for another place or risk being sued.

It worked; Ruth found a new place to live in less than a week. A few days went by, and I emailed the real estate attorney to thank him. But I never received an invoice, so I called his office. It was then I learned it had already been taken care of. He didn't say who, but deep in my appreciative heart I knew it was Ann.

While we waited to move, I decided to rent a small van to pick up some things from our storage units that we no longer needed, or had room for, and drop them off at a donation center called Savers, which benefits Big Brothers and Big Sisters. I really liked that my used things could be recycled. Our new place was less than a thousand square feet and we needed to pare down desperately—cull the herd, as Stenmark always said.

I drove us to the U-Haul rental center and parked out front. Of course, my husband hadn't driven since his first diagnosis with Dr. Skuster, so when I hopped out of the driver's seat, I said, "Babe, I will be right back. I'm just going to pick up the keys to the moving van and then we will drive to the storage unit and get busy."

Stenmark answered, "Okay dear, you know where I'll be."

I smiled as I closed the driver's seat door.

I ran into the building, quickly got the keys, and ran back out the door. I looked around, puzzled. No car, no Stenmark. I was in there less than two minutes. To save time, I did the rental online. I stood there staring at the empty parking space, frantically looking around for my car. I drive a Hybrid, so the key was in my purse, which was on the back floorboard behind the driver's seat, along with my cell phone. I stood there in disbelief feeling oh so utterly helpless.

What the hell do I do now? I'd read that they can roam around with this disease, but he was literally gone from my sight.

My mind was spinning, I couldn't figure out where to go, or what to do. I had no vehicle, no purse, no cell phone, nothing. Oh, dear God...where is my husband and how do I find him? Please keep him safe, I mumbled to myself, hoping God was listening. I need to call someone to come and get me, but I had no phone. I was freaking out and shaking like a leaf. He's not supposed to be driving. What if he hurts himself or someone else. This was so dangerous; I could barely wrap my head around the fact that he had driven off. I couldn't believe he was gone with the car.

This is when my knees hit the pavement and I put my hands over my face and screamed as loud as I could.

I needed to pull myself together for the sake of my husband. I must try and find him or get the police involved to issue a Silver Alert.

In a quick flash, I envisioned everyone in the State of Utah's cell phones blasting at the same time with that deafening alert. But nothing else mattered, only his safety.

I closed my eyes and took some deep breaths...five in slowly, eight out slowly. Then I opened my eyes and walked back into the U-Haul building.

I was a complete panicky mess when I saw the large, buxom lady that helped me before still sitting at her desk. I quickly walked to her, told her my situation and asked to use the phone.

This was a big *no*, since we were in a global pandemic. But she saw my face, my horror and desperation, and she took pity. She offered to call a number for me.

I drew a blank. I don't really know anyone's phone numbers anymore because of these silly cell phones. I thought hard. Please dear God, help me remember someone's phone number, please anyone!

I finally thought of Sean, my eldest son's phone number.

She dialed it as I prayed it was correct, then quickly hung up and said, "I think this is a wrong number. I got voicemail for a boat business."

"That's it! That's his business," I said, excited that I remembered it correctly. But damn! He didn't answer.

She tried a couple more times, still no answer.

Finally, I asked her to please leave him a message and tell him where I was.

She was such a big help. She not only called Sean, but she also called the guys on the U-Haul lot and gave them a description of my car and my husband. They all combed the huge lot but had no luck.

I was beyond frantic.

Then at last my son returned her call. She answered and explained what was happening.

His work was only a couple minutes away, so he arrived fast.

Sean said, "Mom, I called your phone and Kenny answered, he's at Costco."

I couldn't believe it. I silently thanked Dr. Smith for giving him that Viagra prescription!

We drove there and I went in while Sean scoured the parking lot. My car was not there, and neither was my husband. Then we drove to the storage unit, just in case. Still no luck. He took me back to the U-Haul place. Maybe, *just maybe*, he would remember he left me there. I was hoping but was disappointed once again.

I knew he wouldn't remember leaving me.

Just before moving into the rented condo while we were staying with Dusty and Kacy, I went out to my car, which was parked in the driveway, to get his phone charger. Without realizing it, the door locked me out. Our friends were asleep downstairs, and my phone was inside. There was no doorbell, so I pounded on the door hard over and over. No one heard me, and worse yet, my husband didn't even realize I never came back.

I ended up sleeping in my car, until Kacy awoke about five am. But not before I tried to go around to the back door in hopes it was open in the pitch-black dark night and fell face first into a large pile of topsoil, wet topsoil. I was muddy from head to toe, because I couldn't see it. Did I mention it was raining and cold and the sliding door was locked anyway. *Ugh!*

When she opened the front door and I told her what happened, she was mortified. I had brushed my teeth and put my retainer in before I went outside, so as I was frantically telling her my story, I sounded funny due to the retainer, so much so that she was worried. She asked if I had my retainer in my mouth and I said yes. She grabbed her chest and said, "Oh, thank God, I thought you were having a stroke." She probably thought if that was the case, we would be there forever!

When Stenmark came upstairs, he kissed me on the forehead and asked how I was. I said, "fine," no point in telling my sad tale again, plus I was beyond tired.

But then Kacy blurted out that I slept in my car. He had a concerned look on his face as he asked me why. I was so exhausted as one might be from sleeping in the car all night long. All I managed to say was that I got locked out and no one could hear me knocking. Stenmark was mortified, I guess the

Heart Get Ready

"less than one percent" executive part of his brain kicked in, as he did show bits of compassion.

But he was curious why I didn't call him or answer my phone.

My phone did have a couple of messages from him asking me where I was and he was mad at me because I wasn't home, so there was that.

Oh, sweet baby Jesus, I am too tired for all of this.

So, thoughts of him remembering he left me today, were slim to none.

Sean called my phone again and again. I started to cry. I was so concerned he would be in an accident. I was terrified.

In desperation, I blurted out, "We have to call the police."

My son had a much cooler head than I, so he said, "Let's call your phone one more time." Sean picked up his phone and called my husband *yet again*.

Suddenly and surprisingly, Stenmark answered this time.

Sean had such a calm tone when he asked, "Hey buddy, where are you?"

Stenmark answered, "I'm at home."

I nearly fell out. Stenmark had driven all the way up to Park City to the rented condo where we had only been living for a week.

When my son and I arrived, he was outside walking around in front of our building with the car keys in hand, but couldn't remember which one opened our door, and he'd been trying several in the twelve minutes it took Sean to fly up the canyon. Thank God for his radar detector, his good driving, and locked condos. Sean came in to see our temporary place and make sure we were both okay. I'm so lucky I have the best kids.

With tears in his eyes, my son shook Stenmark's hand and then he hugged me tight.

"It's okay, mama, don't worry," my sweet son whispered to me.

Teary-eyed myself, I thanked him as he walked out.

I knew deep down in my soul; it was far from okay.

My Alzheimer afflicted husband had begun the stage when they start to wander and roam. He just drove off in my car with my phone and purse. He left me all alone in Salt Lake City and thought nothing of it.

Our life would never be the same. Our beautiful life of fun filled "romance" had now become a life of plain wandering "roamance."

I turned and walked into our bedroom and sat on our bed. I put my face in my hands and burst into tears. I could no longer control the emotions of built-up worry and complete frustration.

Stenmark walked in and looked at me. I raised my head, sobbing nonstop. There was absolutely no emotion on his face whatsoever. His blue eyes were completely blank and sadly empty. Without saying a word, he turned and walked out of the bedroom.

I was completely shattered. *This was indeed happening.*

CHAPTER 15
Due Time

I've mentioned a couple of times, how handy my husband was before he suffered the effects of dementia. He could literally fix anything. He remodeled our entire house in Holladay, taking the rooms down to the studs. And the results of his efforts were beautiful. I was in awe of what he could do.

But now he was sick, so now everything was all up to me—and YouTube.

YouTube soon became my best friend in the whole wide world.

In November of 2020, we finally moved into our new condo. I tried hard to make it like our previous residence, same furniture, rugs, all our things sitting around. I thought that would make it seem more like home and perhaps not so confusing for Stenmark. Angela picked up dinner and brought him to the condo as a surprise. Note to self…they do not like surprises! I'll never forget the look on my husband's face when I asked, "Honey, do you like our new home."

He didn't know what to think or what to do, so he just stared at everything until he looked at me and said, "We don't live here."

The poor guy was completely confused, especially when I said, "Yes, we do now, Babe. This is our new place."

Stenmark didn't know whether to shit or go blind as he said, "Not here, we live up on the hill in Black Rock." I knew it was best to stop this conversation, remembering not to disagree with him.

Black Rock Ridge was the condo we'd just sold, after living there for over ten years. He remembered us living there as it had only been a short five months since we moved. Although, seven moves later, and an Alzheimer's diagnosis, it felt like an eternity to me. "Well, let's sit down and eat. I'll pour the champagne," I said, acting bubbly, trying to match the beverage we were about to consume.

He will come around, all in due time, Carly, all in due time.

As we ate another one of Stenmark's favorite meals, hamburgers with French fries, we had some pleasant dinner conversation. The time passed quicky as I cleaned up and Angela entertained him. When she sighed and calmy said it was time for her to go home, my husband stood up and started to put on his coat.

"No, no, Babe, we are staying here in our new place," I said cheerfully as I began to help him remove his coat.

"Bennett, I need this on it's cold outside," he said pulling his leather jacket back on. He was right about that. It was November in Park City, and it was very cold. But a leather jacket in the winter? Just another affirmation, like I needed another one. They were now coming at me like bullets. Quick and fast.

"I know, but Angela's going to her home, and we are staying here with the kitties in our new home. But you can leave your jacket on if you are cold.

I soon learned that was part of it. Angela left and I put on *Heartland* once again.

After one episode it was starting to get late. I turned off the television and asked if he was ready to go to bed. He looked at me and asked, "Where?"

I pointed down the short hallway, and said, "Let's go to our bedroom, it's right in there, Babe." I took hold of his hand and began to lead him down the hall.

Stenmark looked uneasy as we walked down the hall, almost afraid, like a scared little boy. *Oh, how I loved this sweet and gentle husband of mine.*

He frowned as he said, "No, we need to go back with Angela. She's probably waiting for us."

It took me close to an hour to get him into our own bed. He flat refused to change into pajamas and insisted sleeping in his jeans, sweatshirt, leather jacket and his shoes. I remember the days when he didn't even own a pair of pajamas. The days of us sleeping naked in each other's arms were long gone.

But tonight, the only way he agreed to get into our bed was if I turned on the television and continued to watch *Heartland* with him, which I did.

I was getting very good at re-directing him.

I was exhausted, so sleep should have come easy. The fact that I had packed up our entire two thousand square foot condo, including a three-car garage, moved us seven times, doing all the moving company arrangements, making several trips to the thrift store so our belongings would now fit into our nine hundred sixty-four square foot condo. Life had run me over. I didn't want to wallow in my sorrow. I can't have a pity party for myself, the time to be brave is now. I thought about how grateful I was for my wonderful children, my bonus son, McLane, my grandchildren and their spouses, along with friends and other family who had helped me so far. I don't know what I would have done without all of them.

The Beatles really got it right, we do get by with a little help from our friends.

I knew I couldn't leave Stenmark alone. Dr. Allison had made that very clear. It wasn't safe for anyone, especially Stenmark, so I changed my work schedule to Wednesday, Thursday and Fridays and I only worked from ten to four. I hired three caretakers, one for each day. They were not trained in memory care or truly any type of caretaking. But they were all nice and very good with Stenmark. They took him places, ran errands with him, and insured his safety while I worked. Even though they were more like babysitters, he liked them and enjoyed the company and my mind was at ease.

I made up folders for each one of them detailing what to expect and what to do and what not to do with someone who has Alzheimer's disease, which is one of the memory related diseases that are all under the dementia umbrella.

Whatever the circumstances, in terms of being a caretaker, you need to keep yourself in the know and above all, sane. You need to be prepared for the consequences of your every move.

There are some big no-no's when it comes to being with a person inflicted with this horrible disease, such as:
1. Never argue, instead agree
2. Never reason, always divert
3. Never shame, distract
4. Never lecture, reassure
5. Never say "remember," instead reminisce
6. Never say "I told you," instead repeat yourself
7. Never say "you can't," instead tell them what they can do
8. Never demand, ask
9. Never condescend, instead encourage
10. Never force, reinforce

These rules, for lack of a better word, became my bible along with many dementias related books, articles and memes. It was hard sometimes, but I knew it was necessary. I wanted our relationship to stay as 'known' as possible so I did my best. I think the hardest thing for me and a lot of others was not to bring up something and say the word "remember." It is such a habit in my speech. It's so hard not to! I mean, truly how many of us say that word before we tell a story?

I had business cards printed with the Alzheimer's purple ribbon and the words, "Please be patient and understanding. My loved one has dementia." Then I wrote on the back, "Thank you for your kindness" with a hand drawn heart.

When out and about, I handed them to people like waiters and such. Sometimes Stenmark would go up to people and talk to them in his *word salad* way. Word salad is a term commonly used to describe the speech of people with Alzheimer's. It is a confused and sometimes unintelligible mash-up of seemingly random words and phrases. Kinda like a salad encased in Jell-O, a word salad doesn't make a lot of sense.

Handing out these cards really helped people to understand that his behavior wasn't his fault.

I remember one day in Costco, while I was looking at something, Stenmark wandered over to a couple with a small little girl in the cart. My husband began touching her head, rubbing her face saying how beautiful she was. Fortunately, I was close by and ran over with a card in hand.

The father looked as if he was going to punch my unaware husband.

I smiled warmly at the couple, handed them the card and took hold of Stenmark's arm. "C'mon honey, let's go and let them get on with their shopping." I looked back as the mother patted her heart with her hand and her lip curled, and the father smiled sympathetically.

I also bought each of us the new Apple Watch with GPS. I ordered two Road ID's for the watches, which are outdoor enthusiasts ID tags that slipped on our watch bands. His was engraved with all the important details, his name, my contact information along with "Alzheimer Disease." A year prior to this, Stenmark decided to get a tattoo. Stenmark loved a saying he coined, "Life is Rhythm, find your Groove." He asked Nash, the talented tattoo artist, at Hearts and Hands Tattoo, to add a single musical note commonly used in country music, which was Stenmark's main genre. Under his Alzheimer's disease, I added the first line of his phrase, "Life is rhythm."

In an effort not to hurt his feelings or make him feel sad, upset or worried, I also made one for myself engraved with "vision issues" (since I have problems with my eyes) and under that I put the second line, "Find your groove" on my watch band.

Stenmark's feelings mattered and were forever at the top of my list.

Stenmark never once asked what they were there for, even though he looked at it and read it. It just never registered in his brain.

So many times, I would just look at him and ask myself, "Why?"

The caretakers I hired were amazing women and I was so grateful for them. I was able to work and get a bit of a break from this new life. Those breaks were so needed. I was back working at the salon, and I welcomed every Wednesday morning. However, it wasn't all peaches and cream with these ladies who "watched" Stenmark, and that was on me. They had no experience with caretaking and Alzheimer's is so tough to deal with. They were nice and tried their best but lacked the knowledge. I was in the exact same boat; I wasn't trained to be full-time caregiver for someone with Alzheimer's. It's a unique skill set, trust me.

I had no clue what I was doing and it was stressful. But in the Alzheimer's world, the caregiver is the one feeling the stress, not the afflicted person.

One day I returned home, and Jude, the Thursday caretaker was so upset as she began to tell me that Stenmark had wandered off in Walmart and was missing for about an hour. While Jude was checking out, he went to the restroom. It was visible from the checkout stands, but poor Jude never saw him come out as she patiently waited.

Jude was brave to take him to Walmart in the first place. I tried to avoid it at all costs, but Kenny always wanted to go. All of the sudden, he loved Walmart.

♡♡♡♡♡♡

I remember one day, in Walmart as I was gathering a few necessities, I found him in the mens department looking at jeans.

Heart Get Ready

"Babe, it's time to go. I will head over to the checkout stand and get in line."

He had a couple pair of jeans in his hands, but he quickly sat them down and said, "Okay." I walked to the checkout assuming he was following. I got in line but no Kenny.

As I stood in the long line, he strolled over with a large stack of jeans in his arms.

I need to approach this carefully. In twenty-five years my husband had never bought his jeans at Walmart. He wasn't lacking in the jeans department; he had a whole drawer full of them. Another Alzheimer's moment.

I asked him if he really needed all of those jeans.

Kenny looked at me and said, "Yes, Bennett I only have one pair," as he pointed to the pair of jeans he was wearing. Don't argue with him, Carly.

"I'll pay for them," he said. I sighed.

I said okay as he sat the stack of jeans on the conveyor belt. I watched as they travelled up to the cashier. I counted them as she scanned the code to ring them up. Twelve pairs of George jeans at $24.98 a pair…cha ching. Over three-hundred dollars.

As we drove home, I knew I would return them the next day. I was hoping that one-time Alzheimer's would be on my side and he would forget about them. It was and he did. I left them in the back of the car and he never once mentioned them.

The next morning as I waited in the return line at Walmart, I carefully looked at each pair of jeans. They ranged in various sizes, anywhere from a twenty-eight to forty-two size waist and the lengths were thirty to thirty-eight.

None of which would have fit my husband.

I moved up the line as I clutched the jeans to my chest where my heart was beating wildly.

"Can I help you," asked the friendly cashier. I sat all twelve pairs on the counter, looked at her and said, "Don't ask," as I handed her my receipt.

Due Time

Jude searched the entire store, had him paged and ended up going to her car and driving around. She finally found him walking along the highway. She was in tears as she told me this story. It was a hard lesson for *both* of us, but we learned not to take our eyes off him *for even one second*.

Then my Wednesday caretaker, Eve, seemed a little off when I arrived home that day. I noticed Stenmark was also upset and quiet. After she left, I asked him about it. "Honey, was everything okay today with Eve?" I should also mention he was giving her guitar lessons on the day she worked.

"No," he exclaimed.

I asked what happened.

"Well, I was playing *Something* by The Beatles, and after I finished playing, I was showing her the chords to start it off."

I was amazed. He was expressing himself just like normal Stenmark! He sounded just like he always had sans Alzheimer's. I looked him in his sweet blue eyes and felt such overwhelming love. I was holding back the tears and managed to say, "Okay..."

Stenmark continued. "She wasn't even trying to play her guitar. I kept showing her over and over. Hell, it was only three chords. She's a smart girl."

I really didn't know what to say, as I could envision myself doing the same thing. I sing, but I am not musically inclined when it comes to playing an instrument, although he was teaching me the guitar before he became sick.

Finally, I said, "Well, did you ask her what the matter was."

Stenmark shook his head, and said in an exasperated way, "Of course I did, Bennett. I'm not a dolt."

Okay... "Well, what did she say?"

"She said she couldn't play it because she didn't know the song, and she never heard it before. Can you believe that shit?"

I stifled a laugh, as he continued to complain. "It was one of The Beatles biggest hits! Who hasn't heard the song, *Something*?" Apparently, Eve hadn't.

CHAPTER 16
Good Memory Gone Bad

There were so many things I was only beginning to discover about this cruel disease. I simply added them to my Alzheimer's list. I decided to just listen to him, nod my head and agree because like it or not this *was* happening. My close friend and smartest woman in Park City, Nancy, sent me a message about a new Alzheimer's study in Salt Lake City.

I called the center where the study was conducted the very next morning. They told me there was a criterion to be met before they would set up an appointment with Stenmark. Was he mobile? Was he under the age of seventy? And was he on Donepezil for at least three months?

Check, check, and check.

They set up an appointment for the following week, and I was told to plan to spend the day with them.

On the day of the appointment, we arrived at ten a.m. Then it began. It wasn't just a battery of question and answers. It was medical testing as well. Blood tests, scans, and an array of other tests. They needed to make sure he was physically fit, and of course he was. They served us lunch and it was very tasty. It was all based on the Mediterranean diet, which has been deemed "The Brain Diet."

Stenmark of course handed me his lunch, so I could remove the cheese off his turkey wrap. He traded me his cheese for my Lays potato chips, his favorite.

After lunch, more tests. The two nurses had fantastic personalities and it was very enjoyable, especially for him. One of them loved to sing and that was a plus. The song, "Lean on Me" was always a favorite of Stenmark's, so when he broke out in this song, she harmonized with him, as he snapped his fingers to the beat. That made both of us smile.

Unfortunately, and fortunately, he passed all the tests with flying colors, and they were ready to set him up in the study. One of the requirements they needed from me was I had to be there with him four to six hours a week. I was told to plan accordingly for the next thirty days, so I did.

This was the end of May in 2021. Stenmark had just turned seventy and I was planning a surprise birthday party for him in Rotary Park, a serene, beautiful location in Park City. I quietly asked if it could be after his party, so it was set for the Monday following Father's Day, June 21, 2021. I approached the thirty days by saying it could help him and others, so he was all in.

The trial medicine was to be taken in addition with the Donepezil and he was also put on the Mediterranean diet while he was there for thirty days. It was a hospital setting and once they found out he was a golf pro, one his male nurses brought in a practice putting green, a putter and some golf balls.

I thought that was so kind and thoughtful, and he loved it.

Stenmark was in his comfort zone and he was happy. I loved seeing him happy, but worried this would soon be a good memory gone bad.

Stenmark called me one afternoon and asked me to bring in one of his putters the next time I came in, so I did. He was funny with the putting green being in his private room. He gave all the nurses putting lessons and before he would take his medication, they had to putt and make it! It was very cute, and it kept him busy and occupied. Which was good, because thirty plus days is a long time.

Stenmark being who he is, made friends with everyone there, even the security guards, because out of necessity, it was a lock down situation. At this time, he had his cell phone and laptop with him and was using both on a regular basis with minimal trouble. He just kept forgetting to charge them!

The study ended and he was discharged on July 26, 2021. He still had another day of testing at the offices, so they could chart his progress, if any. But at least he could come home, and I was so happy to have him here. Even though it was a much-needed break, I missed him especially at night.

His first night home, we slept in each other's arms, holding one another all night long. Just like the old days. When one changed sleeping positions, the other followed. Stenmark lovingly kissed my bare shoulder all night long. Right from the start kissing my shoulder was his thing, and I loved it. And remember, we always slept naked.

Sorry, too much info?

Unfortunately, his re-entry into our home life wasn't as smooth as I had hoped and prayed for. He seemed more agitated and anxious after the month-long study. I can't say for certain that the study, along with the new medication, made him worse, but in my opinion, it certainly didn't help. Maybe it would have worsened anyway, I don't know. My only hope now was that it might help someone else someday in some way. I will continue to pray day and night for some kind of miracle.

Over the next month, I still worked, and the caregivers continued to help. I didn't get much sleep as my husband slipped further away. One Friday, the caregiver had to leave right at four and the traffic was particularly horrible as I was coming home, so I ran about fifteen minutes late, which only added to my anxiety. Those who know me, know that tardiness has always been a pet peeve of mine. I absolutely hate to be late.

But I was worried for nothing, because when I arrived at home, there he was sitting on the couch watching *Heartland* with our cat Lola on his lap.

Stenmark rescued Lola from Nuzzles and Company, a wonderful rescue and adoption center, located in Park City. He got her as a surprise for me for my birthday several years ago, but she instantly preferred him. We still had our sweet boy cat, Newman, aka Newbie, also rescued from Nuzzles and Co., who quickly became *my* little boy. So, we each had our own kitty and we were very attached to both little "hairballs," as Stenmark lovingly called them.

Our sweet caretaker, Becky, had dinner in the oven, and the dishwasher going, which wasn't required for her to do, but was greatly appreciated.

My work may seem easy to some but trust me sitting hunched over in a chair all day long, with strong readers on making sure I see every single little thing as I do nails takes a toll on my eyes.

I would arrive home exhausted, and my back would be killing me. And my eyes were always tired and sore. Stenmark was so sympathetic in the past. He couldn't wait for me to retire. He knew the toll doing nails was taking on me then, but those days were slipping away right before my tired eyes, and there was not a thing I could do about it. This was my new normal now and all I could do was try and deal with it. The biggest mistake we make in life is thinking we have all the time in the world.

Heart Get Ready

Although I've never been a complainer and I do love my job, the fact was I was aging, it was getting physically harder for me to sit all day. But it was also rewarding to look at my work after an hour and see the difference. However, truly the best part of my job was my clients. They were my friends and right now they were saving my life, whether they knew it or not. And I loved every one of them for it.

Stenmark and I ate the delicious dinner that evening and settled down on the couch next to each other for more episodes of *Heartland*. We had *our* shows we watched before this, but now they were also a thing of the past. Stenmark just couldn't follow or understand what was going on with those anymore. For whatever reason, *Heartland* just worked.

Before going to bed, he decided to take another shower. This was going to be his third one that day, but who's counting. I do love me a clean man. It was okay, I learned not to tell him he'd already showered, he simply didn't remember. I now knew I must accept the fact that certain things just weren't worth it. One of the biggest lessons I've learned this year was not to force anything anymore. *"Pick your battles"* had taken on a totally different meaning now.

I was in bed reading when he came bursting in the bedroom.

"The water is all over the floor," he said wringing his hands buck naked.

I jumped out of bed and followed him into our only bathroom. The toilet was running and had overflowed, because that's what happens when you use an entire roll of toilet paper in it. I shook the handle, but no luck.

I ran downstairs frantically searching for a plunger when I remembered it was at the salon. *Damn!*

I grabbed a box of rubber gloves as I ran up the stairs and opened the linen cupboard. I grabbed every towel we had and began soaking up the water. Stenmark just stood there staring at the huge mess. I kneeled on some towels by the toilet, pulled the metal garbage can next to me. Putting on a pair of rubber gloves, I pulled out what toilet paper I could, silently crying as I quickly began to fill up the can.

What a sight that must have been. Two people in three or four inches of water, one crying her eyes out and one blankly staring not knowing what to do. Oh, and stark naked. Time to get Stenmark dressed and head to Walmart for a toilet plunger at ten-thirty at night. I can't leave him alone with this mess. I can't trust what he might do to *"fix"* it.

CHAPTER 17
HeartBent

Little did I know, that was just one of the many things to come. Soon my unaware husband began urinating in the kitchen sink, then occasionally in his wicker laundry basket. It was about two weeks after the toilet paper incident I found him walking down the middle of the busiest road in Park City, Highway 224, at four a.m.

This is a time when I was so grateful, we had splurged on the watches with the GPS. I woke up and found he was not in bed. I searched the entire 964 square feet of the condo and garage. Stenmark was nowhere to be found.

I grabbed my cell phone and opened my Blink camera app. My son, Rick had installed them at the front door and the garage door after a client, who then became a close friend, gave it to me as a housewarming gift. I was so happy, but also very scared to open it up and see Stenmark walking out our front door thirty minutes earlier. *Thanks, Cutie Judi, for your invaluable gift!*

I jumped in the car and with the help of my phone app and his watch, I was able to track him. Being four in the morning it was also helpful that there was literally no traffic.

There he was right in the middle lane, with two coats on, a pair of boots and two pairs of his favorite shoes in hand.

I parked next to him, put on my flashers, jumped out and began to quietly coax him to the car. My heart was pounding out of my chest, and I felt sick to my stomach. "Honey, where are you going," I asked trying not to sound hysterical.

Stenmark answered, "Back home."

I took hold of his arm gently moving him next to me towards the car.

"Well let's go together, it will be faster in the car," I said ever so sweetly.

It worked and as I opened the door, he turned towards me and kissed me.

"I love you, Bennett," he said.

"I love you too, Babe, now let's go home."

As I flipped the car around, he immediately told me I was going the wrong way. Once again, I started to explain how we moved into a new place.

Stenmark began to get irritated, and I was desperately trying to tell him *something* that might help change his thinking. "Well, the kitties are waiting for us at the new condo, and I bet they are hungry by now."

Stenmark sat there for a few seconds and then responded, "We better go and feed them."

Whew! It worked. I just never knew what would make some kind of sense to him, but that did. It resonated and I felt a huge sense of relief and I didn't even have to lie. As soon as I pulled in the garage, I opened the door. We both laughed because there were our cats, Newbie and Lola, at the top of the stairs looking at us waiting for their food, just like I said.

Stenmark fed them and we all went back to bed, but stress was taking over. I couldn't fall back to sleep. What happens now? My mind played the *"What if?"* game, and I couldn't stop the scenarios jumping around in my brain.

I began to silently cry. My husband was my rock. I could always count on Stenmark to make everything better. He always had the answers and knew all the right words to make me feel safe, secure and above all, so loved. *Now it's all up to me and I don't know what the hell to do.*

It's not like I am a helpless woman. I've always been fiercely independent, and let's not forget, I was single and lived alone for six years before I met the love of my life. I knew how to take care of myself and the little things that come along with being a single woman. I had four grown kids who were always willing to help me with the *not-so-little things* that popped up.

When did I become so dependent on a man?

I know exactly when it was—June 6, 2001—the day the man of my dreams moved in with me. Stenmark made it easy for me right from day one. I depended on him and I am not ashamed to admit it. He had become the rock that I leaned on for so many things for so many years. But more importantly, we depended on each other, without a doubt. We were a team and I liked it that way.

We used to joke about our "boy jobs and our girl jobs," which I playfully started when I came up with those names. As an example, our meals were one of my "girl jobs" and him crawling under the house to install our sprinkler system, was one of his "boy jobs." I am sure you get the picture.

If we made a purchase, whether it be a blender or a hot tub, it was discussed, and Stenmark researched it to death for weeks, finding the best product and the best possible deal on whatever it was. I loved that and so many other things he did for us. He made our life so perfect.

Yes, we were a team and a good team at that. But now it's all changed.

"We" has now become "me."

First things first, I bought an alarm that attached to his side of the bed. It would alert me when he got up. There was only one drawback, he was up and down all night, which kept waking me up when he was only going to use the bathroom. But it didn't matter, it felt safer and that was my main priority.

I couldn't have him wandering off again, so I would happily deal with it.

My clients and friends started to notice this taking a huge toll on me and one day my close friend, Alix recommended a caregiver's support group to me through Jewish Family Service. This group was non-denominational and met every other Monday via Zoom at three o'clock. *Perfect!*

I would highly recommend a caregiver support group to any person who has stepped in or been thrown into the role of a caregiver. This group literally saved my life and I am eternally grateful to my dear friend Alix.

There were so many things I didn't know about this disease, and I just had to learn, or this landslide would have taken me down more than it already had. This was truly the hardest thing I'd ever been through, and to me it wasn't over yet. Not even close.

My heart was in pieces as I thought of facing the future without Stenmark in it. I knew that absolutely nothing in this life had prepared me for losing him…*nothing. I knew I was heartbent, not badly broken yet, but with a heck of a dent…but heartbreak was coming fast.*

The next morning, I woke up and as I looked over at my sleeping husband, I felt the tears well up. He looked so peaceful as he slept, so sweet and childlike. Almost like an innocent little boy. Stenmark doesn't deserve this as I gently kissed his cheek and thought to myself again *why?*

I got out of bed and forced myself to pull it together. What else could I do? I was already wishing, hoping and praying for a better outcome. I had even began resorting to my superstitions and "woo-woo" beliefs—Stenmark's cute name for the things there were no logical explanations for. I could no longer throw horseshoes over my left shoulder; I was aging and one day I might knock myself out, metaphorically speaking of course!

I still had to use my humor before I lost my own mind. I couldn't have us both going down the drain. Plus, if I didn't laugh, I would surely cry. I had my macular degeneration eye shots later in the afternoon and crying wasn't the best thing for my eyes. I made myself a cup of black coffee and sat down on our leather loveseat. I looked over at Stenmark's empty leather chair and the thought of this being a reality someday was almost more than I could bear.

The thought of losing my life partner, my best friend and my soulmate was in so many ways such a different kind of wound. In the wheel of life, we all lose our parents and as difficult as it is, it's the circle of life.

But this is my lover, my other half, the person I thought I would grow old with, *but not like this*. Stenmark was my life, and every day I had to watch him slip further away from who he was, slowly but surely losing himself to this unfair disease.

I pulled up the soft fleece blanket with the Alzheimer's poem printed on it. The words probably echoed how my sweet hubby feels, but is no longer able to express:

"Don't ask me to remember, don't try to make me understand.
Let me rest and know you're with me,
Kiss my cheek and hold my hand.
I'm confused beyond your concept,
I am sad and sick and lost.
All I know is that I need you,
To be with me at all costs.
Do not lose your patience with me,
Do not scold or curse or cry.
I can't help the way I'm acting,
Can't be different if I try.

Just remember That I need you,
That the best of me is gone,
Please don't fail to stand beside me.
Love me until my life is done."

This was becoming a daily read for me. I couldn't let my own feelings and emotions get the best of me. Stenmark needed me to remember this, even if he didn't realize it. Being a caretaker is so difficult. There are no words to explain just how difficult it is. It's so easy to lose patience, but I had to always remember to pause and take a deep breath before answering or reacting. When I was a young girl, we were visiting my maternal grandmother who was very intuitive and wise. She noticed how impatient I was at age eight. Being a strong Catholic, she called her priest who came over and blessed me and gave me a beautiful glow-in-the-dark rosary. The kind priest also gave me a copy of the prayer for patience he'd blessed me with.

I have always felt it worked because I am usually very patient. But that too was being tested regularly.

I'll be the first to admit it when I have a knee jerk reaction, and I am not proud of it when I do, but I am human.

The feelings I had when it did happen shook me to my core. I loved this man and he can't help it. What is wrong with me? The last thing on earth I would want to do was make my sweet hubby feel bad. He was so good to me and loved me like nobody ever has. I would be so hard on myself, and always would end up in tears. I would think I can't take much more of this. I've always been so compassionate and caring; this is not me. I hung my head and I was ashamed.

Do better, Carly.

CHAPTER 18
Lucky For Me

It was Friday afternoon and I planned for Shelby, (a part time caretaker who filled in when one of the three caretakers couldn't come) to sit with him while I went for my eye shots. My close friend, Dagmar, always takes me for my monthly appointments, because I can't see to drive. Of course, my husband used to take me, but those days are now in the past. I warmed up some pizza leftover from last night's dinner, and once again put the television on his favorite show, *Heartland* and gave him a kiss. Dagmar pulled up right on time as usual, but the caretaker had not arrived yet. I tried calling her, but no answer.

Shelby was like most young people these days. She was not one to be very good about answering her phone and preferred text messaging. I'm sure she was driving at the time, so I chalked it up to that. She was usually very dependable and I knew I could count on her, so I didn't worry too much. I had to get to my appointment, so Dagmar and I left, thinking Shelby would arrive very soon.

Upon arrival at the doctor's office, Dagmar dropped me off and went to run an errand. Today was a shorter appointment, anywhere from a half an hour to forty-five minutes, usually.

I called to check on Stenmark while I was waiting, and he told me Shelby wasn't there yet.

What? I asked him if he was okay.

He said he was fine, just watching *Heartland*.

"Okay, honey call me if you need me. I'll be home in one hour. That's just one episode of *Heartland*," I said, then hung up and said two quick prayers, one for my husband, and one for Shelby. This wasn't like her and I was worried. I sent another quick text to her.

I went in for my shots and it was very quick. I called Dagmar as I made my next appointment at the front desk. I walked out and there she was at the front drop-off and pick up point. I can always tell it's her SUV by the big red U on her front license plate. Do you know how many white SUV's there are in Utah? I'm grateful her son played football for the University of Utah and that she's a fan!

I shared my concern with Dagmar as we drove up the canyon. She told me, "It will be okay, don't buy trouble."

I smiled at her very direct, cut and dry German way. I found her words comforting and reassuring. Dagmar never sugar coated anything, and I loved that. She always made me feel better.

We were just approaching the Park City exit when my phone rang. Siri announced, "Loverboy" was calling. My pet name for Stenmark in my contact info. I answered, "Hi honey, everything okay?"

His voice was shaking as he said, "No, I burned a pan."

I felt my stomach turn and panic started to overcome me. "What do you mean you burned a pan," I asked terrified of knowing the answer, but knew I needed to know it.

Dagmar stared at me in inquiring wonder.

Now, this is a man who *never* touched the stove in twenty-four years. That was one thing he didn't know how to do or chose not to do. I've always enjoyed cooking, so it didn't bother me at all. Besides that, I had child proof knobs ordered specially for the new range. Hell, I could barely figure them out. I knew he only used the microwave, so I assumed he put a pan in the microwave and it was popping and shrieking like metal does in a microwave.

Note to self; one should NEVER assume.

So, I asked, "Is the microwave still on?"

Stenmark answered a quick no.

I then told him to close the microwave door and leave it alone. "I am almost there, and I will deal with it." We were literally around the corner from our house. Thank the Lord.

He asked, "What should I do?"

I said, "Just go sit down and watch TV. I'll be right there. We are out front."

Dagmar asked if I needed help and I said, "No, it's okay. I'm sure it's just a pan in the microwave." I hugged and thanked her as I hopped out and ran up the seventeen stairs to our condo. I opened the door to find Stenmark standing over the stove watching wild eyed as two-foot flames were burning the white plastic cutting board sitting on both right-side burners. They were still turned on as the plastic melted into the two slices of pizza he tried to warm up.

Holy shit!

And that's not all. He had a plastic pitcher filled with water and he was just starting to pour it on the flames as I yelled, "Honey, no!"

He pulled the pitcher up quickly, but not before a few drops landed on the flames, which shot up higher as the plastic cutting board was popping like a firecracker. I ran to the pantry and grabbed my large Tupperware container of baking soda that I just so happened to fill early that morning! I threw the lid off and dumped the baking soda all over the shooting flames until they were doused. It was such a huge mess, but at least it was out, and my husband was safe and unharmed. I couldn't say the same for the brand-new Jenn-Aire gas range. I just left the whole mess sitting there until the next morning.

Frankly, I just couldn't deal with it tonight and of course I couldn't see.

I got up the next morning and began to clean up the mess. I replayed yesterday over in my mind.

Then I called Shelby. She didn't answer, so I sent her a text asking if she was okay.

I got a "yes" back via text and that was it.

Do I really have to pull this out of her? Guess so.

"What happened yesterday," I wrote.

"What do you mean," she texted back. *Seriously?*

"You never showed up," I wrote.

"Oh, I forgot. Sorry."

That was it! Then that was *really* it. I knew what I had to do. This was simply too much for my hired babysitters.

So, I just went back to cleaning up, thinking that was not money well spent on the child proof knobs. I never texted Shelby again and she never texted me either. I wondered if I should have told her what happened, but then I thought is it really my job to school her? I decided to just let it go. Plus, that was just one more fucking thing. I was so frustrated.

I turned on the stove only to find those two burners would not light.

I looked and discovered all the little holes were plugged with plastic. How do I resolve this problem? I guess the only thing to do was to order a new right side. I began searching the Jenn-Aire site and discovered they had replacement burners. *Yay!*

However, they were four hundred dollars and did not have them in stock. Then due to "supply chain issues" (which was common during the pandemic) they were backordered and no date as to when they would be in. *Boo!*

I had a handyman friend who told me he could probably blow all the dried plastic out with a blow torch. He came over and picked up the burners and returned them to me the very next day all cleaned up. I gave him a hundred dollars, cancelled my backorder through Jenn-Aire and called it a day, another fucking day.

The range worked perfectly, thanks to my handy man friend.

Funny thing not once did Stenmark ask about it. It was as if it never happened. He completely forgot about all of it.

By then, I'd pretty much stopped being surprised at these things. I was becoming angrier at the disease. It was just another hard smack right in the face.

♡♡♡♡♡

I thought about my life with Stenmark, caring for him at home. He was getting worse, even though it was just a little over a year from diagnosis. As of late, I felt we had dodged a few bullets. One, when he was walking down the middle of the highway; one when the caretaker lost him in Walmart; and now this last event, the fire. I thought if the fire had been more serious, I have elderly neighbors on each side of me. *What if? What if? What if?*

It was clear that I couldn't leave him in the hands of the untrained caretakers I had coming in the three days a week while I worked. There was an upside to placing him in a facility: I could work more, go back to five or even six days a week, which I would probably have to due to the cost of suitable places. I would need to investigate these things, find out how it all works. My siblings and I had put my dad on Medicaid when the time came for him to go into a skilled nursing facility after my mom passed away. That was a possibility, after all we are not wealthy. I don't know…

But I realized what needed to be done. It was crystal clear; I didn't have a choice now. It was too hard to depend on untrained caretakers as his disease progressed and took more and more of him. It was becoming too hard even for me. I sent out a group text letting them know and reiterated how beyond grateful I was to all of them. They were here for me and my husband in every way that they could be.

I didn't want to put my sweet husband somewhere else. The thought made me feel so much guilt. I loved him so much and I was so torn. Is there another way? Perhaps a different solution? I racked my brain with other options or solutions, but there were none. I had to figure this out myself before anything else happened. I can just hear it now, "You left your husband with Alzheimer's disease alone for over two hours while you went to Salt Lake City?" Lucky for me, my eye doctor was on time and Dagmar was a rockstar getting me home.

Not to mention that he was a danger to himself and to others. The HOA probably wouldn't want to pay for any damage caused, there could be lawsuits or worse yet…funerals. It was no longer safe for us, and it was now time for me to think about the dreaded next step. A care facility was in our near future as much as I wanted to keep him here with me, it no longer would work. More guilt began to set in.

My heart ached at the thought of living without my sweet man. I knew the days would not be as difficult as the long, lonely nights staring at the other side of our empty king-sized bed.

CHAPTER 19
Warm Place to Hide

These thoughts consumed me for the next few days, but I watched him like a hawk. It was now a golf day for us and I made up my mind to enjoy this time with my hubby. We decided to play eighteen holes of golf and then go out for dinner. We arrived at the golf course forty-five minutes before our tee time. *Got to practice before we tee off, you know.*

That was something he never forgot, and I found that a very interesting part of this disease. Some things stayed while some things left. There was no rhyme or reason whatsoever.

Once we were out on the golf course, it quickly became more interesting. I let him drive the golf cart and he did just fine. I just couldn't take everything away from him, so when he hopped in the drivers side, I was silent. After a couple of holes, we teed off on number three. I had a decent enough hit, and Stenmark's hit was more than decent enough.

It was out of sight, but in a good way. As he drove along the beautifully well-maintained fairway, he passed my ball. Now this was not all that unusual.

Often when I play golf with not only Stenmark, but other men, it's like they have "tunnel vision" and can only see their ball. They often pass mine up and I must remind them that I want to play too. That was the case again today. Stenmark turned the cart around and began to drive towards my bright greenish yellow golf ball.

This was an ocular color I was told by my eye doctor. Stenmark leaned down and picked up my ball and handed it to me. Without taking it from him, I said, "Well, I need to hit it, Babe." He looked at my ball, then at me and in a very strange and puzzling way he said, "Oh! You want to hit *this* ball, well okay," he said as he threw it about ten feet back in the fairway.

Now, this is not at all like my husband. He is by the book when it comes to golf. He knows the rules inside and out. *And there are no gimmes, either.*

I stared at him not believing what I'd just witnessed. He's just messing around I thought. Then I thought, why are you surprised, Carly?

I got out of the golf cart and was about to grab my three-wood club, when I asked him half-jokingly, "Why are you acting so goofy, Babe?"

He didn't answer, or even look back at me, he just drove off. *That's weird.*

Normally, my golf pro hubby would watch my shot, and if it was a decent shot, he would say, "Bet you'd take that one, wouldn't you?"

Then if it wasn't decent, he would ask if I wanted to know what I did or throw out another ball and tell me to do it over again, but he watched and *always* counted it.

There was none of that this day and it was clear to me this part was now gone, too.

We barely finished nine holes and it was painful. So much so that we stopped there. My poor hubby had no idea. He didn't even realize we were stopping early. Stenmark would always tell me, "It's an eighteen-hole game, Bennett." That certainly wasn't the case that day.

But interestingly, he could still teach golf to his loyal fans! Of course, they'd text him and he would show it to me, because they knew I would have to drive him back and forth. Often,

Vaughn would need him to run golf carts for him and then he would offer to bring him home. I know there will be a special place in heaven for that man.

Monday came quickly and it was fast approaching three o'clock. I put on Stenmark's favorite show, *Heartland*, put in my air pods to tune into my therapy session via Zoom. I sat on the bed as we all took turns talking about our week. It was my turn, so tearfully I told the "fire story."

Our facilitator, Rosemary, sympathized as I told her I probably need to start thinking about a place for Stenmark.

I couldn't even believe those words were coming out of my mouth. Was I really going to *abandon* my wonderful husband? Even though I knew it wasn't abandonment, it still felt like it. What else is there for me to do? What else can I do? There must be something else, some other way, something! The mere thought of it totally wrecked me and I broke down and cried like a baby. Right in front of my entire support group.

Rosemary consoled me as best she could, telling me how hard it is, but she had a woman who worked for Salt Lake Aging Services that would help me find the perfect place for him. I called her the next morning, and she assured me I was doing the right thing, not only for Stenmark, but for both of us. I was in a fog as she made mention of making appointments for me to see these places in a couple of days.

Dear God, is this really happening?

The woman Rosemary referred me to was Alicia, and she was wonderful. She had five places we would see and could I meet her at ten o'clock.

Yes, was my answer. I texted McLane and Retta and I asked if they could watch him for about three or four hours, telling them the reason. They were happy to help, and I was very grateful. I dropped him off and of course, he was so happy to see his son.

The first place was in Sandy, Utah, just about fifteen minutes from his son. My children were all in that area as well, so that was a huge plus. The place was clean and smelled nice, which isn't usually the case in those places. It also had been recently carpeted and nice new leather furniture dressed up the social area. I was shown the room that was ready for him to move in. It was a double room and even though it was empty, I was told that he would eventually have a roommate.

I honestly didn't love that idea and I knew Stenmark wouldn't either, at least *normal Stenmark* wouldn't want that at all. Then I met Casey, the director and he was friendly and kind. I liked him instantly. He introduced me to the head nurse; Liz and she was the same way. That really made an impact, coupled with the fact that it was only a memory care facility. The skilled nursing facility was a separate facility across the street, and I considered that another plus.

I was given all the imperative information, and we were onto place number two. This one was closer to his son, but it wasn't as warm and cozy feeling. In fact, the person we had the appointment with was nowhere to be found so a handyman showed us around. He knocked on the door of a resident, and asked if we could see her room.

The frail woman smiled sweetly as she walked out of her room without uttering a single word. I was told by the handyman this is what his room would look like. It was nice enough, but no carpeting, just hard, cold but beautiful Mexican tile. I envisioned Stenmark falling and cracking his head open on it while frantically searching for a warm place to hide. That thought scared the hell out of me. I was disenchanted with the staff. There were no smiles or even hellos as we walked past. I also didn't like that the memory care was mixed in with the skilled nursing care people. That bothered me but we would let the handyman finish our tour.

There were shadow boxes next to the doors, on the wall of each entrance to the rooms. I was told the staff made them for all the residents. All I needed to do was bring in the memorabilia. That was nice, but I'd read that memory care people were very fidgety and liked to mess with things. I thought and wondered to myself how long that would last on the wall. And not just his shadow box, but everyone else's too!

I realized relatively quick that this place was a hard no.

The next place was out in South Jordan, so I threw the flag on it being too far away from not just me, but everyone else. My thoughts kept going back to Alta Ridge Memory Care in Sandy. As hard as this decision was going to be, I had a good feeling about Stenmark being there. Alicia had two more places left, so I told her how much I liked Alta Ridge and she completely agreed with me. It was her favorite as well and said it was no problem for her to cancel the others, which is exactly what she did.

We drove back to Alta Ridge and told Casey, the director the news. He was happy about our decision and started the paperwork. I gave him the deposit on the room and paid for the remainder of September and October. It was then I found out that the guidelines had changed since my dad was in care eight years ago.

I had to pay out of pocket for the first year, then Medicaid would start October of 2022. I was assured by Alicia that was the norm everywhere these days. But damn, that sucks. *Shit! Shit! Shit!*

I felt I had no choice, and this was a nice place and right in line with the other places as far as monthly rent goes. "Yes, there were other places," said Alicia, "I wouldn't put my dog in any of them, not to be rude, but I feel you deserve the truth."

I was thankful for that, but knew I had to put my husband in a nice place. Stenmark didn't deserve this awful disease, but this is where we are now and dammit, he deserved to live in a nice, clean place. A place where the staff was kind and friendly. I felt they would take good care of him and I would not settle for anything less.

We set up a time the following Monday for Casey, the director, and Liz, the nurse to come to the house and do an evaluation and meet Stenmark. I suppose they must make sure people aren't just wanting to send their person off somewhere else, just to get rid them. I'm just being silly. Humor is still a very close friend of mine, but after doing nails for over forty years there are some women willing to do whatever it takes to get rid of their husbands, trust me.

I had five days to break the news to my husband. I played out several scenarios in my mind, trying to figure which one was the best way to tell my kind, sweet, and wonderfully intelligent man that he was going into a care facility. I was nervous as hell about it and my stomach was in knots. It was something I couldn't put off and Monday was fast approaching.

I knew I had to find the right time, but truly is there ever a right time for bad news? Of course not.

I had a lot of time to think about it as I was driving Stenmark to his son and ex-wife's house on Saturday and Sunday morning. I had to furnish and get his room ready. It was to be set up as if he was moving into an apartment without a kitchen. My children and my adult grandchildren helped me, and I needed their support. I don't think they knew just how much. They have always seen me as an independent and strong woman through their entire lives, and they were used to that.

But now... now was very different. I was barely keeping my head above water, as I tried to deal with the hardest thing that has ever been thrown at me. Plus, I still needed to talk to Stenmark about it. Prayer has now sped past humor as my best buddy. On the way home, we stopped at Meir's Chicken to pick up dinner. I think deep down I was hoping to get his favorite meal, open a bottle of Chardonnay and get the ball rolling with a conversation I was dreading.

The evening was going well as we finished our meal and retired to the leather love seat in the living room. But no television until I got through this. I didn't want him distracted.

"So, honey." I said as I put my hand on his thigh. He responded with his usual, "Yes, dear heart." *Ohhhhh this is not going to be easy.* Those words melted my heart every time as they were always said with such pure love. I'd replayed this conversation over and over in my brain and although I was nervous, I thought I was ready. But I was wrong. I took a deep breath and suddenly my well-practiced and polished words came flying out tumbling across my lips and I said something I'd never rehearsed, "Honey, did you like being in that study?" *What the hell, Carly, where did that come from?*

CHAPTER 20
Cheating Was Part of the Game

This wasn't any part of my speech. I thought I had it memorized, I'd rehearsed it over and over. Stenmark looked at me and answered, "Yeah, I guess." But he didn't ask me why, so I quickly continued. "Well, they have another study at a different place. Some people are coming over to talk to us about it in the morning. Are you okay with that?"

The words flowed and there was no stopping them now. I had to be ready and willing to play along.

This was an out and out lie, but Rosemary had taught us in our support group that these types of lies were called "love lies" and that was okay. I didn't know if that was true, but I went with it. I still felt like I was playing a game somehow where cheating was a huge part of it.

It didn't feel good to me at all. Stenmark answered, "Sure, it wasn't that bad and if it can help somebody, of course I will do it again." I was happy with that answer, but I wasn't surprised.

Stenmark was always about helping others. One of the many things I loved about this music man of mine. I smiled and gave him a tender kiss as I thanked him. I turned on *Heartland* and I fell asleep in his arms, which was always my favorite place to be in the entire world.

Monday morning, I sent Casey a heads up about my love lie. I'm banking on that being okay under the circumstances when I get up to the Pearly Gates to meet St. Peter!

The doorbell rang promptly at ten o'clock. I opened the door while Stenmark stood behind me.

"Hi guys, come on in," I said cheerfully. I turned to Stenmark and began to introduce him to Casey when out of the blue my husband said, "Hey buddy, how have you been?" That question was returned with a very quick, "Ken!" from Casey. My eyes felt like they were going to pop out of my head as I stared at both as they shook hands.

"You guys *know* each other," I exclaimed, still in shock. Stenmark replied with his usual.

"Sure."

Then Casey said, "Ken was my boss at the Canyons for the three years when he was a supervisor there." He went on to say, "He was our favorite. We all hoped we would get on his team every morning. He was the best supervisor. He approached us with such compassion and kindness. If we made a mistake, there was no yelling or scolding. It was always, 'what could we have done to handle that differently?'"

Then Casey looked at me and said, "I didn't put it together, Carly. I had no idea. I'm so sorry." The look on his face and the tears in his eyes said it all. He knew my sweet husband when he was at his very best and he was about to get to know him now that he wasn't, and that was heartbreaking to all of us.

It was no surprise that he "passed" the evaluation with flying colors. At one point he asked Casey, "When does this study start?" *Thank God, I gave them a heads up.*

Casey replied, "You will come to the facility next Monday." Stenmark shook his head and said, "Okay." Casey didn't lie and he just went along as he looked at me with a sympathetic smile.

Stenmark was happy to know that Liz, the nurse, was originally from Minnesota. He began speaking like a Minnesotan, saying to her, "Ah, sure, *dern tootin.*" That lightened the mood at our kitchen table.

Stenmark was always proud of the fact he was born and raised in Minneapolis and loved that he was Swedish.

"I'm a *Svenska Poika*," he used to say. *Swedish boy;* even naming the internet in our homes, even this new place *Svenska Poika*.

Stenmark never forgot his heritage and I found that not only interesting, but also very endearing. The things that leave the brain and the things that stay are mind boggling.

Anyway, the wheels were in motion now. We said our goodbyes and about an hour later, I received a text from Casey that read, "Carly, we have moved Ken's things into room number one, the gentleman's suite, and it is a single one-person room. Normally it is one thousand dollars more per month, but I am keeping it at the same rate I quoted you and it will remain at that rate until you get him on Medicaid, October 1, 2022. It will show as a 'promotional credit' on your statement each month."

Is this cheating or just part of the game.

I couldn't believe my eyes. I knew Stenmark would be so happy to have his own room and bathroom. I was not only thrilled, but I was also so grateful to Casey. I was so proud of my husband. He made an impact when he worked with Casey. What Stenmark did and said mattered and I knew it. My husband was such a rock star!

Now the real work began. I had one week to set up his "apartment." McLane and Retta were a huge help to me during this time. I would drop Stenmark off in the morning and work all day getting his room ready. I made it look as if he was walking into our bedroom and his private bathroom, right down to the pictures on the wall. For the first time in almost twenty-five years, I even set up his television. I also brought in his favorite blue Washburn acoustic guitar and hung it on the wall. Right where he could see it.

I set up his bathroom with all his personal items, his electric razor, electric toothbrush, the towels he picked out last year from Costco which were his favorite. All his familiar things. I needed to make sure my sweet hubby felt *at home* in his new home.

A home he will probably never leave. That was the harsh reality of this new "study," unlike the last one that ended thirty days later, this was his home until it wasn't. We all know what that means without speaking the words. This was no longer a hard smack in the face, this was another hard gut punch. Thinking of that reality truly took my breath away. Monday morning, we were to be there at ten o'clock. That seems to be the magic time everyone chooses for some reason, but we were driving down from Park City so that was just fine with me.

Upon arrival, the handful of residents were in the social room which was a big room with a big screen television mounted on the wall, a DVD player, record player, and lots of things to keep everyone busy.

It was then I was introduced to an angel.

His name was Phil, and he was the activity director for the care facility. I'm not kidding when I say he was heaven sent. This man was amazing. Not only could he play the guitar, piano, and a variety of other instruments, he could sing as well. But one of his many talents and strengths was the ability to connect with the memory challenged souls. Phil just knew what to say and do in any situation that would arise.

Such a gift. He genuinely loved these people, and they loved him. It was so clear, crystal clear. Stenmark sat in a chair with his guitar at a large table next to Phil, who was seated at the piano, and they began to jam together for the residents. I knew by the intro what song it was, *Freebird* by Lynyrd Skynyrd.

Isn't that ironic? *If I leave here tomorrow....* I couldn't stop the tears. Music is so moving and is probably the one thing I need now and will always need in my life.

I watched as my sweet husband stopped playing his guitar and pointed at the shoes of Ralph, one of the residents there. Stenmark always had a hankering for shoes. The last golf trip we took to Mesquite, when I knew something wasn't right in his brain, he brought along twenty-three pairs of shoes. In the evening while we watched television, he would bring them all out and sit them on the floor in front of him and proceed to try them on. He would mess with the shoelaces, pull out the inserts and switch them to other shoes repeatedly. I sat there and watched. What goes on in the Alzheimer's brain? What was he thinking? I had no answers, I just let him do it.

A couple of hours later, it was lunch time at Stenmark's living facility. The plan was I'd spend the first day there with him, and then leave without him before dark. Because of my poor night vision, I no longer drive at night, except where I am completely familiar, like around Park City. I've been driving around this small ski resort town for over forty years, so yes, it is very familiar to me.

Lunch was served by a very friendly, bubbly Asian woman named Lee, and of course Phil helped get everyone seated and ready. We sat at a table consisting of all men. Ralph was one, Tony was another, and finally another man named "Princess." I learned something about each of them from the angelic Phil.

Ralph was the great grandfather of the head nurse, Emily who was a wonderful, kind and thoughtful person. She was sensitive to not only her great grandfather's needs, but everyone else, as well, in the facility. Ralph was such an intelligent man with a heart of gold, and big friendly smile. Plus, he was a huge golfer. He once told me, "Never trust a golfer with an eraser on his pencil." That made me chuckle.

Heart Get Ready

Those golf days were in the past for Ralph, as he was now in a wheelchair, but he still loved talking about it. Once I found out he loved golf, I started bringing in Stenmark's Golf Digest magazines (that still arrived in the mail monthly) for Ralph to read; after the hubby was finished with them, of course.

Ralph seemed to enjoy the magazines, and he did read them. I don't think he was as far into the world of dementia as Stenmark was. He was probably there because of Emily. I could carry on a normal conversation with him. He reminded me of my dad; just a sweet big teddy bear who wanted everything quiet and peaceful.

Now Tony was a different story. He was a physically healthy, rather tall man, who wasn't overly friendly. Originally, he was to be Stenmark's roommate once they got to know each other and became friends. Well, that never would have worked out, as Tony didn't like my husband right from the start for whatever reason. It was plain as day.

Last but certainly not least was "Princess," a very flamboyant cross dresser. He was a small man in a wheelchair with long blonde hair and not a tooth in his mouth. His shirts were all cut off midriff style and he loved his "things." He had hair clips and ties, make up and his special comb all that tucked into a small purse he carried on his lap as he wheeled around. He became very angry if anything was missing. He would shout out obscenities and want to know who took his stuff.

I have to say, lunch was delicious. I gave the chef the heads up on the three things that Stenmark did not like: fish, eggs, and cheese. And she abided by that at every meal. After lunch, we all made our way back into the social area, and it was completely decorated with balloons and a huge sign that read, "WELCOME STENNY!" It was all very welcoming and made me confident I had chosen the right place. Stenmark had been asked what name he preferred at the evaluation, Stenmark,

Kenneth, Kenny, or Ken? He answered with, "Stenny," the name he was called at the golf course, so Stenny it was.

We were then surprised with a beautiful homemade chocolate cake from the chef. Stenny's favorite. I thought that was such a nice touch.

I stayed until a movie was put on for the residents to enjoy. I remember that was *West Side Story*.

My thoughts drifted back fifteen years prior, when Stenmark was in *The Park City Follies*, an annual, local, live performance variety show that lampooned the culture of Park City. That year, they did a spoof on the East and West side of Park City, and who inhabited which area. Stenmark was a "Jet" in the comedy sketch that year, *and I chuckled thinking Park City has good and bad sides of town? If only…*

CHAPTER 21
Never Blue

We were only part way through the movie when most of the residents fell asleep. However, Stenny was wide awake. As he and Phil talked about music, we learned that Phil was in a band which didn't surprise me, he was a very good musician. My ever-so-humble hubby didn't mention his background in music, so I did! I was extremely proud of my music man and his many, many musical accomplishments and told Phil I would bring in a CD of his music next week.

As part of Stenmark's transition process, I was not to come and visit for a week. I was sad that I was leaving him there and he wouldn't see me for that first week. What will he think? What if he thinks that I have left him for good? Or for an Uber driver? (Like he thought before.) I didn't want to agree to a week of absence, but I resigned myself to the fact that they knew better. I know the plan was for him to get used to his new surroundings without me. However, he could use his cell phone so that was a plus.

But they kept him so busy all day long he didn't have much of a chance to talk on the phone, at least during the day. Which meant he had time to call me only at night. I have to say, those two, three, and four am phone calls weren't conducive to a good night's sleep, for either of us. But I always answered and talked to him for however long he wanted. I knew deep down the day would come when I would miss them.

The week dragged by. Phil gave me his cell phone number and I promised not to abuse the privilege of being trusted with it. Even so, I texted Phil every other day just to ask how Stenny was doing. But often Phil would text me first, and I would get a video of Stenmark participating in dancing, playing ball, or even just saying he loved me. These kind gestures kept me going until I could spend time with Stenmark in person. I missed my sweet husband so much. *We were so connected; I felt like I was missing a limb, which would have probably been easier.*

I truly couldn't wait for Monday to come. This was the longest we had ever been away from one another. When he was in the thirty-day study, I was down there all the time, as required in the guidelines, so this was new to me.

When the time finally came that I could see Stenmark, I was so excited. On the drive down, I had my happy music on turned up loud. When I walked into the lobby, I was greeted by Emily. "We just love Stenny!" she exclaimed; he is so funny."

I agreed with sweet Emily. He had the best sense of humor. I thanked her as I entered the code to the locked door that opened into the social room.

Stenny saw me and stood up to greet me.

I smiled and said, "Hi honey!" I stood on my tip toes and threw my arms around his neck. I stand a good five-foot-eight, but Stenny is six foot three, so I needed tippy toes to be face-to-face with him, or as we preferred, lip-to-lip.

Stenmark picked me up and twirled me around, held me up to his face, and kissed me smack dab on the lips. Although, he never verbally expressed how much he missed me unless I asked him, his actions spoke louder than words, and I'd like to think he missed me. We sat down on a leather couch and as people walked by, Stenny would introduce me. "This is my wife, Carly, but I call her Bennett." He couldn't remember their names and sometimes they couldn't either, but I soon got to know all of them by name. It was easy considering there were only sixteen residents.

I would always make sure I included them in every conversation, asking them questions and complimenting them on their hair or attire. There was a salon in the facility and a hairdresser came weekly and kept up their appearances. I cut Stenny's hair so there was no need for him to use that service, but he could if he wanted to. It was all included in the $3,400 monthly fee, and so were the Monday and Wednesday field trips that Phil took them on. They went on picnics, went to get ice cream, or just simply drove around checking out various places in Salt Lake City.

After I'd been there for a couple of hours, it was time for lunch. As we walked over to the men's table, we were redirected to a table located behind the men's table. There were three women sitting there, Jackie, Ava, LaMonte and an empty chair for Stenny. I had to laugh to myself. My husband had been moved to the women's table, which was comical because he was always better with women than men. That's why he oversaw the Women's Nine Hole Golf League in Park City for over twenty years. He loved all those golf women, and the feeling was mutual. Yes, Stenny was in fact a ladies' man and now he was in seventh heaven at this lunch table. He loved it and so far, was happy at this facility. I was relieved, because that was the goal.

Eventually I got to know all of Stenmark's lunch ladies. Jackie was an Asian woman who was very soft spoken and kind. It scared her when Princess or anyone else was upset and vocal about it. If any of the residents got into what I like to call a "dust-up" she would shake her head in disgust. She had also been a concert pianist when she was *normal* Jackie.

Then there was Ava, a beautiful and kind Hispanic woman who owned a very popular Mexican restaurant in Salt Lake

City. She was always "done up" as my mother used to say. I never saw her without makeup including a beautiful shade of red lipstick. Her dark hair was always up in a chignon-like bun, and she dressed in very stylish clothing. When I met her, she only spoke Spanish. I could understand a little, but fortunately we had a young Hispanic male nurse who would translate.

Finally, there was LaMonte. She was an attractive petite woman. She informed me that her name meant mountain in French, and she could never understand why her parents would name her *Mountain*. "There must have been something wrong with them," she told me. LaMonte was a friendly sweet woman; that is, until she wasn't.

A couple of months after Stenny arrived, she got it in her head that he was her husband. And after that, life there with LaMonte would never be the same. There was incident after incident with her. The first time I experienced the wrath of LaMonte was one afternoon when I was visiting my husband. We were sitting on the leather couch, and I was showing him pictures of our kitties, Newbie and Lola when LaMonte walked over with Jackie and stood in front of us.

"What are you guys doing," asked Lamonte. I detected a bit of anger in her voice, which was out of character.

Stenny just stared at her, and I responded happily to her. "We are just looking at pictures of our cats. Do you want to see?"

I'd come across a picture of Stenny's cat Lola, who was standing on her hind legs like a lemur. "LaMonte, look how cute Stenny's kitty is. Look how she is standing up." I turned my cell phone towards her and Jackie. LaMonte frowned and said in a snarky way, "That's nothing, they all do that." She rolled her eyes at me. Jackie just stood there not saying a word. I guess she was moral support for LaMonte.

I tried to bring LaMonte back to liking me when I said, "She is a cute kitty, isn't she?"

She replied again in a rude tone, "Well, you're the worst kitty of all, you trollop."

Trollop? I hadn't heard that word in a very long time!

Then she tried to kick me on the leg, but my reflexes are still pretty good.

She missed. Then she took a swing at me, missed again, leaned down and tried to bite me. Even Ken's ex-wife wasn't violent with me, and she had a good reason to be. (Just adding a little levity to the sad situation.)

Time to get a nurse before she hurts someone or herself.

The next time I went in, all was thankfully forgotten, but it didn't stay that way. These situations are sad, and I knew she didn't know what she was doing. Afterall, Stenny was the best-looking man in the place. I would have picked him too! Anyway, a few days later when I went to visit, we were on the leather couch and LaMonte walked over. I patted the other side of the couch and asked her if she would like to join us. It changed her whole being, she smiled and sat on the other side of Stenny. She held his left hand, and I held his right and that worked; until it didn't.

It was Stenny's first Christmas in the care facility and he had been in care for three months. My daughter, Megan purchased a small Christmas tree and brought it in fully decorated. The facility had a nice Christmas party a few days before Christmas, complete with Santa handing out wrapped gifts we each purchased for our resident. Stenny's gift was a pair of UGG leather slippers. He had a pair that were worn, so these new ones would be something useful that I knew he would really like.

Unfortunately, nothing really seemed to excite Stenny these days. It was as if he was just along for the ride. But he was happy there, not once did he ever ask to come home. Not like when he was in the study.

Our anniversary was two weeks before Stenmark went into the care facility. At the time, a close friend of mine, Lynn Stith, who was a brilliant photographer, offered to come take some pictures of us in various places around Park City. She had been the professional photographer at our wedding, so it was only fitting she captured us again sixteen years later. The pictures turned out beautifully. I had one made into an eighteen-by-twenty-four size canvas portrait to hang on Stenny's wall in his room. I wrapped it up in Christmas paper and drove down that snowy Christmas morning. Funny, when I walked in, he was sitting right next to Tony on the end of the long leather couch. You know like little kids do. It was sweet and touched my heart. I thought they disliked each other, so this was good to see. *Merry Christmas to me.*

I handed Stenny his present, kissed him and told him, "Merry Christmas, Babe." He looked at me and asked, "Is it Christmas?" as he carefully began to unwrap my gift to him.

"Yes, it is," I said.

"But I didn't get you a present," Stenny said with a look of sadness in his eyes.

I rubbed his leg and said, "This is my present, just being here with you."

Then he made a funny face like he used to when I said something that he thought was corny. Often, he would say or do something that was "so him" and this was one of those times. *He was still in there...somewhere.*

I think Tony grew tired of watching him slowly unwrap his present, because he reached over and started to tear the wrapping paper off. Stenny didn't mind, he just watched him until it was completely off. Then Stenny stared at the picture, and I asked him if he liked it. "You are so beautiful, Bennett, but who is that you're with?"

I was surprised, so I said, thinking he was being silly and teasing me, "Honey... that's you."

He furrowed his brow and said indignantly, "That's not me."

Then I made the number one mistake and big no-no in the Alzheimer's handbook. I argued with him, acting like I knew better. "Yes, it is you, Babe. That's our anniversary picture that Lynn took, remember?" Oh, shoot another big no-no. Don't ever say "remember" to them. Carly, you *do* know better.

Well, he went off. The picture was mainly of our chests on up and the light was reflecting off Stenny's balding head, (he always hated losing his hair.) I noticed it when I received the canvas print. It was not that way in the original photograph at all.

I got the wrath of Stenny, "That shiny, bald-headed motherfucker is not me, Bennett! Have you gone crazy? What the hell is the matter with you?"

Pardon my French, but that's what he said verbatim, and changing the verbiage just doesn't have the same impact. I was in disbelief once again, so I just said softly, "Okay, honey."

Then he looked down at the picture again and said, "I don't know who that is with you, but I really like his shirt." You see, that was Stenny's favorite shirt.

❦ ❦ ❦ ❦ ❦

I brought it in the next day and his response was for me to tell my new boyfriend "Thanks," which made me so sad that I chose to ignore his comment. But my mind drifted back to his song, *"I promise you, never blue."*

I beg to differ, Stenmark.

CHAPTER 22
Loving You is the Only Place to Start

The next day when I came back to Stenmark's new home, I brought in a ring that was in his safe and was given to him by Patti, his first love, his high school and college girlfriend. I had it on my thumb and I asked him if I could try his ring on. His nice, engraved platinum wedding ring. He took it off and handed it to me. I handed him the one I was wearing. I watched as he put on the ring from Patti and we went about our day at the facility. Stenmark never mentioned it again, but a few weeks later it went missing, and I was so happy we had traded. I would have been heartbroken if it was his real ring, but this was one I didn't care about losing. That wasn't the only thing that went missing. I was constantly asking the staff about his belongings. I remember this being a common occurrence at my dad's facility.

It was then I decided to bring home his blue Washburn guitar that he played when he was on stage in front of twenty-thousand people. Yes, he was a real music man, a real musician. I was told by Phil that he really didn't play the Washburn anymore. I swapped it with his travel guitar, a small but very nice guitar, and he never mentioned the expensive Washburn. Stenny never skimped on much, particularly his music equipment. It was all top of the line, best of the best. I get it, that was his business. I didn't get where I was in my business by using cheap-ass stuff, either.

We were now approaching Spring in Utah. I had really started to find my own spirituality through this journey, which I'm told is not uncommon. Stenny was a Lutheran and proud of it, and I am LDS. The care facility had Sunday services at ten-thirty in the morning, so I started making a point of being there so we could attend together. Stenny was already up, dressed and had his breakfast when I arrived.

The days rolled by one after the other as I continued to drive the canyon from Park City to Sandy, Utah to see my husband in this expensive new home. I am so thankful to my friend, Nancy, who started a GoFundMe account to help pay the expenses that first year. I was really embarrassed when she suggested it, and I said, "No, I can't do it, Nance."

"Well then, how are you going to do it, Carly. Your friends love you and Sting (her pet name for Stenmark). They want to help you. Please let me just write something up."

It took more than a ton of persuading to talk me into it, but she was right.

I realized I couldn't do it without help that first year. This damn disease. It ruins people's lives, their relationships, and their bank accounts. I didn't have the forty plus thousand dollars needed for that first year, and it wasn't safe or feasible to care for him at home. Nancy was right, as usual, I had no choice. That's what happens when you're close friends with the smartest woman in Park City. That was a long-standing joke between the two of us. We would laugh and joke, but there's always some truth in humor. That's what makes it funny.

I lived in the mother-in-law apartment above Nancy and Barry (soon-to-be husband's) house for about five years. They were the first to meet Kenny, or as they both called him "Sting."

He did resemble the talented, good looking former member of The Police, so the nickname stuck all these years later.

When we attended their wedding, and the reception began, we walked over to the happy couple to congratulate them. I asked Barry, "How does it feel to be married to the smartest woman in Park City?" Nancy laughed and Barry answered, "It feels pretty damn good."

That was almost twenty-five years ago and they are still happy together.

Nancy did as she promised. She wrote up something that was beautiful and heartfelt with a picture of Stenmark and me.

In fact, it was the canvas picture I gave him for Christmas, without the shiny bald head. I opened a separate bank account for the donations to be automatically deposited in from the GoFundMe. I was so grateful as they started to roll in at a rapid rate. I even had two anonymous donations, one for ten thousand dollars and the other for eight thousand. Those saved me for sure and I wished I knew who they were so I could properly thank them both. It was now July and I started the fun process of completing the Medicaid application.

♡♡♡♡♡

The large anonymous donations came in right after Vaughn, the manager of the golf course and Kenny's close friend, sent out an email to the entire men and women's golf league, calling Stenny a huge part of the golf family with a plea to help and included the link to the GoFundMe account. Nancy instructed me not ask her the names of the anonymous donors so I didn't. I was just so touched by the generosity of everyone who donated.

The amounts went from ten dollars and up. I was so thankful because it meant just how deeply we were loved and thought of, especially Stenny. The amount didn't matter, it all added up and helped me more than I can say.

But I was also beyond grateful, and it made me smile to know how deeply Stenny had touched all these wonderful people, in one way or another. He was just that kind of man, and everybody loved him—except Tony in the facility. Thank God, Tony was not the violent type, as he stood six foot five and was in excellent shape.

It was still so apparent that Tony didn't like Stenny, so I was happy he was not violent, as my once big, tall healthy husband was becoming a mere shell of what he used to be. Stenny was rapidly losing weight, even though he was eating. I brought him lots of treats and told everyone else to do the same. Especially after I found out, he was going into the other residents' rooms and eating their treats.

But back to Tony.

One day I watched as my sweet husband tried his hardest to talk to Tony, making jokes, being his usual comedic self. He reminded me of the boy wanting friends so badly that he would give them his lunch money. We have all known a child like that, I'm sure. Tony would just walk off and sit somewhere else. It was heartbreakingly sad. I almost cried when I witnessed these attempts. This was so hard on my heart.

I would always run to Stenmark, kiss him and tell him I loved him before Tony could hurt his feelings by rejecting him once again…I loved my sweet man and that was the only place to start. *But, oh my poor heart.*

One day I went into the facility and there were Stenny and Tony walking around with the nurses' clipboards in hand. They were talking to the other residents and jotting down their nonsensical "word salad".

It was then that I found out *normal* Tony was a physician.

The one thing about this disease is, it does not discriminate. Then here was Stenny who had his master's in psychology and worked in a care facility out of college in Minnesota for a couple of years, and after moving to Salt Lake City to ski, he enrolled as a law student at the University of Utah. He also worked in the Psyche Ward at LDS Hospital when it wasn't snowing.

It was kind of amusing that he thought he worked in the care facility. Our close friends, Mark, Genevieve and Donna, often went to visit him, which McLane and Retta also visited, as did all my kids and grandkids. But the first time that Mark, Genevieve and Donna went in, Stenmark told them I lived in Park City, and he lived and worked there now. But just until this job was finished.

He never asked when the study would be over, when he would go home, or anything remotely resembling him leaving. I think that made it easier for me, even though I missed my husband terribly. So much so, I cried every single night as I longed for him to be "normal Kenny" and I prayed this nightmare wasn't true. I would have these dreams that I would walk into the facility the next morning and I was there to pick him up because he was "cured." But upon waking up and realizing it was only a dream; I would cry my heart out.

This morning I walked in, greeted by a somber Emily.

"What's wrong, sweetie," I asked in my own sympathetic way.

"Tony passed away yesterday," she said tearfully. I could hardly believe my ears. Big Tony was gone? I thought he was so healthy.

It was then I realized the physical body could give out at any time and I really could lose my husband with no warning. That thought broke me even more. I couldn't stand the thought of losing him, I just couldn't. I loved him so much. He was my world.

It was a tough realization for me. It was as if Alzheimer's was speaking directly to me and cruelly mocking me saying, *"Let me introduce myself, Carly. I'm the cold, hard truth."*

CHAPTER 23
No Me Without You

I had friends tell me I was in denial at the beginning of this journey.

Of course, I was. I didn't want my husband, life partner and soulmate to have this dreadful disease. Stenmark was such an awesome man, so full of life and had so much love to give. I was the blessed recipient of that heart, a heart full of love and kindness.

How was I going to exist without him? Would I even be able to? How do I get through this, how do I deal with my own feelings and emotions, let alone try to see and help Stenmark battle this new unknown enemy. How do we win against this unforeseen enemy? But there was no winning, not with Alzheimer's disease. I know that now as I thought about how much I hated this fucking disease.

I shook the stress, and thoughts that were making me worry, from my mind. I had to stay somewhat sane, not just for myself but mostly for my husband. I drove to Kenny's facility with the music blasting. My favorite rock song *Hold on Loosely* came on and I turned it up even louder. My thoughts went back five years to when I surprised Kenny with tickets to a singer/songwriter festival and three-day music festival up in Eden, Utah. The festival featured several *back-in-the-day* bands and singer-songwriters we both liked, including Emmylou Harris and Rodney Crowell. We got to see Jim Peterik, the founder of the rock band "Survivor" and vocalist and guitarist for The

Ides of March. Peterik co-wrote *Hold on Loosely* and a bunch of other songs for 38 Special, so we both were excited for that.

After the last day of the festival, we went back to our Airbnb. We had an early tee time at Wolf Creek Golf Course the next morning. As we drove to the course, Stenmark stopped the car and turned around. "There's Jim Peterik," he exclaimed. Sure enough, there he was walking on my side of the street, still decked out in his purple outfit from head to toe, his iPad in hand.

Stenmark pulled up next to him and I rolled down my window, "I love your song, it's my favorite," I said nervously.

"Which one?" he asked in all seriousness. *Boy, do I feel stupid.* He had written and co-written so many!

"*Hold on Loosely*," I said, feeling weak in the presence of this huge rockstar.

Peterik then commented, "Well, you and about a million or two other people."

Then we all laughed as he shook my hand. I was so star struck I forgot to take a picture.

Maybe that story will be in *his* book one of these days. *Hah!*

When I pulled up to the care facility and opened the door, cute Emily was cheerful as she told me that Stenny was on a bus ride with Phil and some of the other residents. They wouldn't be back for a couple of hours, so I decided to get a pedicure. I usually do my own or swap with my friend, Lori from the salon when we have time. I found the place my daughters both go to and decided to give it a try. And to my surprise it wasn't half bad. I am *very* picky when it comes to manicures and pedicures. But then so are my daughters, having grown up with me as their mom made them that way. They knew the difference between quality and sloppy nail work.

After my pedicure, I arrived back at the facility just as the bus was pulling in. I parked my car, got out, and watched as

No Me Without You

angel, Phil, patiently helped everyone get out and go back into the facility. Safe and sound behind the locked door once again. Phil put on a movie for them and in true form they all started to fall asleep.

Even Stenny began to nod out.

That's when Phil came up to me and said he had a funny story to tell me.

There was a new resident named Eleanor. She was tall, thin and always dressed to the nines, including hair, makeup and nails perfectly done. Once she found out I was a manicurist, she wanted a certain color of nail polish and would always ask me as soon as I walked in, "Did you get the polish?"

When I would answer, "No, they didn't have it, Eleanor, I'm sorry." She would give me a dirty look and storm off. *Supply chain issues, Eleanor!*

With that in mind, Phil began his story with, "You know how Eleanor always asks everyone what church they go to?"

I was very aware. I'd been asked several times myself and had witnessed her asking the other residents and the staff. The *only* right answer according to Eleanor was the LDS church. Phil continued, "Stenny and LaMonte were sitting together on the bus, eating their ice cream when they were approached by Eleanor with her usual question."

I grinned because I knew the question.

Phil said, "Well, after Eleanor asked her question, LaMonte said to her, My husband (meaning Stenny), and I are Jehovah Witnesses."

Then Stenny said to me, 'Will you please tell my wife (meaning LaMonte), that I am a *Lutheran*?

Eleanor said that was wrong, in a sharp tone, and stormed off."

I was a bit crushed by my husband's remark, and I must've looked it. Because then Phil said, "I'm sorry Carly, but I found that funny."

It was funny, sort of. I just had to remind myself that it was the disease, not my music man. He couldn't help it, dammit. I know he loves me, and I love him, but Tony's sudden departure was weighing heavily on my mind. I am so scared going forward. I can't be without my love, my one and only true love. *Who will I be without him?*

After about an hour or so, our neighbor Bob walked in. We lived next door to them when we were in Holladay. They were the best neighbors, and we soon became fast friends. He was an attorney for the Utah State Attorney General's office and his lovely wife, Barb, was a junior high school teacher...*bless her!*

Bob was also a musician and played in a band with some other lawyers. I was surprised to find out he came weekly. I wondered how many others visited him that Stenmark never told me about because he couldn't remember.

This visit, Bob had a baseball cap with the name "Bennett" on it and a small light blue pin that read, "It's all about love" and put it on Kenny's head. I found Bob's gesture so thoughtful. And after Phil's story, I secretly hoped maybe my man would know *I was his wife*, not LaMonte.

Stop being so childish Carly, LaMonte can't help it either.

I thought about the time I was sitting with Stenny, and she walked up to us. She began wiggling her finger at us asking, "What's going on here?"

I answered saying we were just sitting there listening to music.

Her eyes went to my hubby. "How do you know her?" LaMonte asked.

Stenny just stared with that blank look, so I piped up, "We're married, LaMonte." I hoped that might snap her memory back, but in hindsight I should have known better.

It didn't work, of course it didn't.

Then she asked Stenny, "You never told me that. What about the children?"

I just sat there wondering if I would make it worse by taking another stab at the truth. I decided against it. I didn't want to add to her confusion.

"I will have your things packed when you get home," was the next thing out of her mouth.

Again my poor husband didn't know whether to shit or go blind. He just stared, as she walked away. My heart ached for her. How sad that she felt I was taking her husband away. I could feel the tears forming in my eyes as I laid my head on Stenny's chest.

Damn this disease!

CHAPTER 24
Old Lovers

Sadly, it didn't end there. There was incident after incident with LaMonte. I went from being a trollop to being a harlot. I really don't blame her for latching onto Stenny as I said, he was the best-looking man in the place, but then again, I am slightly biased.

But then a new couple moved into the facility, Rick and Kate. He was like Stenny and all the other residents there, but his wife had what they called Covid Dementia. So apparently that's a thing now. Rick was worse than Kate by far.

She was a very skinny woman with a mean face. I only saw her smile when she sang, and she did have a beautiful voice. Her husband was a huge man. He was much taller than Stenny and had about sixty or seventy pounds on him, at least. He was a retired doctor and Kate was a former singer with the Mormon Tabernacle Choir.

I loved hearing the back stories of these residents. It was so amazing to me how this disease can take over the brightest of brains. Stenny was living proof of that—as were all the residents in the facility.

There were also two other women who moved into the facility with their memory-challenged husbands: Dawn and Alice. They were both in their early nineties and although Dawn was healthy, Alice was wheelchair-bound. But both were completely with it mentally.

Often when I came in, they sat and chatted with me. One day, as I was talking to Alice, she was under the impression that Stenny was an attorney. So, I told her he was enrolled in law school but dropped out to become a singer/songwriter in Los Angeles. I played her one of his songs and she was very impressed, just like anyone who had ever heard him sing. His voice was amazing.

Alice told me how much she and her husband loved music and asked me for one of Stenny's CDs. I told her I would bring one in for them the next day when I visited. I asked Stenny if that was okay and he said, "sure!" My husband was very protective about his music and chastised me once for giving one of his CDs to a friend of mine, stating, "...they had not been mastered or registered yet."

I totally understood. What if someone heard them, liked them and passed them off as their own. That would not be good.

After that, I always asked his permission. After all, it was his work and I had to respect that. It was then that I asked Alice how she was handling things in the facility.

Her answer was something I completely understood. "Every day I sit here and look around at everyone and I feel like I'm in *One flew over the Cuckoo's Nest*, but I do it for my husband."

The next day was Sunday, and the LDS church services were being conducted. I sat next to Stenny. I remember it well. That was the day he forgot he was a Lutheran and began taking the Sacrament. It was also the day that he had his first hallucination. Yes, that's also a thing. During the sacred and quiet Sacrament services, he leaned down and began snapping his fingers calling out loudly for our cat, Newbie. This had never happened before and I was near tears.

I shook my head no and quietly said "Newbie isn't here, Babe."

Stenny looked at me like I was from Mars. "Bennett, he's *right* there," he exclaimed as he continued to snap his fingers and call out to the non-existent kitty. It was then I realized the quick progression of his disease. I just looked at the couple who conducted the service and smiled. They both smiled back. I simply let my husband live in his world for a few more minutes realizing I'd said the wrong thing. He was, for the first time since moving in, acting annoyed with me. I knew better. I broke the first rule of Alzheimer's Land, *again*. *Don't argue with them or correct them…ever!*

It was so hard for me not to try and "help" him remember, but I had to stop doing it. The last thing I wanted was to upset him or worse, make him feel stupid or hurt his feelings. I bit my lip. Little did I know there would frequently be blood in my mouth from biting my lip repeatedly.

I had to remember this was our new normal now.

After the Sacrament service concluded, the woman who was conducting with her husband began to deliver the lesson that week. As a Mormon I knew what to expect, but as a Lutheran, my sweet hubby… *not so much*. I remember it clearly; it was a lesson on the joy that comes from reading the scriptures. She had been speaking for about three minutes when Stenny leaned over to me and said, *not using his inside voice*, "She's driving me fucking nuts." *GULP!*

She looked at me along with everyone in the place. *Shit! What do I do now?* I managed an uncomfortable smile as I spoke quietly to Stenny, trying my best not to correct him. But how do I do that? I am just learning the drill. I managed a soft, "Let's not say that during the church part, Babe."

He strongly replied to me in an irritated tone, "Well, she is," as his brow furrowed. I just rubbed his leg, trying to distract him. From what I don't know. The I mouthed a very soft "sorry" to the woman. She gave me a sympathetic smile, and I let it go.

We had quite a few instances during the church services, but it wasn't just Stenny all the time. We had a new resident when I walked in on another Sunday morning. He was also in a wheelchair and looked grouchy. I asked him his name and he replied, "Norm." I smiled and lightly rested my hand on his broad shoulder. "Hi Norm, welcome. We are happy you are here."

Norm answered, "Well, I'm not!"

Okay…time for me to walk off and sit with Stenny and LaMonte. I walked over slowly not knowing what to expect from LaMonte this Sunday morning.

"Is that your husband or just one of your *old lovers*," LaMonte asked me, pointing to Norm. *Oh, Lord please help me.*

I leaned down and gave her a hug and asked her how she was doing. *Redirect!* I wasn't in the mood for a fight from LaMonte this morning. *God bless her.*

♥♥♥♥♥

The services began and we all took the Sacrament. The Mormon, the Lutheran and the Jehovah's Witness. I focused on the lesson. It was about how magical music was. Whew! That should keep Stenny's interest, and it did. In fact, all the residents were very interested.

The woman played a beautiful piano song on her iPhone. She held it up and some residents closed their eyes and listened intently. Some swayed back and forth, but they all had smiles on their faces. It was so beautiful and so moving to watch. They all looked so happy, even my *old lover*, Norm.

(That was another one of my attempts at humor.)

When the song ended, the woman asked, as she raised her hand, "Wasn't that a beautiful music piece, how many of you like music."

Mostly everyone including me raised their hand, everyone except Stenny. We all put our hands down and then he raised his. The woman smiled lovingly at him and said, "Oh, Stenny do you like music?"

He answered, "I like girls!" *Okay, then.*

She just smiled and I chose to simply let it be.

They had to know what they were getting themselves into when they accepted this new calling, didn't they?

After the service was over this couple always walked around and spoke to each resident and their family members. I thought that was so kind. They extended their hands to all of us. As they approached Norm, arms outstretched, they welcomed him and asked how he was doing.

"Not good," Norm replied.

The kind woman rubbed his back softly and asked him what was wrong.

"I have to take a dump, okay?" was Norm's reply.

She patted his back and smiled as she approached the next resident.

At least it wasn't Stenny with an inappropriate comment this time.

The staff, as shorthanded as they were, particularly on the weekends, put on a movie before lunch. I made a point to stay until it was lunch time. I sat with him holding his hand with LaMonte on the other side most of the time, holding the other hand.

I talked with both, showing them pictures from my phone, and asking them questions, as I listened intently to their word salad. It is just the way Alzheimer's afflicted people speak and I was getting used to it, sadly.

I helped get Stenny into the lunchroom and noticed he was no longer at the table with *the girls*. He now sat with Princess at the first table as you entered the lunchroom. It was an effort on the part of the staff to keep LaMonte and Stenny separated, which worked.

But as I sat there with Stenmark at lunch, the arrows still flew!

CHAPTER 25
Anywhere But There

We still owned our timeshare in Mesquite, Nevada, and we now had two weeks this year, thanks to the pandemic. I invited my closest friend, Janice to take a golf break with me for a week. It had been snowing so much and it was now April of 2022, and we were both more than ready for some relaxation, golf and sunshine. I decided I would drive down early on Friday and she would come on Saturday. This would be my first time at the condo since Ken went into care. I knew I needed the break from work and the stress of adjusting to my new life.

I was apprehensive about being in the condo alone that first night, but Janice had to work on Friday. As I packed my car the night before, I had to chuckle a bit remembering the last time Ken and I went down with nearly every pair of shoes he owned thrown in the back of my car. They took up so much room since he had a size thirteen shoe and there were twenty-three pairs! *Yes, I counted them! I am funny like that.* As I sat on the bumper of my car, my thoughts drifted to how he dressed for golf that first day. The head pro at the golf course was a friend of Stenmark's and had made us a tee time for early in the morning.

He walked out of the bedroom in a pair of wrinkled up plaid shorts that looked like he'd slept in them. At least they were golf shorts, and a striped tee shirt that he *did* sleep in. Now remember, Ken was a golf professional who *always* dressed like a golf professional. He had such great golf clothes and they were expensive, top of the line, always.

I said, "Honey, where are your nice golf clothes?"

He looked down at his wrinkled-up attire and said, "Right here."

"But Babe, that isn't a collared golf shirt," I said as kindly as possible.

He looked puzzled as he answered, "I can wear this, Bennett."

I sighed and thought, oh my poor husband. I know I can't argue with him.

But I absolutely cannot let him go to the golf course dressed like that.

As I rifled through his suitcase, I searched my mind trying to find the right words that would convince him to change his clothes. I found a nice golf shirt and another pair of golf shorts. I drew in a very deep breath as I pulled out the portable ironing board and iron. I quickly pressed them both.

I walked into the living room of the condo where he was sitting in the leather recliner watching television. "Hey Babe, look what I found in your suitcase. I'm so happy you packed this outfit. I love you in this blue shirt, so I pressed it for you. It's my favorite."

Kenny stood up and amazingly he took the shirt and shorts from my hand and smiled, "You're so sweet. Thank you, Babe."

It worked! I said a little prayer and thanked the Lord.

I jumped up off the bumper of the car and decided I better finish packing the car, as I knew six o'clock in the morning would be here sooner than I wanted it to.

I was right. The next morning the alarm went off and I jumped out of bed and into the shower. I prepared for the five-hour drive to Mesquite, alone for the first time in over twenty years. I was so thankful I'd taken the cats to the boarder the day before as I began my long trip.

For whatever reason, I decided to drive through Salt Lake City instead of Provo Canyon, which is the way we always drove. Mindlessly, and deep in thought, I mistakenly took the exit as if I was going to see Stenny.

I'd made the decision to get on the road by eight o'clock and since I had been with him after I dropped off the cats, I wasn't going to stop. But here I was on the road to the care facility and feeling like I should stop and give Stenny a kiss. It was such a strong prompting, for lack of a better word, that I knew better than to ignore it. My mother taught me to never ignore my intuition as a child and it had always paid off.

I pulled into the parking lot, turned off my car, and said yet another quick prayer. My usual routine before entering the facility. I walked into the main door and there was Emily with the phone in her hand, just as my cell phone rang. I looked at my phone, "Alta Ridge Memory Care." She hung up quickly,

"Carly, I was just calling you. Stenny is not doing well at all this morning."

She came around to the locked door as I asked anxiously, "What's wrong with him." My heart was not ready for what I saw when she opened the locked door. I thought it was going to explode right out of my chest. My knees shook and I felt weak as I ran over to him. I was scared to death.

There he sat, my sweet husband, slumped over in a wheelchair that he had never needed before. I dropped to my knees next to the wheelchair and called his name, "Stenmark!"

His head was down and he was drooling profusely. The nurse wiped his mouth and face. I noticed his right arm was limp and his hand was shaking. I feared that he may have had a stroke. I grabbed the box of tissues from the nurse as she ran to get a towel. I sobbed uncontrollably as I wiped his mouth and chin with the tissue. They were soaked immediately. The nurse took over with the towel.

I threw my arms around this wonderful man of mine. To see my sweet husband like this was so heart wrenching, I couldn't control myself. I screamed out the words, "What the hell has happened to him, he was fine yesterday."

Poor Emily. She looked scared as well, but she was calm when she answered, "He woke up this morning and didn't want his breakfast, so we let him sleep a little. When we went in after breakfast, he couldn't get up or walk, so we put him in a wheelchair. It looks like he may have had a stroke so we gave him an aspirin. We've called his doctor and I am waiting for her to call us back, unless you want us to call an ambulance and have him sent out."

"*What the hell, Emily?! Of course, I want him sent to the hospital!*"

I guess she must ask, but I truly wanted him anywhere but there at this moment in time. I was freaking out and I was not going to wait for a doctor to call and then wait again for her arrival. I'm sure sweet Emily was just following protocol, but *hell no!*

The ambulance was there in record time and I chose a hospital that was close to his son's house, but not too far away from the care facility. I wanted to make it easy for McLane to come and see his father. The paramedics loaded Stenny on a gurney and then put the oxygen mask on his pained face.

One of them told me I could follow them in my car and there would be no siren as he was stabilized and they didn't consider it a life-or-death situation. "We just need to get him to the hospital and have him evaluated, and find out what's going on, and why he is unresponsive, but he is stable."

"Well, should I drive him to the hospital?" I asked remembering from my father's ambulance ride, that ambulance services were not covered by insurance.

"No, it's against the care facilities rules for him to be transported in a personal vehicle to a hospital in an emergency situation," the paramedic replied.

I thanked him and said OK. Then I went to my car and again I prayed. But this time it wasn't for my strength; it was to help my sweet husband. The paramedics went into the facility, so I pulled myself together enough to make some calls before starting the car.

There were things I needed to take care of as I waited. First, I called Retta, as I knew McLane would be at work and she'd know how to get ahold of him. Then I quickly emailed Jennifer, my friend at Master Villas, where our condo was, and told her I had to cancel the makeup week and explained the situation. Jennifer was so kind; I knew she would understand.

Next, I called my oldest daughter, Channy, and told her to let the rest of my children know. Being "my little weeping willow tree," (our pet name for her growing up) she had always been such a sensitive soul. Channy began to sob as I knew she would, and she wanted to come to the hospital.

I told her to wait until I got there, to let me see what was happening and I would call her as soon as I had some news.

Then I called Janice to let her know the trip was off. Of course she understood. My last call was to "Saint Angela," our realtor friend in Park City. We were both in tears as I told her I was on my way to the hospital. I told her what I told Channy and Janice, that I found him unresponsive when I popped in this morning, an ambulance was called, and I honestly didn't know what was wrong yet but he was stable.

I gave Angela permission to tell two of my closest friends but asked her to wait on telling anyone else until I had more information.

I told all to stay tuned and I would be in touch when I knew more. Then I drove to St. Marks Hospital, parked my car in the large parking lot, and realized I was grateful for three things that morning. The first being that I'd listened to and trusted my gut. *Thank you, Mom.* The second was that the paramedics eased my mind by telling me the siren wasn't needed. I was not ready to lose my husband, but right now it was apparent he needed hospitalization. Which made me weepy and scared shitless, no doubt about that.

And lastly, I was so thankful for my kids and friends. I knew I could always count on them.

CHAPTER 26
Is There Enough

I grabbed one of my black covid masks before I got out of the car. This was a hospital and I knew the rules. As I locked my car, I saw the large blanket that covered up my golf clubs and all my other belongings I needed for the week. Kenny had taught me that when we first began travelling together. I learned so much from him. He *has to* be okay. I am not ready to lose my husband…*again.* Alzheimer's disease had already taken him once from me.

I ran quickly to the emergency entrance. I noticed several signs stating *"no visitors allowed"* in the emergency room. I sent a quick text to Channy telling her to let the rest of the family know they were not allowed in the emergency room due to Covid.

Stenmark was in one of the ER rooms and a nurse was there administering a blood test for Covid when I walked in. She smiled from behind her mask and I said, "I am Kenny's wife." I took a seat as she explained what she was doing. She then asked, "What medications is he on?"

I knew them, but my mind wouldn't let me remember them, not even one. I told her I would call the care facility and find out.

Emily texted them to me immediately and the nurse wrote them down. There wasn't much except his vitamins, a low dose of an anti-anxiety medication and another medication called *Risperdal,* widely used to treat some mental mood disorders helping to restore balance of certain natural substances in the brain, the nurse explained.

Wait…that sounded familiar, I remember that name.

I thought back to a phone call I'd received a few weeks ago from Stenmark's doctor, Dr. Bran-Dee and she told me he was having some problems with hallucinations and focusing. She said the dose he was already on was low and felt this would help with clarity, sleep, etc. I remembered asking about the side effects. I was told they included dizziness, light headedness. But drooling, shaking (tremor), difficulty swallowing, muscle spasms, mental and mood changes and interrupted breathing during sleep were the serious side effects.

Dr. Bran-Dee was uncertain about whether he might or might not experience the light side effects and assured me the nurses in the facility would be on the lookout for any appearance of those and the serious side effects, so I agreed to allow her to increase the dosage.

A few minutes later, someone from our insurance company called me, concerned about approving this new dosage.

I told them about my conversation with Dr. Bran-dee.

The insurance company still sounded skeptical, but said they would approve it based on the doctor's recommendation, but for one month only.

I felt sick to my stomach as I looked at Stenmark. I gave him a kiss on the forehead and he opened his eyes ever so slightly and smacked his lips together indicating to give me a kiss back. I laid my head on what used to be his big strong chest as I held his hand waiting in the emergency room.

It had been over two hours by then, and I knew everyone would be wondering and waiting with anxiety. I decided to send out a group text saying I was still waiting and to stay tuned… Then the texts started to roll in, texts from not just my family, but close friends and they were all so sad. They all wanted to help, asking what I needed and how terribly sorry they were. It struck me as odd, but I thought it was because of the situation, so I chalked it up to that. I just 'clicked' a heart on each one and focused on my husband.

I was weepy when the doctor entered the room about a half an hour later. Stenmark patted my arm and quietly shushed me, which I thought was so sweet. I thought with that he was coming around, but we still needed to find out what happened to cause such a dramatic change in less than twenty-four hours. Not to mention, I needed some reassurance that my husband wasn't going to *leave* right then and there. Stenmark gave me the assurance I needed with a simple *"shhh"* and the pat on the hand. He always knew how to make everything better and I felt so much more at peace. I calmed down and honestly, I felt I could breathe a bit easier now.

Dr. Olsen, the emergency room doctor, was a very nice man, seemingly sympathetic and kind as he told me Stenmark did not have a stroke (thank God) and his Covid test was negative. He was now able to open his eyes briefly when he heard his name. The doctor called him Kenneth, as they do in any official setting. Stenmark whispered in a frail, softer than normal tone, "Stenny."

I told the doctor that was his preferred name.

"Okay, Stenny, we will be transferring you upstairs until we see what is going on," Dr. Olsen said as he patted his arm.

Nice touch, I thought. Time for me to let everyone know he was being admitted to the hospital. We were now almost at four hours in since I left his care facility and followed the ambulance. I never dreamt what could happen and the damage that can be done in just four hours, but I would find out soon enough.

I spent my week of vacation in the hospital sitting next to my sweet husband. Lucky for me, this was a planned trip and I

Is There Enough

was already marked out from work for the week. The hospital let me stay that first night and I was grateful. After that, I was kicked out at seven p.m. every night but was allowed back in at eight in the following morning. I didn't want to leave him alone, but I had no choice. Hospital rules. As I drove back up to Park City, I thought about how much I loved my music man and wondered is there enough time for all of our love? Every single little bit of it? *There just had to be more.*

During that week, he had three different doctors checking in at eight each morning and I made sure I was there to hear their findings.

The first was Dr. James, a general doctor, the second was Dr. Peterson, a neurologist, and the third was Dr. Francis, a pulmonologist. Stenny couldn't swallow easily and they were worried he could aspirate if he ate any food or drank liquids. So, it was a water-soaked little grey sponge on what looked like a popsicle stick. That was scary as he would cough and kind of choke just on the water.

Dr. Francis called in a respiratory therapist to help support his breathing. They were concerned with him developing aspiration pneumonia.

Several tests and x-rays later, Dr. James confidently informed me that it was the medication, Risperdal, that has caused the trouble. He called it a "stacking" of the medication. He went on to say that this drug had built up in his system and the increased dosage didn't do him any favors either. I sat and listened to his explanation telling me it just had to get out of his system, which is why they stopped all his prescribed drugs, including his vitamins, until they figured it out completely.

I just stared at him, feeling sick by what I heard. The guilt consumed me as I listened.

"Let me get this straight," I finally said. And then repeated what he had just explained to me, focusing on it being the Risperdal.

Dr. James solemnly nodded his head and said, "Yes."

I couldn't hold back the tears and I began to cry. I told him how bad I felt for not questioning Dr. Bran-Dee about the increase. "The insurance company even called me and questioned the prescription. I just took the doctor's word for it and went along with her."

Dr. James looked at me and asked, "Did you go to medical school?"

"Well, no," I answered.

"Look, Mrs. Stenmark you are not a doctor and there is no way you are expected to act like one." I gave him a half smile and thought how true that statement was. He's right. I'm a nail technician and let's say he needed a manicure...that I could manage.

But the guilt still swept over me like a tidal wave. I said, "I know but I should have been smarter about it. Stenny is sick. He has nobody else to advocate for him and now here we are. That is *my* job. I am supposed to help him. He can no longer help himself."

Dr. James said calmly, "But you're not a physician, Mrs. Stenmark. Now let's focus on getting Stenny better so you can *both* go home, shall we?"

I guess that means I better pull myself together.

"Thank you, Dr. James," I said appreciating his kindness more than he probably realized.

But screw you, Bran-Dee!

CHAPTER 27
Rebels & Outlaws

The next morning as I drove back to the hospital, I knew what I needed to do. When I went into Stenmark's room, he was asleep. I kissed him and this time it was him that gave a half smile. "Are you still sleepy, Babe?" I asked.

He nodded his head yes. I rubbed his sweet face and told him I would be right back in a few minutes. Then I walked out of his room, down the hall and sat in the empty waiting room. I called Dr. Bran-Dee and left her a message asking her to call me. I looked at my watch and figured it was likely before office hours.

Well, that's okay, she will get my message as soon when she arrives at her office this morning.

I went back to Stenmark's room and I waited…and waited…and waited. Hours passed and still no word from Dr. Bran-Dee. I called three more times and left messages with her receptionist and one with her nurse to please call. *Nothing* the rest of the day. I was trying to give her the benefit of the doubt. Maybe she was busy with patients. Maybe she worked straight through lunch and took no breaks like I did at work. I was really trying…but my patience wore thin.

The hospital made an announcement that visiting hours were over. I was talking with Stenmark when one of his nurses came in. "I'm sorry Mrs. Stenmark, but it's time for you to go home and get some rest. We will take good care of Stenny, I promise." Before I could respond, he said, "Why is everyone calling her Mrs. Stenmark? That's my *mother's* name. Her name is Bennett."

I smiled and gave him a kiss as I told him I would be back early in the morning.

"You better be," he said as I walked out the door and thought to myself, *this sweet man of mine is coming back.*

I woke up early the next morning. I honestly felt such relief. I knew he wasn't going to leave me anytime soon. The doctors had assured me of that right form the get go, but seeing him lying there unresponsive, mostly sleeping took a toll on me. But now he was joking with the nurses and back to teasing me. Yes, he was still in the depths of his Alzheimer's disease, but he was recovering well from the "stacking" of that medication.

Dr. James had referred it to being in a drug coma.

As I drove up the canyon, I rehearsed the message I was going to leave for Dr. Bran-Dee, since I had still not heard one word from her or her office. It really infuriated me, but I decided to practice and stay calm when I gave her a piece of my mind.

At least that was the plan. I turned off my music so I could really focus on my words. I tended to break out in song when I listened to music while driving, especially these days. Music was indeed my savior.

I arrived at St. Marks Hospital and walked up to the elevator. It was a little after eight in the morning when the door opened. The elevator was crowded, but not jammed full. As I hopped in, I asked cheerfully, "You got room for another friendly soul?" I was welcomed with head nods, smiles and the positive answers of "yes" and "sure."

When I got to Stenmark's room, he was still sleeping. As I said, being a musician, he was never a morning person, so I walked over and softly kissed his cheek. He needed his rest, so I sat down with my iPad and waited for the doctor. I knew the nurse would come in first with his breakfast of his first soft foods. I smiled because it was a signal to me that he was improving, and the breathing treatments were indeed helping.

It was about nine a.m. when Dr. James came in with his clipboard in hand and told me that Stenmark was progressing well. But it was going to take some time until the medication was completely out of his system. "Stenny, can you wake up for me" Dr. James asked a couple of times.

Stenmark's eyes began to open and Dr. James asked him how he felt.

"Tired," Stenmark replied.

"Well, I want you to wake up, because the nurse will be in to help you with breakfast. But first I want to listen to your heart." He took out his stethoscope as Stenmark sat up. He grimaced as Dr. James put the metal head on his back. "Damn that's cold! Good God, Doc!" Stenmark cringed and said sharply.

No apology from Dr. James.

I chuckled and thought, *'He's back to being his outlaw/rebel self!*

When the nurse came with his breakfast, she gave Stenmark the choice of applesauce or pudding. He reluctantly chose the applesauce. Stenmark was never one for diary. No ice cream, puddings or milk-based products. He had a few small bites of the applesauce, then he grimaced and handed it back to her. She tried to coax him with a few more bites, but he flat refused.

"I will be back in a few minutes to do his sponge bath, and get him changed," she said. "Then his respiratory therapist will be in." After that, she hustled out of the room.

I decided her return would be my cue to make the phone call. I thought about how *everyone* at the care facility was calling and texting me daily for updates. They were all so worried and genuinely concerned. I knew for certain that Dr. Bran-Dee received my messages and yet not a word from her. This alone made my blood boil.

I walked down to the family waiting area and this time it was partially vacant, just a few stragglers here and there. I called Dr. Bran-Dee's office for the fifth time. I tried so hard to give her the benefit of the doubt, but my patience wore thinner with each call. This time I got her receptionist. "Hi Samantha, this is Carly Stenmark *again*. Is Dr. Bran-Dee around?"

Samantha told me she was there, but was busy with patients and did I want her voicemail?

"No. I have already left her several messages. Has she received any of them? I asked. "Because I have not heard one word from her about my husband who has been in the hospital for five days. And this is my fifth call."

"Um, I think so. I'm not sure but let me check," she said cheerfully as she put me on hold.

Of course, she isn't going to say anything bad or negative about her boss but I can!

Samantha came back in record time to let me know that Dr. Bran-Dee had been very busy, but she would make sure to have her call me by the end of the day.

That was more than a voicemail could do for me, so I thanked her and hung up. Hope springs eternal, I guess. I responded to my other concerned friends, clients, the nurses at his facility and our family before heading to his room.

I had some interesting texts from some of our closest friends in Park City, along with some people from the golf course. They were all so damn sad. But my mind was elsewhere right now so I just chalked it up to them being concerned about Stenmark and me as well.

I walked back to the room and found Stenmark asleep. I sat with him watching him sleep the remainder of the day. My mind kept racing back to the morning I walked into his care facility and saw him in that vegetative state. That visual would bring me to my knees if I dwelled on it too much. I blinked back the tears.

I am strong-willed person, but honestly that was almost more than I could handle. The day wore on, and before I knew it, it was almost time for visiting hours to be over. But now an even bigger realization occurred to me—not a word from Dr. Bran-Dee.

I thought about my close friend Zena who had, to cheer me up, sent me a photo of her next to a camel in the desert of Egypt, with the caption, "Car, here is a picture of me walking like an Egyptian." That did put a big smile on my face. I could always count on Zena for that. I've always said she is the epitome of honesty, good advice, humor, and the voice of reason.

The announcement came over the PA system that visiting hours were over. As I kissed my husband goodnight, I was so thankful he was in a place where the nurses and doctors truly cared. I walked the long hallway and paused as I reached the family waiting area. It was empty and I took that as a sign. It was seven p.m., and Dr. Bran-Dee's office was closed, so she certainly had time to call, but still nothing! I spotted *my* chair in the corner, and although it was past office hours, I knew what I had to do. I went to my recent calls and pressed Dr. Bran-Dee's number for the sixth and final time. I listened to her outgoing office voicemail message and my heart was calm as I heard the beep and then I let her have it.

"Dr. Bran-Dee, this is Carly Stenmark, Ken Stenmark's wife calling you for the last time. Since you have not bothered to return my calls, I am forced to leave you this message. Ken is in the hospital and has been for almost six days. The competent doctors here have diagnosed him with an 'over stacking' of the drug you prescribed, Risperdal. In case you are interested they have taken him off everything including his vitamins, to try and get his system back to normal. This is the same drug that I not only questioned you about, but that the insurance company did as well. This call is a courtesy call to let you know that you are no longer my husband's doctor. You will not be seeing him in or out of the care facility. I find your lack of professionalism and lack of concern for Ken, *who is your patient*, disturbing at best. Furthermore, if you go anywhere near my husband, I will sue your ass."

And yes, that is a threat, Dr. Bran-Dee.

Then I added sarcastically, "And if the reason you haven't called me back is because you are dead, then I apologize. Goodbye."

CHAPTER 28
Long Time Lonely

Then I called Gary F. Holland, MD. We met him at the care facility the first week Stenmark was there. He seemed like a good doctor, but I didn't stick with him due to our insurance. The facility had recommended Dr. Bran-Dee instead, and she was in our network, so we went with her.

Dr. Holland called me back and couldn't have been nicer. He told me to call him when Ken was back in the facility, which I did and he met us there that very day. I would pay out of pocket for his care if I needed to, but soon found out he was now with our insurance.

It was a plus that Stenmark remembered and really liked Dr. Holland.

I felt like it was meant to be.

After our hellish week, I went back to work. Stenmark's physical health slowly continued to improve, under the care of Dr. Holland and the care facility staff. Dr. Holland suggested we call in a hospice nurse. That word scared me, but he reassured me that hospice no longer meant an automatic death sentence. It just meant more care, such as showers and they would even shave him. They would also bring in a wheelchair, a shower chair, pull-ups, wipes, and a hospital bed complete with bedding.

Three times a week, he would be showered and it was all covered by Medicare and that was good news.

Another thing I found curious about this disease was the patient's lack of caring about having "nice things." The hospital bed was twin sized, and the mattress was made of foam covered in thick durable rubber and was only about five inches thick, but it had a guard rail so that was a plus. But as soon as I laid eyes on that small uncomfortable mattress, my mind went back to the first thing Stenmark bought for my condo.

♡♡♡♡♡

Stenmark called me at work after we moved in together and told me we had to go down to a furniture store because he wanted to buy a new mattress for my bed.

I was surprised and wondered why but decided it would be a *"glass-of-wine-and-then-we-would-chat-about-it"* kind of night.

"Honey, I'll be home in about an hour, can we talk then?"

Stenmark's easy-going personality went along with my suggestion.

I arrived right on time and walked in the door of my condo to find the music on, two glasses of chilled Chardonnay wine, a single red rose in a tiny vase, and a lit candle sitting on the coffee table. I sat down as we picked up our wine, kissed and toasted to us before taking the first sip. I loved this ritual.

"Okay so why do we need a new mattress?" I asked and really didn't expect the answer I got. "Bennett, you've had a couple of boyfriends since your divorce and I don't want to sleep on a mattress that you've been sleeping on with other guys."

Wow! I guess he had a point, but it was a surprising point. That was something I never thought of. I reminded him that I was single for many years before I met him, with only two long term relationships. Sure, I had dates, but my rule of thumb was always at least three months of dating before I felt comfortable and safe enough to let anyone in my bed.

Stenmark was always so cute and witty.

He smiled as he said, "That's a long-time lonely Bennett." Then he added, "Why did you make me wait so long?"

"Wasn't it obvious, Babe?" I replied slyly.

Then he winked at me.

Of course it was, I didn't need to remind him. Time to change the subject.

Stenmark told me he had a couple mattresses picked out and wanted my opinion. "Oh, Babe, I trust you. I don't need to test the mattress. You just pick the one you want." He took a big sip of his wine.

"Bennett, I lived a long time with someone who didn't want to participate in things Ike this, and I don't want to do that again. In fact, I *won't* do that again. I want your opinion. This is a partnership, and I don't want it to just be me taking charge and making the decisions."

"Oh, okay. You know, Babe, when Clark and I were married, I wasn't included in these kinds of decisions. When our house was built, he took a ski instructor friend with him while I was working to pick out the counter tops, sinks, fixtures and such. He even picked out all the appliances and the furniture for our house. I liked all of his decisions, so, I guess I just got used to that. I'm sorry, Stenmark."

That's how Clark and I ended up with a waterbed, which I promptly got rid of when we divorced. I hated that damn thing. There is no way to get your rhythm going on a waterbed. I don't care who you are.

At that point, Stenmark walked over and put his arms around me. I thought to myself how different we are with different people. I realized I was a completely different version of myself now in my sixties, than I was at twenty, thirty, forty, fifty. Not to take anything away from the other important loves in my life, but I realized I was trying to love, while trying to grow, while trying to live, while trying to learn, while trying to raise a family. All at the same time.

There were times when I'd juggle everything better than other times, that's for sure. But I do accept my part and take responsibility for the failure of my "practice marriages."

So, Saturday morning, we were off to Granite Furniture to pick out a new mattress. After laying on more of them than I care to remember, we decided on the perfect one for both of us. They sure don't give them away, because twenty-five hundred dollars later, we owned one be both liked. They agreed to deliver it on Monday and haul away my old *tainted* one.

♡♡♡♡♡

Seeing my picky hubby on a flimsy, clearly uncomfortable mattress provided by hospice was even more heartbreaking as I thought of how things used to be. Stenmark once loved nice things and made sure we had the best that *our* money could buy. He lived within his means and that was another thing I loved about him. Now it didn't register at all.

"Is your new bed comfy, Babe?" I asked him earnestly.

"Well, of course it is, Bennett," he replied flatly.

Creature comforts no longer mattered to him, thanks to his Alzheimer's disease. But it was killing me to see him lying on that twin size bed with the mattress covered in thick dark blue plastic. I understand the reasoning behind it, but it still broke my heart. I wasn't even allowed to bring in new sheets.

I told my friend, Zena, about it the following Friday morning.

"The saving grace is he doesn't know, Car," she replied empathetically.

I agreed with her and told her about Dr. Bran-Dee and the message I left her.

Zena was appalled at Dr. Bran-Dee's lack of concern. She shook her head and then said, "Well, with a name like *Bran-Dee*, she probably slept her way through medical school."

I laughed, but then thought about my niece who had a double master's degree and was brilliant. My apologies to my niece, also named "Brandy," but it was funny! *Oh, Zena… maybe it was the spelling!*

I continued to spend time at Alta Ridge Care Facility. After what happened the last time, I was scared to leave for any length of time. I realized that anything could happen and that scared me to death.

I was there nearly every day I wasn't working. I found it interesting how some people would tell me I shouldn't go so often.

Wait…what?

I got everything from "He probably doesn't even know you're there" to "This must be so hard on you, Carly." I thought about that very first week he was in there I wasn't allowed to visit, and that was tough. I missed him so much, because I was so used to being with him. The nights during that week were particularly lonely.

Was he different from when he first entered the care facility? Of course, he was. This disease might hide the person underneath, but there was still a person in there who needed my love and my attention. So while he was in there, I would continue to go see him as often as I could.

I decided to just ignore other people's comments. From then on, I kept the frequency of my visits to myself. Did I do it the *right* way? Is there even a *right* way? I don't know, but what I do know is this was *my* journey and I would do it *my* way. I know they were all well-meaning, and people's opinions weren't intended to hurt me in any way. It's easy for people to judge, share their views and offer advice when they haven't been through it. Dagmar sent me a gentle reminder that read, *"Don't let anyone who hasn't been in your shoes, tell you how to tie your laces."* I love that!

Truly, unless you have experienced this, you have no idea how you would do it. I know I didn't. It's not the same as caring for an elderly parent, elderly grandparent or elderly aunt with Alzheimer's disease, as hard as that must be. I'm sorry, but it doesn't even compare, or come close, to going through the same journey with your life partner and soulmate. It is so different when it's the person you love most in the entire world. The pain I felt daily was nearly unbearable. To watch my sweet husband's mental and physical health deteriorate right before my eyes every time I saw him was more than I could stand.

But I did it anyway. I went through the motions, as I watched him slowly become a stranger that I hardly recognized. I tried to stay strong, kept my composure, and did the best I could. I did it my way, and that's the only way I knew how.

But I did appreciate my close, well-meaning friends and their concern for me and my health, along with the love and support they showed me on a regular basis.

That's not to say there wasn't invaluable advice along the way. There was, that I did take and it helped me immensely. I also realized the huge importance of taking care of myself. We couldn't both go down the drain at the same time. I needed to have some self-care on this journey. Otherwise, who would take care of him? The thought of my husband being in his memory care facility with nobody visiting him made me cry.

We have kids and grandkids, but they all have lives, jobs and children of their own. I was happy that they visited as often as they could. It pleased me when they made time in their busy schedules. A handful of friends would also visit him on a regular basis, but most found it too difficult. "I want to remember Kenny like he was," was the comment I got the most. I get it. Seeing him in his new normal was not for the faint of heart. It was damn hard. He didn't look, or act, like the man we all knew and loved.

Alzheimer's disease somehow erases the personality and filters the person had for a lifetime prior, leaving only the basic self. But who my sweet hubby was at his core remained, and occasionally he peeked through. And I could see it. Sometimes it was only a glimpse, but I knew the man I loved was still in there, somewhere, and I smiled whenever he told me he loved me. He still wanted to hold my hand, still teased and joked with me, winked at me and wanted a kiss. All that made seeing him so meaningful to me.

Plus, I wanted him to always remember me. The thought of me being completely erased from his mind killed me.

I wasn't going to give him the chance to forget me.

CHAPTER 29
Read Between the Lies

It was the end of April 2022 and I was invited to the birthday party of a close friend who was turning seventy. Donna had lost her husband of forty-five years a couple of years before and naturally she was still in deep grief. It was a small intimate group of friends at her daughter's house. I'd been to see Stenmark that morning, and he was doing well since the Risperdal had finally been out of his system for nearly two weeks. I was excited to celebrate Donna and kick back with a glass or two of wine. A little relaxation couldn't hurt.

I walked into the party and noticed the usual suspects seated close to a beautiful buffet table. It was quite the presentation. I grabbed a wine glass and a plate of yummy appetizers, then found a spot amongst the friendly faces. Of course, they all asked about my husband's health, and they asked the important questions.

We all chitchatted for a few minutes and then Angela made a strange, random comment. "That was a bad doctor," she said.

I found it odd, largely because I never told anyone about Dr. Bran-Dee. But as intelligent and lovely as Angela was, she's been known to have an awkward moment occasionally, so I let it go.

We all have something, don't we?

The next day was Sunday and I drove down to the care facility. I went in and sat next to Stenny on the leather couch.

"Hi honey," I said cheerfully as I kissed him and began telling him about my week.

He listened and after I finished speaking, he said, "...and you are?"

But that was something he joked about on a regular basis, so I played along like I always did and answered, "Mrs. Stenmark."

Without missing a beat, he said, "That's my mother's name."

I kissed him and said, "I know, but I am Mrs. Stenmark too, because I am your wife."

To which he replied, "No shit? Damn I'm lucky."

I hugged him and told him how cute he was, as we both laughed. I'd like to think he did remember me. I left the care facility feeling so loved because after all, I am still his loving wife and I felt in my heart that he knew it.

My work week began and my first client of the day was another close friend. *Let's be real, aren't they all, after all these years?*

Beth was fun and she usually brought in vanilla lattes! As we chatted over the tasty lattes, she asked me about Kenny and his health. Suddenly, Beth picked up her phone and began scrolling, then she turned her phone towards me. On her phone I read a text from Angela that was sent *one hour* after the day he was hospitalized. It was a group text to about six of our friends and it read, "Kenny passed away this morning. Please don't call Carly. Her children are with her."

I sat there staring at this foreign text message and could hardly speak. Finally, I managed to say, "What is that about?"

Beth told me to wait, she scrolled on her phone some more, then turned her phone back to me. Angela had sent another odd text less than an hour after that first shocking one, and it said, "The doctor was able to revive him."

HEART GET READY

I couldn't believe my eyes and I didn't understand.

Then it clicked... *the bad doctor comment! Now I get it, but what the hell was happening?*

Beth, believing the first text, told me she let a few other friends know the sad news. I finished Beth's gel manicure and she apologized saying, "sorry sister." When I had a break, I called our mutual friend, Kacy. She told me that's why she called me at the hospital asking if my children were with me. She told me she didn't want to upset me while I was with Kenny. She was making sure Kenny was alive by asking how he was doing.

That's a good, considerate friend. Testing the waters first.

My two o'clock appointment came in. Sarah was also a friend and a golfing buddy. She'd received a similar phone call and was so upset, because she trusted she'd received the sad news on good authority. Sarah confessed that she'd sent out an email to Vaughn (the golf course manager and Stenmark's boss). Then she went into the course and told me they were all crying about his passing. Apparently, the news went out by email to the entire men and women's golf leagues.

Must have been before the doctor revived him, UGH!

Sarah was mortified and I didn't know what the hell to do. Angela was such a close friend, and I was so confused. This was very serious and in my eyes was more than just an *awkward moment*.

About this time texts to me began to roll in on my own phone.

Donna sent a text apologizing profusely for the strange text she had sent me. Also believing the news of my husband's death was credible, she called two close friends who lived out of state. Since Kenny was the head of the ladies golf league, this affected everyone, and indeed left them heartbroken at the thought of that he had passed. In her text Donna wrote, "You probably thought I was nuts when I sent you that text, and I am in Whole Foods crying my eyes out."

I laughed, because honestly, I had no words as she continued, "I called Genevieve and Barbara to let them know and I apologized profusely."

I shook my head. Donna told me after she'd shared what happened, Barbara asked, "Do you think someday we will laugh about this?"

Again, a sense of humor is paramount in situations such as these.

There were so many thoughts rushing through my brain. Should I call Angela? Should I text her? What did I say to make Angela think such a thing? What did Angela hear? How did this happen? I silently hoped and prayed for a logical explanation. After all, Angela was my friend, *our* friend. Kenny and I both loved her dearly.

I thought about how I called her on the way to the hospital. Naturally I was worried and very upset, but there was literally nothing I could think of that would've led her to believe that my husband had passed. I racked my brain, wondering if I had said *anything* that could possibly have been misunderstood.

Still nada!

I went over and over my conversation until finally I had to stop because I was making myself crazy. I decided it was better just to wait until she came in for her nail appointment in a couple of days and I could talk to her about it then. But during this self-imposed waiting period, I had several other clients tell me they had heard the same thing. Park City is a small town and Kenny and I were very well connected, with a large circle of friends, so the untrue sad news had spread like wildfire.

Finally the day came, and Angela arrived her usual ten minutes late for her manicure and pedicure appointment. I'd

Heart Get Ready

become used to it and had allowed for her tardiness over the last twenty years. *Just book out an extra half an hour…* Sure, I lost money, but she was my friend and I loved her.

I was ready for her when she arrived. I gave her a quick hug and she sat down in the pedicure chair. "Is the water, okay?" I asked as she stuck her feet in the warm pedicure bath.

"Perfect," was her reply.

We were about halfway into her appointment when I decided it was time to find out what was going on. Surely there was a reasonable explanation.

I dove right in and asked Angela about the texts she'd sent the golf girl group.

Her face went red and she asked me, "What texts?"

It was apparent from her look that she knew *exactly* what I was talking about, and realized she was caught.

Do I really have to spell this out for her?

We just stared at each other for a long second, and it became painfully obvious that's exactly what I was going to have to do. I told her the contents of her text…*as if she didn't know!*

Angela just sat there with a very mean look on her face, a look I'd never seen before and didn't speak a single word. She literally offered no response. I didn't want to hurt her feelings, but what else could I do.

Was I really going to have to read between the lies here?

I called her out this time asking, "Why would you send that out to everyone?"

Angela's flippant remark completely stunned me. "Because that's what you told me, Carly, you kept screaming he's gone, he's gone, he's gone, over and over."

I almost fainted. *Wait…what?* I took a huge breath in, paused and said calmly as I looked her straight in the eye, paying no attention to her bright red face. "Angela, that is *not* how I speak. I'm *not* dramatic like that. If, in fact, Kenny *had* passed away I would have said something like…he didn't make it. I would never yell those words, that's simply not me."

Angela was seething as she said, "Carly, that's what you said!"

I couldn't believe she was arguing with me about this, telling me what I'd said! *Are you kidding me right now?* I went on to repeat what she wrote in the first text. "You had the chance to clear the air, but instead you perpetuated the lie by telling people not to call me because my children were with me. They weren't even allowed in the emergency room; nobody was, due to Covid, and I told you that when you called."

Angela's mean look just got meaner. But at that point, I didn't care. I couldn't stop. "Then you had another chance to correct it all, but instead you sent out yet *another lie*. You texted that the doctor was able to revive him. What the hell, Angela? I don't understand where that came from, either."

By now she was so red-faced and there were big red splotches on her neck. But still she stuck to her guns, telling me that's what I said.

OMG that's annoying! To be told you said something, when you know damn well you didn't, is maddening.

The whole thing was senseless and I was beyond confused, unable to say anything more. I just continued with her pedicure, applying her favorite toe color, Pink Flamingo, as I heard the door open. I looked up from Angela's perfectly polished pink toes just as Barbara from Arizona walked in. I was surprised to see her, as I didn't know she was in town. I stood up to hug her as she pulled up a chair. I dropped the conversation and sprayed Angela's toes with some quick dry. She said a quick hi to Barbara as she gathered up her belongings and left saying another quick "bye" to me this time. *No manicure today, I guess.*

Obviously, I had those few extra minutes and Barbara asked me about Kenny. She had been on that infamous golf girls text thread, and poor Donna had confirmed it with a phone call. I shook my head and told her Angela was insisting that's what I said.

Barbara asked me, "Well, why did she send out the text about the doctor then?"

Exactly!

"You tell me, Barbara." Then she laughed and said half-jokingly, "If you ever get a text like that about me from Angela, please call me and make sure I'm dead before you tell people."

I can always count on Barbara's quick wit. I burst out in uncontrolled laughter and so did Barbara.

When I got home, I poured myself a glass of wine, a *big* glass of wine. I thought about the distress that text caused so many people in a matter of two short hours. Then my phone *pinged* and I looked down to see it was a text from Angela. *"I'm so sad that things got so messed up that you felt that you had to tell me about what a mess I caused. I'm sorry."*

I stared at the message and honestly didn't know what to make of it. I gulped down the last of my wine. Obviously, Angela had thought about it.

I decided it was a start and felt confident that we would be able to work through this. After all, she did apologize at the end of her text. So now I was hopeful we could move forward.

CHAPTER 30
Love is Talking

It was Saturday and I drove to Alta Ridge to check in on my man. This time, I brought some cookies from our friends, Dagmar and Jeff. I knew that cookies were something he probably wouldn't forget. He loved his cookies, and Dagmar's were some of his favorites. He ate about three or four before I took out my phone and began to record him. "Tell Dagmar thank you for the cookies she made with love," I said to him as I pointed to the red heart drawn lovingly on the bag.

He replied with the usual word salad for a few seconds, while I just nodded my head, acting as if I understood everything he said.

"Dagmar made those for you, Babe. You know Dagmar."

"Sure," he said.

I quickly added, "and Jeff."

Stenny nodded, then turned to me with a puzzled look on his face and said, "Well, of course! Do you think I went nuts in here?"

I started to laugh quietly and said, "No."

Then he added, "Good God Almighty, Bennett!"

Then I really laughed and told him how cute he was and how much I loved him.

"You better," he replied.

It made a very cute video which I sent to Dagmar and Jeff, who really got a kick out of it. That was love talking right there and I knew, in that moment, Stenny really did remember them.

HEART GET READY

As his physical health improved, he didn't need to use the wheelchair anymore, so that was a plus. I preferred he walk on his own accord, and so did the staff at the care facility. And most importantly, so did Dr.Holland. I went to visit one morning, and as we were sitting there, I realized that my husband needed to be changed. Since the pandemic the facility was so short staffed, and there was a huge turnover. I bow to the caretakers of Alzheimer patients. That's one tough job. And I believe it takes a special kind of person to do it. I know firsthand, that it's an emotionally and physically exhausting job that comes completely from the heart.

I looked around the social room and didn't see anyone and thought they must be caring for other residents. I stood up and reached for Stenmark's hand. "Come on honey, let's go to your room so we can get you cleaned up."

He stood up and we walked into his room.

I learned right from the get-go to carry a small kit in my purse. In that kit was a tiny pair of scissors, a pair of latex gloves, a small jar of Vicks VapoRub and a leftover Covid mask. I would rub the Vicks all around my nose, put on the mask and gloves. Then with the tiny scissors, I would cut each side of his pull up. That made it so much easier and a lot less messy than trying to pull them down. Upon arriving home, I would replace what needed to be replaced and stick the kit back in my purse.

This day I knelt beside him as he stood up. I cut the pull-ups as usual and discarded them in the bathroom waste basket. I used the wipes to clean up my husband, when out of the blue, he put his hand on the top of my head. "I'm so sorry, Bennett," he said ever so softly.

I looked up as a tear slid down his cheek.

"Oh, Babe, it's okay. This doesn't bother me at all."

He patted me on the head as I continued. "This is what we do for the people we love. You did it for your sister, and I know you would do it for me, if the situation was reversed. It's no big deal."

Then that was it. Not another word as I finished up. That just reinforced what I already knew; he was still somewhere in there. And from time to time he would surface, *briefly*. I just witnessed another glimpse of the man I fell madly in love with.

I know to some people, this little story is probably more than you might want to know, but it's all part of the progression of this terrible disease. Before this, I never had a clue about this part of the journey, so I do feel the need to share.

It's not disrespectful to my husband to share it with you. It's what happens. They can't help it and I was being completely honest when I told him I didn't mind. I changed him many times, and it really did not bother me. True love at work. It was talking and I was listening.

And when I say, "I didn't have a clue," when it came to knowing what to expect while caring for a loved one with Alzheimer's Disease, I really mean it. Before all this, how would I?

By now, I've learned so much, I am listing the stages of this disease (according to Dr. David Wolk, co-director of The Penn Memory Center at the University of Pennsylvania) in the hopes that it might help someone else, who doesn't have a clue about what to expect. The timing and severity are different for each person, and it can be difficult to determine what stage your loved one is in. Stages may overlap and are only meant to be a guideline.

THE SEVEN STAGES OF ALZHEIMER'S DISEASE:
Stage One: Before Symptoms Appear

Alzheimer's begins before symptoms are noticeable. The risk of Alzheimer's increases with age, so it is important to keep up with your regular doctor visits. By the time you notice a loved one beginning to slip, they could be entering the second stage of Alzheimer's disease.

You will probably notice your loved one's forgetfulness or change in personality before they do. If so, you may be able to get them treatment sooner to slow down the progression.

I feel badly because I did notice a very slight bit of forgetfulness in Stenmark, but I never in a million years thought that my bright, well-educated husband had Alzheimer's! It never crossed my mind. I naïvely thought it was just us getting older, or him being a "man" not paying attention to things. Now I feel badly for believing that famous line in Tammy Wynette's song, *Stand by Your Man*, when she sings, *"...cuz after all, he's just a man."* I feel like a bad wife, but I know what's done is done and unfortunately, I can't turn back the hands of time and the clock has no sympathy. But hopefully I can help others.

Just like Dr. Skuster told us after reading Stenmark's MRI: Her words were, "I'm sure this began *ten to fifteen years ago.*" My sweet husband was doing his part to stay healthy. From the moment I met him, he went to his yearly physicals and was the one who insisted I get yearly physicals just like he did to circumvent any problems that may arise with our health. Before meeting Stenmark, I only went to the doctor when I was sick. I often joked that he went to see his family care physician when his hair was parted crooked, which was difficult as he only had four hairs on top!

But apparently Dr. Smith never noticed a change in Stenmark, neither nor did he believe me when I tried to tell him that I knew something was not right with him. Instead of listening to me, Dr. Smith treated me like I was some kind of *know nothing* bimbo.

Stage Two: Basic Forgetfulness:
We can all be forgetful at times and it may become more frequent as we age. These early stages can look just like normal aged forget-

fulness. *Our loved ones may experience memory lapses, forgetting people's names, or where they left their keys, wallets or phones. But they can still work, drive and be social. Eventually these memory lapses become more frequent. Once I began to take notice that something was off, I started to seek out treatment to slow down the progression.*

Looking back, this stage was very hard for me to notice, almost an impossibility. We were both aging, and I would be forgetful now and then so I chalked it up to that. I had friends and clients who were older than me and I heard stories about their husbands misplacing things on a regular basis. They would sit across from me at my manicure table and let loose about how it drove them crazy. I listened and even laughed at some of the stories, and those stories never ended with Alzheimer's.

Instead it was just memory lapses, and as we age, that's common. We misplace our keys, forget someone's name and even forget to buy that loaf of bread that we went into the store for in the first place. So, as we grow older, forgetfulness happens more often and we usually brush it off. It's easy to start to question what's normal, but unless you have previous knowledge or first-hand experience, or some family history with Alzheimer's, most of us don't think our forgetfulness is a sign of Alzheimer's disease.

Stage Three: Noticeable Memory Difficulties

This stage usually brings noticeable changes and it is no longer easy to blame it on age. This is when the person's daily routine becomes more disrupted, as when Stenmark was no longer able to work in the golf shop. This stage goes way beyond forgetting names and misplacing things. In this stage, Stenmark would forget something he recently read in the paper or in a book or his golf magazine. He would also forget making plans with others, even with McLane. I thought he was being extra messy, because he became so unorganized. But at this point I was still in denial, which I read was perfectly normal feelings. With this stage also came increased anxiety for Stenmark as his symptoms became worse.

This is the stage I really noticed more than a few things. I was promoting my first book with the Utah Women Writers and was carpooling with a friend and fellow author. While I was waiting in the parking lot for Bonnie, my husband called me and asked if I'd seen his wallet. As I said previously, this was the beginning of many times he'd misplaced it.

I told him I would search my car for it, though I had not seen it. I looked all through my car, in the glove box, in both side pockets, on the backseat and the pockets attached to the back of the front seats, and under both seats. I even opened the back and looked around. I thought because it was a dark brown, I could have missed it when I loaded my car up to promote my book at the street fair. It was not there, and I called him and told him so.

"Bennett, it must be in your car," he said, frustrated, "It is not anywhere in this house and I must get to work before one o'clock." (Again, he didn't want to drive without it.)

"But Babe, it isn't here," I replied, "I've torn my car apart and now my ride is here, and I have to go and load my things into her car." I told him to keep looking around.

I shared this and a couple of other things he'd misplaced with Bonnie on our ride together to the street fair. He was always misplacing his things. I honestly thought it was a guy thing. My clients and I joked about it years before this.

When my husband was first diagnosed with this dreadful disease, we were told it had already progressed to Stage five Alzheimer's disease. I promptly looked up the stages only to discover there were only seven and that it will eventually rob the patient of his or hers cognitive and physical abilities. And (worst of all) that there was no cure.

While memory loss seemed to be part of the normal aging process, Alzheimer's is far from normal. It is serious form of dementia, which I learned can be aggressive. There is a big "dementia umbrella" and Alzheimer's disease is just one of many types of disability under that umbrella, along with vascular dementia, Lewy Body Disease (LBD), Frontotemporal dementia, Chronic Traumatic Encephalopathy (CTE) dementia, alcohol and down syndrome Alzheimer's disease, and HIV associated dementia. Not to forget TBI (traumatic brain injury) dementia, Parkinson related dementia and now Covid related dementia.

I have a close high school friend who is in the middle of dealing with his wife, Debbie. She has Parkinson related dementia. Poor Mark. He is really struggling. Fifty wonderful years of marriage, and it ends like this?

Life truly isn't fair.

All seven stages are listed in the Dementia Stages Chart, which is a valuable reference chart not only for healthcare professional caregivers, but also for caregivers like you and me. It offers insight into what to expect and how to provide the appropriate care for each stage. Since Stenmark was diagnosed at stage five, I started there so I could deal with what was happening in that moment, and what was to come. But I did go back and read up on the stages prior to stage five, and it opened my eyes big time. I now realized there were things I did notice, but at the time it never occurred to me that my husband would ever get this dreaded disease.

Stage Four: More than Memory Loss

This is the stage that impacts more than just the memory. Some begin to have trouble with language, organization and calculations. Daily tasks start to become more and more difficult. Big changes in sleeping patterns, distinguishing day from night, choosing appropriate clothing for the weather conditions and the risk of wandering off and getting lost. Also during this stage, your loved one will experience major difficulties with their memory. They might remember significant details such as what state they live in or who they are married to. But another interesting factoid is their memory of the distant past will usually be noticeably better than their memory of day-to-day information. Go figure!

This is the stage where Stenmark began to drain his bank account leaving him financially bankrupt. I remember noticing at the time he would get the days of the week confused and his sleep patterns were definitely changing, which is common in stage four. Things that require a lot of thinking, such as social gatherings were beginning to frustrate him and he became a little moody, almost withdrawn at times, which was not like him at all. And his personality was changing, as he became increasingly suspicious of others.

In researching this stage, I realized this was where I really began to pay attention to Stenmark and his changing behaviors. Although my realization came late, I was no longer chalking it up to age or him just being a guy. I flashed back to the small, glass plated key holder I had bought for him on our third anniversary, because it represented a glass or crystal gift, which is the third-year anniversary gift. It had a picture of a set of keys on it with the saying, "Honey, where's my…"

He threw it away one day, which was completely out of character for him. I'm not even sure he remembered that I had given it to him.

I began watching his every move like a hawk. His behavior no longer made sense to me. This was the stage where I told him I'd noticed things about his behavior and that we should see a doctor.

His response was the first time in twenty-five years that he raised his voice to me. This is also when I found out he had been searching the internet for the signs of Alzheimer's disease and memory loss related articles.

This is when I felt my heart break in a billion pieces for the very first time.

Stage Five: Decreased Independence

Up until now, your loved one may have been able to live on their own with no huge changes. Now, they are really unable to function without regular assistance. They will likely have trouble remembering people, even the ones that are important to them. Then they will begin to struggle with learning new things and those basic everyday tasks such as getting dressed become too much for them.

Also at this stage emotional changes come into play such as delusions, paranoia and hallucinations.

Up to this point, Stenmark could drive with me in the vehicle and he drove very well. I could leave him home for small, quick errands and he just watched television with no problem. He was truly able, up to this stage, to function without regular assistance from me. However, it was this stage that I began to notice he was having trouble remembering people that were important to him such as close family and friends. Stenmark loved learning, hence his many degrees, but learning new things became too much for him, such as learning to drive my new hybrid car. He also became well skilled in pretending to recognize people, including family and friends.

Stage Six: Severe Symptoms

This stage was tough… well, truly aren't they all? You may be noticing the list getting longer as the disease progresses into the latter stages. During stage six, Alzheimer's becomes very difficult for the person with the disease. They begin to experience significant and obvious symptoms. They absolutely cannot manage their own care and they become more and more dependent on the help of others. As your loved one's independence decreases, they can become more frus-

Heart Get Ready

trated as their personality changes in a big way. *Please remember that these monumental changes are not universal. Some afflicted with Alzheimer's disease are content throughout the course of the disease.* But it is very important to remember when these changes occur, your loved one is unaware of what they are doing at this point, so please try not to take it personally.

During this stage, Stenmark never heard his cell phone ringing. He no longer responded to things like phones ringing or fire alarms blaring, even when he pulled them at Alta Ridge at three in the morning. These things never phased him because he didn't have the slightest idea what to do. He no longer could manage on his own and became increasingly dependent on me and others to get him through his days. Communication became more difficult in this stage, especially communicating about specific things, such as experiencing pain. Personality changes are huge in this stage, Stenmark still used some words and phrases he always used but he had increasing anxiety, hallucinations, paranoia and delusions. His independence became nonexistent and he became more frustrated, even with me. So much so, that he had to be medicated with anti-anxiety medication. But it did help him and in turn it helped me too. I think it's important to remember they are not aware of what they are doing or saying at this point so try not to take it personally. That's tough as well.

This is the stage after Stenmark was diagnosed by the neurologist, Dr. Skuster. I was surprised by how quickly he went through the stages and asked her about it at that first visit. She gave me the *"everyone-is-different,"* speech, but she did say deterioration could happen quickly. That didn't make me feel better at all. But she was being honest.

This is also the stage during which he was prescribed, Donepezil, the medication to slow down the progression. I looked up the side effects and watched closely for any of them to rear their ugly heads. Side effects included diarrhea, nausea, headache, sleepiness during the day. The only thing Stenmark complained about while he was on Donepezil was a stomachache, so I gave him Pepto Bismol and that seemed to alleviate that problem, but then again experiencing pain is a problem, so who really knows. I would catch him swigging Pepto Bismol constantly. It could have been the bottle of Viagra he took in three days' time because he didn't remember taking any of it at all. Thanks again, Dr. Smith.

From that time on, I hid all medications. I had to or he would self-medicate. They forget what and when they take medications, even vitamins, so all medications need to be supervised. I started setting out everything he took morning and night, including his vitamins, and handing them to him with a huge glass of water.

This is also the stage where Stenmark went into his care facility. It quickly becomes too much for the caregivers to deal with. Once he moved into the care facility, the staff didn't complain at all, and they took great care of him. But when I was home alone with him, it was a lot for one untrained person. Part of the reason that I made the decision to move Stenmark in a care facility. One of the toughest decisions I've ever made.

And that is when my severed heart completely broke into a billion more pieces.

Stage Seven: Lack of Physical Control

In this stage, the decline is rapid, and you cannot miss it. Since this disease destroys brain cells, it can cause serious mental and physical impairment, where a person's mind is no longer able to communicate and delegate tasks effectively.

Alzheimer's disease destroys brain cells and eventually this causes severe mental and physical impairment and their body will begin to shut down as their diseased brain struggles to communicate and delegate tasks.

During this time, your loved one's needs significantly increase and they will need round the clock care. They will need help with walking, sitting and eventually swallowing. Mobility has decreased so much that their body becomes venerable to infections, such as pneumonia. At this point, it is vital to avoid the chance of infections at all costs.

During this stage, Alzheimer's had taken its toll on both Stenmark's mind and body. He was no longer my big, strong handsome husband. He was now a frail, thin and fragile old man. Along with his beautiful brain, Alzheimer's had taken his incredible posture, and his good looks, but of course he didn't know, and that was another check in the plus column. Stenmark would have hated his ravaged Alzheimer's mind and body; I was thankful that he didn't know. Of course, I still loved every inch of him. He did indeed need round the clock care at this stage and I was happy he was getting the wonderful care he needed. They all helped him immensely as he struggled with walking, sitting and eventually swallowing. Unfortunately, Stenmark's body had become vulnerable to infections due to his decreased mobility. In this stage it is vital to keep their teeth and mouth clean, which is also a struggle because they don't brush their teeth regularly. It's also important to treat cuts and scrapes with antibiotic ointment right away. The competent staff took care of those things. And flu and Covid shots were given regularly.

It got to the point that when I went to visit Stenmark, it was always something. His hygiene was deteriorating, and he flat refused to brush his teeth. One day I walked in and sat next to him and asked how he was doing.

When he answered I noticed he was missing a tooth. I asked the nurse about it and she didn't even realize it was gone. Before his Alzheimer's, Stenmark was a freak about his hygiene and brushing his teeth. He had three implants, and we had every kind of tongue scraper, mouthwash and dental stick that anyone could ever need. All important to him.

Now, he was missing one of his incisors and nobody even noticed. Where did it go? Did he swallow it? When I asked about it, the young, certified nurse assistant (CNA) went to his room and checked his bed but it was nowhere to be found. She informed me that she had just come on shift and would text the night nurse to see if she knew anything about it. She had no idea one of his teeth was gone and neither did my husband.

All part of this wretched disease.

It's important to remember that Alzheimer's affects everyone differently. The severity and the timing may be different for each person, and sometimes it's hard to determine which stage your loved one is in because they can overlap. Alzheimer's disease is the most common form of dementia. And it's heart wrenching to hear these four words; *there is no cure.*

Our journey was closing in on the final stages of Alzheimer's and I found myself floundering, because I felt like I didn't belong anywhere. I lived my normal life, but my poor hubby no longer lived it with me. And there was no chance of him coming back.

Just another emotional blow.

CHAPTER 31
Am I Losing My Place

Alzheimer's has a big reach, and it consumes everyone around it, even if family members try to stay away. They are only fooling themselves that distance will lessen the anguish they feel. In my experience, all staying distant does is increase guilt, especially when the end draws near and finally arrives. I know firsthand how hard it is to walk into a care facility only to see how much your loved one has changed while being there. It brings you to your knees in an instant. Trust me.

But I am also smart enough to realize that I'd be curled up in an emotional ball if I didn't go see my husband. The guilt would consume me and I would be no good to anybody.

So, I continued to drive to the care facility as much as possible, and I am so happy I did. I have no regrets. I also felt it was important to be seen regularly by the staff. I wanted to know exactly how my sweet husband was being treated and make sure his needs were being met. I would also suggest you change up the days and times you visit. That's what I did. I think it's a must. Let's face it, there truly is no perfect place as far as these facilities go. I have friends who have put their loved one in the most expensive care facilities and still had the same problems and complaints that I had. It's unfortunate, but no matter how high end these facilities are, they are usually understaffed and the staff is often overworked.

One day, I walked into Stenny's facility and went over to the chair he was sitting in by the fireplace. I sat on his lap, which was getting harder because of his weight loss. He was so thin and frail. I could only sit there for a couple of minutes and he would start to squirm and give me a slight nudge meaning he wanted me off. He was done. I learned to read the cues pretty well.

I would get up and then pretend pout, teasing him by singing a line from one of his songs, "Am I losing my place after all this time? Has LaMonte taken the love that was mine?"

Stenny would just roll his eyes and shake his head unimpressed with my attempt to tease him. But then he would smile and kiss me.

But today as I sat down and put my arms around his neck, I noticed he had a black eye. I stood up quickly, put on my *strong glasses,* lifted his chin, and looked at his eye closely. "Honey, what happened to your little eye?"

I asked my heart pounding.

He looked at me and said, "Nothing."

I started to react feeling my heartbeat at record speed. "Babe! You have a black eye!"

Stenny reached up and touched his eye...*the other eye.*

I lightly touched the correct eye and asked him if it hurt.

He shook his head, "no."

I couldn't believe it didn't. The blackness was all under his eye and on the side of his handsome face. Plus the color was such that I knew it wasn't recent.

"Honey, I will be right back," and I walked over to the CNA as Stenny's eyes turned to the big screen television. I asked the CNA, "What happened to my husband's eye?"

She had no idea and told me she just got there.

Apparently, I need to come before shift changes...note to self.

But in her defense, she rushed over to Stenny and examined his black eye, took pictures and told me she would find out. She was on it and I was grateful.

Then I noticed Rick and Kate, two other residents, as they entered the social room. I sat down next to Stenny and put my arm around him, as he carefully watched them. I softly asked him if Rick and Kate were mean to him.

Stenny gave me a stunned look as he furrowed his brow, and said, "Of course not, Bennett, they are nice people."

After a few minutes the nurse returned with some info. "I spoke to the night nurse and I guess Stenny wandered into Rick and Kate's room last week and Kate started to scream, which Rick took as her being in danger and started a fight with Stenny. So that explains the black eye." Both night nurses had to break it up but it was only Rick doing the fighting. Stenny didn't fight back at all.

That made me feel worse. My frail husband was getting a beat down by this big ass gorilla, and he just stood there and took it. It's probably because he no longer knows how to defend himself and I'm sure he didn't even begin to grasp what was happening and why.

This was a tough situation. Alzheimer people wander into each other's rooms. All. The. Time. This I know. But Rick is three times the size of Stenny. But he is also demented and was just protecting Kate, his wife.

My heart ached for Rick as well. But regardless, I had to make sure my husband stayed safe. That was my number one priority.

I texted Phil, the activity director, the pictures I'd taken of Stenmark's eye.

Phil called me immediately and was so upset. He informed me this was not an isolated incident. Apparently, Phil had stepped in between Rick and Stenny quite a few times. The story was always a similar situation; Rick hitting Stenny, and Stenny not ever engaging back. Phil also told me that this happened a couple of the times when Stenny was not even in Rick and Kate's room. Rick would just walk over to Stenny and punch or push him. Often Kate would join in, even throwing a pitcher of water at him one day.

I was livid, but not at Rick or Kate. Why wasn't I hearing about these problems with this couple? They had only been there a couple of months and never were there problems with physical altercations with Stenny ever before. The only other potential threat was Big Tony, but Big Tony just ignored my husband and would walk away.

I stayed awhile longer and told the nurse I'd called Phil to see if he had witnessed anything. I told her about Phil's several comments. She informed me that she had notified Emily, the head nurse, and I thanked her for doing so. Emily was going to reach out to Leah, the new director of both the memory care facility and the skilled nursing facility across the street.

I was near tears as I walked over to kiss Stenmark goodbye for the day. I honestly wanted to scoop him up in my arms and bring him home with me.

As I entered the door code, I looked back at him, smiled, and blew him a kiss. He smiled back ever so slightly and winked at me.

That's when I knew I really wasn't losing my place in his heart.

On the forty-minute drive home, my brain was reeling. If the staff was aware, why didn't they call me immediately and inform about this? I shook my head, sickened with horror. I thought about my next move. This is a serious situation that needs to be dealt with ASAP.

Heart Get Ready

After I arrived home, I texted the staff myself. I had questions and I needed answers. I sent out a group text to Emily, Leah, and to Lindsay, Stenmark's hospice nurse, stating I knew this was not an isolated occurrence and asked why I wasn't called. The texts all included the pictures of his eye as well. Lindsay returned my text right away privately. I knew she, like Phil and other staff, did not work weekends. Then she added, "I bet it was Rick." I didn't even have to tell her. She was very concerned and upset. The rest of the night, I had no other responses from my group text.

I hardly slept and when I did, I dreamt that Rick and Kate were both ganging up on Stenmark. It was a horrible, fitful night. I finally gave up on the Sandman visiting me anytime soon and got up. I hoped I would have reply texts from Emily and Leah, even though neither of them was ever prompt in responding to texts or voicemails due to their work. But I really thought I'd hear from them on such a serious matter that could truly mean life or death! It wasn't like I was wondering if my husband was out of Diet Pepsi, for hell's sake. But still, I held out hope as I picked up my phone and opened the messages—but saw nothing from Emily or Leah.

Utter disappointment set in.

However, there was another text from Lindsay saying how sorry she was and wishing me a peaceful night's rest.

I thought about this whole situation while dressing for work. I normally do not work on Mondays but was feverously trying to clear my waiting list to keep my weekend open. I liked spending the entire day with my husband on the weekend, especially knowing they were so short staffed on weekends.

On the weekdays they not only had more staff, but the incredible Phil was there, and he kept the residents busy with music, playing ball, going on bus rides, doing arts and crafts, and so many other things. It really was amazing how busy he kept them during the week.

There is a saying amongst Alzheimer care givers; *"If you don't keep them busy, they'll keep you busy."* True story.

Speaking of being busy, my day was nonstop, which was a good thing. That kept my mind focused on doing nails, which kept me from driving myself crazy by checking for texts that never came. After work, as I was driving home, I wondered why I got some of my best ideas while driving. I always heard that running was the best way to jumpstart creativity and spark the creative flow and I believed it. I guess like driving, running gives you the uninterrupted space for inspiration, time to clear and sort out your thoughts. You can even let your mind wander, *but please not while driving!* I find myself working through work and life's problems faster than ever when I am driving down the road or running on the track.

But tonight, even though I was perplexed, just like when I had to deal with Dr. Bran-Dee, it was so clear what I needed to do. But I was so exhausted from lack of sleep and working ten-hour days that I just couldn't physically do it that night. I needed rest and a clear head. I climbed into bed and checked *one last time* for a message. I've always been a person who gives people the benefit of the doubt and trust their actions are in line with their own moral compass.

In this case, I was right on with that. There was a text from angelic Phil detailing Stenny's day, assuring me that all was well. My heart could now rest easy for the night.

I fell asleep quickly and slept until three-thirty that next morning. Since I climbed into bed at eight, I had reached my goal of sleeping for seven or more hours. I woke up refreshed and ready for the day. Gone were the days of putting pen to paper when I woke up early. I sat down at my computer and wrote a rough draft to the three women, Emily, Leah, and Lindsay. I read and reread making sure it was exactly how I wanted it. Then I went to the gym and hit the track before work. I became inspired as I ran. I knew I needed to do some finetuning when I returned home from another busy day. After all, I truly liked all three of these women very much. I thought they did a tough job very well. Although I had to admit, I hadn't spent much time with Leah, because she was new, but I still liked her.

I sent out a text to the three of them again and just wrote a simple, "Thoughts or solutions anyone?" with a purple heart emoji. That purple heart had become my *signature* over the last two years anytime I sent a text, due to purple being associated with Alzheimer's disease.

Very shortly, I heard from Lindsay separately. I explained to her that I thought it was best to include her in my texts or emails concerning this matter, and she agreed.

Next, I heard from Emily, saying that she was sorry, then she offered up her set of excuses. One of which was them talking about solutions like they did with me and LaMonte. *We see how well that worked!* I finally just gave up and tried handling LaMonte myself. I was still getting verbally spanked by LaMonte, which included her physically trying to attack me. And oh, the name calling! First, I was a trollop, then a harlot, hussy, tart, kitty, scarlet woman, and even a woman of easy virtue! Some of those names I'd never heard before. As I said before, even Retta never resorted to name calling that I knew of.

But this was LaMonte's reality now and she believed I was all those things.

Deep down what I really was, when I left Stenmark's care facility (and all that occurred there), was the emotionally walking wounded. There was always something I had to deal with, and it seemed to be never-ending.

And the beat goes on…forever it seems.

Still, I had heard nothing from Leah, the director. Finally, almost a week later she sent me a chapter length text full of her own set of excuses, which included, "…*I oversaw a huge birthday party at the facility for one of the residents and she was a friend of the family, then I had a flat tire, then I ran out of gas, and then I had to deal with a resident in the assisted living facility across the street…*"

But truthfully, the reason was much more than all the above. Leah was in way over her head with both facilities and was unable to run either of them effectively. I knew it and so did everybody else—except Leah. As I said earlier, I liked all these women very much, but my husband came first.

Since July I had been working nonstop on getting my husband qualified for Medicaid with a company in Lehi, Utah. The paperwork was overwhelming and I was happy I started early in July. Our year would be up the first of October 2022, and the donated money would run out at the same time so this was beyond important.

I gave the owner of the company, Mark Haslam and his assistant Kathy all their contact information with phone numbers and email addresses. Emily and Lindsay had completed their parts in record time, but we were still waiting on Leah.

What a surprise.

I went home and began my fine tuning and although the finished email was crass in places, I felt it was important to get my point across. I was so tired of excuse after excuse and we were now the end of November 2022. I was forced to pay October and November's rent to the facility. I had a client who saved me by writing the facility a check for the two months, or else I would have had no choice but to bring him home.

Again, I didn't want her to do that, it was embarrassing, but she shook her head as she took out her checkbook without looking at me as she wrote the check payable to Alta Ridge Memory Care, almost ten thousand dollars.

My plan was not to charge her for her services. I would be doing her nails till I was one hundred, but that was ok by me.

But she wasn't having any of it. "Absolutely not," she said.

After that she paid me only in cash when I did her nails. "I know you won't tear up cash," she said, as she took out cash and handed it to me.

I smiled when she added, "I know you, dear Carly. You would tear up a check the second I walked out that door."

She was spot on. *I absolutely would have...*

CHAPTER 32
Now and Forever

After much writing and rewriting, agonizing and consideration, here is the email I finally ended up sending to Emily, Leah, Lindsay, and Phil. It gets rambly and emotional at times, but I decided to leave all that in.

Dear Staff of Alta Ridge Memory Care,

I am very upset with your lack of responses to my texts and emails, and particularly upset by ALL the excuses from Leah and Emily as to why no one gets back to me. The fact that my husband's beating by Rick seemingly happened during the day LAST week and NO ONE noticed that Kenny had a black eye and severe bruising on the side of his face and cheekbone is COMPLETELY unacceptable. Not to mention, NO ONE called me.

I'm sure his black eye had faded in the few days before I saw it and was much worse than when I arrived yesterday. I have macular degeneration and very poor eyesight due to this genetic disease and it was very noticeable to me immediately WITHOUT glasses.

What the hell, you guys? Do your damn job!

When I finally received your text full of excuses, I had to let them sit before I responded because I was so furious and utterly upset. I tossed and turned and cried all night thinking about this horrific incident happening to my sweet husband.

When I took Kenny into the lunchroom and first saw his bruises. I asked him about his eye, and if it hurt. I softly rubbed his bruised eye and cheek with tears streaming down my face.

We all know he speaks in word salad these days, but often I can pick up on the underlying message he tries to convey. Yesterday, I assumed he had fallen so I wasn't thinking about ANYONE hitting him there, for crying out loud!

But then I realized he was trying to tell me about Rick and Kate being mean to him. Because when I asked him if LaMonte was being mean, he got a bit frustrated with me and furrowed his brow as he shook his head no. Then he looked directly at Rick and Kate sitting at their table. I even said their names and pointed to them. They both looked over at us.

I am so upset with myself that I didn't pick up on this yesterday. I just thought Kenny was confused. And I thought he'd fallen. I never entertained the thought of him being hit by another person in the facility.

My sweet man.

NOW I MUST VENT AND GET EVERYTHING OUT:

From Day One, I've had to deal with LaMonte physically and verbally attacking me almost every time I visit my husband and now this, which is far more concerning. Nothing has really ever been done about LaMonte. In the very beginning some of the nurses, Leah and Emily specifically, did separate us from her. But now all that has stopped. I've had to deal with her on my own for the last few months. And trust me it's not pleasant, especially the name calling.

Nobody but Lindsay responds to my texts and emails in a timely manner. All I get is excuse after excuse—no solutions—when I do hear from the staff. And when I go in and happen to see Leah or Emily, that's when I get apologies for not responding and more excuses.

Also, I've been trying to get you to respond to Mark Haslam's and his assistant Kathy's several emails and messages for WEEKS now, so I can get Kenny on Medicaid. I can't imagine you don't see this as important. You are all very intelligent, and hello, this is part of YOUR JOBS. You guys referred Mark Haslam to me back in July and working with him remains important unfinished business.

I can't help but feel as if there's no sense of urgency on your part to help us get on Medicaid, now that you have received anonymous donations into Kenny's account. Apparently, there's no big hurry now that you have our money. But that will be used up come October 1, 2022.

I also had to pay Mark's company five thousand dollars out of my measly savings account just to get this ball rolling. They are doing their part and so am I. But your facility is not. (I'd like to add here that my husband received final approval two days before he passes away…ugh!)

I understand that everyone is busy, but so am I. I understand the excuse of being short staffed and trying to hire people. But then I get a text last night from Leah assuring me that you are not short staffed?

Seriously, which is it?

Mark's offices are calling me at work, leaving texts and messages saying nobody at the facility, except Lindsay, returns any of their calls or messages.

This has gone on way too long. I applied July 18, 2022. It wasn't until recently that Leah asked me to have Mark send her an email, which I did. I thought it was all completed, then I received another phone call and message from Mark's office which I forwarded to the three of you.

Lindsay was the ONLY one of you who responded to me.

I can't help but wonder if I had not decided to go down yesterday and discovered Stenny's abuse with my own eyes, would I have ever known about it?

I know Stenny wanders into the residents' rooms. Everyone that lives there does. It's part of the disease and I would hope you know that, as well. I've witnessed several other residents come into his room when we are in there and even when we are not. I began to lock his door and then they will knock. I open the door and its usually LaMonte with her back up forces, usually Jackie, wanting to know what we are doing. Then it begins. The name calling and dirty looks while sweet Jackie just stands there. LaMonte calls Stenny a pig and tells him she will have his things packed when he gets home. My poor hubby doesn't know what to do or say. I will never forget the look on his face or the hurt in his eyes in that moment.

But do I call you guys about any of this? No. I notify you only when it becomes more than words. Otherwise, I handle it myself, asking them to leave. I try to comfort Stenny by telling him she didn't mean it.

I know Stenny is hard at times due to his disease, but I rarely hear anything about him in a negative way. He isn't mean or rude at all. I know he wanders around all hours. I know he goes into opened rooms and takes food as well, especially treats. But I've been trying to help with that by making him his own treat box. I try my best to keep it well stocked. I know he's not the perfect resident, if there is such a thing in a memory care facility, but I do know he's damn close. At least that's what I've always been told. As we all know, Alzheimer's is a disabling and cruel disease. I know the shopping, aka stealing, wandering, and confusion is all part of it.

Dealing with Stenny's disease has truly wrecked me and left me completely heartbroken. But the lack of communication on these hugely important issues from the staff, excluding Lindsay, is disturbing at best. I have my phone near me 24/7. I have a sick husband and I know anything could happen at any time. Of course, I realize there are small windows when we can't respond in a nano second. I know that. However, not getting back to me on weekdays is inexcusable, not to mention downright rude. Especially in your field. My clients communicate with me by text all the time and I answer them quickly even if it's just a thumbs up emoji or a quick stay tuned, and its only fingernails.

I want these issues handled yesterday and I want the communication improved one hundred percent when it's a matter of great importance. Please know I will not contact any of you for petty reasons.

I want the Medicaid issue resolved and I want this incident with Rick and Kate fully investigated and resolved immediately. When you have all the facts, I want their family notified. I would want to know if the situation was reversed. They need to be aware of Rick's violent behavior towards Stenny. He is a big strong man and this could have been so much worse for my frail husband who can't defend himself if his life depended on it. And oh, guess what? It does.

I also don't trust Kate as far as I can throw her. She is very dramatic and theatrical. She screams and Rick comes running. I want both of them kept away from Stenny beginning now. I would like an incident report filed about Rick's abuse, and I am demanding I be contacted immediately with anything regarding this and any future incidents concerning my husband.

With all this said, I will do whatever is necessary on my part to make sure Stenny is as safe and happy as he can possibly be, taking his illness into consideration. I know I am emotional, stressed and upset beyond belief right now. I always try my best to be a kind soul, but please do not confuse my kindness with weakness, especially when it comes to Stenny. Like all of us, I do have it in me. I will continue to protect Stenny now and forever, make no mistake.

Thank you, Carly Stenmark.

Shortly after this email went out, they did notify Rick's family and Kate's family, as it was a blended marriage. They also told them if anything else happened, Rick would be "sent out," which means the police would be called and he would be taken to the hospital for a two-week evaluation.

A week later, unfortunately it did happen. Kate began screaming when Stenny walked over by her and Rick thinking he was protecting his wife, rushed over and pushed my sweet husband as they both yelled, then Kate stood up as Stenny was walking away and began pounding on his back.

The staff kept their word and called the police who took Rick to the nearest hospital which happened to be across the street. Fortunately, Stenny was not hurt badly this time, but I wondered if this was going to be a forever thing with the two of them. I don't know how much more of this we can take, especially my kind-hearted hubby. But as I said before, I will always protect him and do what I need to do to make sure he is safe...

I think I could easily take Kate, but Rick was another story! Of course, that's a joke...I would never!

These past few months have truly left me sad and lonely. Why did this happen to my beautiful man was the question that swirled around my brain. It was on a twenty-four-seven loop playing over and over, day after day, week after week. Then of course I have the guilt of putting him in the care facility in the first place. I know it was for the best, but my heart ached thinking of him being there and me being here in our place without the love that I missed so much.

Why? Why? Why?

Every time I confided in my sister, Bren, about my frustrations dealing with the care facility and the issues surrounding Kenny, she told me to trust in the Lord. Four months before I discovered Stenny's abuse at the care facility, Bren lost her own husband just a few months shy of their fifty-year anniversary. No practice marriages for either of them! She was so strong in her core beliefs. She knew beyond a shadow of doubt that her wonderful husband Dan was indeed up there in the arms of Jesus. And she was now waiting patiently for her own *promotion*.

I was a bit envious of her strength of faith through all the years he was so ill to when he finally lost his battle with ankylosing spondylitis (AS, commonly referred to as bamboo back or bamboo spine). She was so brave, just like when we lost our parents.

Bren visited me just four months after Dan's passing. I opened the door to my beautiful blonde, blue-eyed sister standing there with her rolling suitcase. She flashed me a smile and asked, "You got room for an orphaned widow?"

CHAPTER 33
Nobody Else

I laughed and threw my arms around my sister and gave her a sympathetic hug. Bren had the same dry humor as the rest of us and more than once it had saved me during hard times, especially now. During this time in my life, I needed to laugh or I would have continually cried non-stop. Let's face it, there were humorous things along the Alzheimer's path.

But now my sister was here and she always made me laugh. My brother Jeff used to say, "Deep down, Bren is still a Gautney," which was our last name.

The first thing Bren and I did was drive to the care facility so she could visit with Stenmark. Not only was she so good with my husband, but with the other residents as well. Bren spoke to each one of them. She agreed with me that Ralph, the golfer, reminded her of our own father. She walked up to Ralph's wheelchair, put her hand out with a very friendly "Hello Ralph", and began singing the Beatle song, *I Wanna Hold Your Hand*.

Ralph let out a soft chuckle and said, "Is that right?" as he extended his hand to meet hers. We both smiled at each other, because his response reminded us so much of our dad.

Bren's visit helped to ease my loneliness and pain. Bren was very smart, she had degrees in her own right, just like her daughter, Brandy. But she was also so strong in her own faith. It was impressive how she could quote line and verse from the Bible. Her scripture recall was amazing. I do not have that gift.

I was also blown away her ability to speak such comforting words to people, at just the right times. She knew just what to say, and then would top it off with an appropriate scripture that made my broken heart swell.

I was excellent at recalling song lyrics, but not even close with her recall of the scriptures. Nobody else in our family had that gift, but then she was the wife of a preacher man. Yes, Dan was a preacher for many years and he was a good one. He was well loved and held in high regard...and he was surely missed by everyone. I introduced them when Bren was only fifteen and Dan was seventeen. He was the security guard and I was a car hop at a drive-in restaurant in Salt Lake City, Utah, called Don Carlos and I thought he would be perfect for my sister. And he definitely was.

Bren stayed with me for four days and we had a blast. She was so much fun to be with and she was an excellent cook. I have a few things I can cook well, but it seemed everything she made was delicious—or maybe it was because someone else made it for me.

Nah...it was Bren.

After a week, her visit was over. The day she left; she got up early to begin her journey home. All too soon, her ride came to take her to the airport, where she'd get on a plane back to El Paso, Texas.

As I closed the front door, the tears began to flow. I love my sister so much and was so proud of the strong woman she was, but was envious of her incredible memory, but she was two years younger than me.

Bren had been with Dan twice as long as Stenmark and me, yet here she was, a pillar of strength, with her comforting me right after her husband passed away. I said a prayer for God to watch over her along her journey home. Afterwards, I chuckled to myself how I'd always teased her about praying.

All. The. Time.

Bren prayed first thing in the morning, at every meal, every time we got into the car for safety, every time before we got out of the car, thanking God for getting us to our destination safely, and on her knees before bed. At one point during her visit as she said, "Let's pray, Sis,"

"Again?" I said.

To which she replied, "Prayers—they're not just for bedtime anymore, Sis."

I giggled. And then we prayed...again!

I knew how I believed in the power of prayer, but as my new realty began to unfold, I found myself questioning the power of God for the first time in my life. I didn't understand his plan with this horrible disease that was gradually taking my wonderful husband away more each day. Our mother always told us that God wouldn't give us more than we could handle, and to pray about it. When I first noticed things about my husband that were not quite right, I did increase my prayers. I learned there were practical and spiritual benefits of prayer.

The obvious reason of course was to get closer to God, but I found praying also helped reduce my anxiety and added calmness to my days and nights. I began to be more grateful and thankful for the things I had been blessed with in my life. I noticed I was shifting my focus to others and looking outward. Prayers also helped me resist temptation, not that I did anything bad, other than a little love lie now and then.

Remember, Alzheimer's "love lies" do not count.

Mom also believed in miracles from God, and said all we had to do was pray and God would hear us. My mom had witnessed miracles in her lifetime and when I thought about it, I had too. So, to me a miracle was more than possible, if I had faith. So, I prayed and prayed for God to send a miracle to Stenmark.

But I was still waiting for that miracle and believe me I was praying for it daily. I guess this was Him not giving me the *no-more-than-I-could-handle* part. But I was still at it, because after all, I am a believer in God.

Nobody else loves me like the Lord, this I know.

But I admit Alzheimer's disease has made me question so many things. I was counting on my faith as being part of this process, *my process*. Stenmark wasn't sad or worried about being there. He didn't know, once he was further into the stages, that anything was wrong with him. He just thought he was working a new job helping people, which I thought was cute and of course I was very pleased about that part.

There was a resident named Faye who would wheel herself over to the locked door and frantically scream that she wanted to go home, pushing the buttons on the keypad and yelling "Let me out!" My heart hurt watching her, what if my husband did that? I felt lucky and very blessed that he didn't.

Honestly, he was happy and content being at Alta Ridge and so was I, if nobody else picked on him. So far so good.

Kate was being the model resident now that Rick was being evaluated at the hospital. I just hoped that once he was back at the care facility, all would be forgotten in his mind and he would be medicated just enough to calm him down. However, I was worried that when Rick returned, the drama from Kate might return as well. I was hopeful that maybe the Covid dementia she had would kick in just enough to keep her memory still. One can only hope.

In any case, I continued to see my husband as often as I could during the weeks, and always spent Saturdays and Sundays with him. That way I could help with his daily needs and take some of the workload off of the two weekend aides. I didn't mind doing that and Stenmark seemed to like it better when I was there anyway. I loved spending any time I could with him and enjoyed sitting in the social room talking with the other residents.

They all loved company and some didn't get many visitors. I know how hard it was. I lived it every time I pulled into the parking lot and walked through those locked doors. Each day is the same, but different - like the film *Groundhog Day*, so it's difficult to tell what they feel when you're there. But the staff told me they always appreciate visitors.

Sometimes visits were tough, especially when I visited and saw drastic changes in my husband. But I soldiered on and tried not to act shocked or depressed. I took pleasure in the little things; the way Stenmark smiled at me, or when he gave me a wink, told me a joke or teased me about some silly thing I said. I loved when he cuddled with me and asked me for a kiss or when I asked him for a kiss and he pretended to be annoyed with a slight sigh. Just like he used to do before Alzheimer's was in the driver's seat.

But I tried my best to live in the moment, because it didn't matter if Stenmark remembered my visit. I like to think it brought some happiness and joy to him while I was there holding his hand. I believe it's important to recognize that this strange evolution is the journey of dementia, and I had to come to terms with these changes in my sweet husband, both physically and mentally.

I am just speaking for myself. I know everyone's experience and journey is different. But it is never easy.

CHAPTER 34
It's You

I was just getting ready to head down to Alta Ridge when I received a call from Leah. "I wanted to let you know that I got a call from Alice (another resident at the care facility) at three o'clock in the morning." Leah was friends with the residents and had shared her cell phone number with Alice. During her call, Alice cried to Leah, "Stenny is in my room and he's eating all of my Fig Newtons."

I was surprised, not that he wandered into Alice's room, but that he ate her Fig Newtons. Kenny hated those cookies. Well at least normal Kenny did. I added those to the list to bring in.

A few weeks later, Phil sent me a picture of Stenny in another resident's room. He was lounging in an overstuffed chair with his legs crossed watching television. Stenny was wearing his black jeans, a nice blue golf shirt, and one of his TaylorMade golf hats.

As I looked more closely, I noticed he was also wearing a women's flowered sweater. I recognized it as belonging to Ava, the very tiny Hispanic woman. The fit of the sweater was perfect for Ava, but for my husband, not so much! The waist was up by his chest with the arms barely below his elbows.

One thing that sticks out in my mind with that picture is, it was one of the last times I saw him in his jeans. After that it was either workout pants, sweatpants or pajama bottoms. I remember crying the first time I saw him without his jeans. I went to my car that evening and just sobbed. Normal Stenmark loved his jeans and would never dress the way he was now dressing.

I had to learn to wrap my head around so many foreign things as Alzheimer's took the wheel. At first, I tried to get him to put on his jeans after his shower one day. He fought me tooth and nail. "But it's you, Babe. You never wear your PJs in the daytime," I told him.

He just looked at me like I was speaking a foreign language. It was in that moment I realized my determination had created more of a struggle than anything else. I also came to the realization I wanted him in his jeans. I wanted him to look like the man I fell for, and that wasn't fair to him at all, so I stopped trying to force my will upon him.

Speaking of a foreign language…about eight months into his "study" at Alta Ridge, Stenny began to speak Swedish. Over the years he would teach me a couple of words and quiz me, but this was different. He was trying to carry a full-on conversation with me in his parents' native tongue. It was wild. This was something I'd never heard of with this disease, but then the brain is so complex I would never even begin to try and figure that one out. I'll leave that to the pros. I just let him ramble on, nodding my head in agreement and smiling.

Repeatedly, on the weekends I would play music from my iPhone for him and other residents that would sit with us. I learned music was the last part of the brain to leave. Several studies have provided evidence that music is stored in the auditory dorsal stream including premotor and prefrontal areas. Research suggests that listening to, or singing, songs helps provide emotional and behavioral benefits for those with Alzheimer's disease and other types of dementia. Musical memories are often preserved in people with Alzheimer's because key brain areas associated with music memory are relatively undamaged by the disease.

I found that interesting, but of course we all know music can relieve anxiety, stress, agitation and depression. It is also beneficial to those of us who are caretakers. It somehow seems to lighten the load, plus it's another way to connect with a loved one who is challenged by Alzheimer's disease.

One day I was playing some of Stenny's music in the facility. He stared at my phone for a couple of minutes and asked me who it was. I smiled and said excitedly, "It's you, Babe, it's you!"

Looking puzzled he said, "That's not me, Bennett."

Without thinking, I told him it was indeed him.

Stenny didn't get upset, he stared harder at the phone while listening intently said, "Damn, I'm good!"

I laughed and whole-heartedly agreed. In the late seventies and early eighties, he had four songs on the Country Billboard charts in the top ten, so yes, he was very good and extremely talented. Stenny had the Midas touch when it came to music. His songwriting skills were remarkable and his voice was mesmerizing. The first question Bob Fead of Warner Chappell Music asked me when I met him was, "Have you heard him sing?"

Yes sir, I sure have.

Stenmark had a unique way with words. He used to say, "There's ways to say I met a girl in a bar…and *I met a girl in a bar.*" Also, he told me that "Including moon, June, spoon in a lyric was a big no-no, because it can't be too *rhymey.*" He was beyond clever with his lyrics. His music was sensitive, and coupled with his beautiful voice, it always pulled me in. I could listen to him for hours. I would arrive home from work to find him in his recording studio. "Sit down, Babe. I want you to listen to this song I wrote today."

It's You

While I clipped toenails and fingernails in the salon, he was writing music and lyrics and had songs ready for me to hear upon my arrival home.

Once when he went to LA to pitch some songs to Bob Fead, he told me after listening to two full CDs of Kenny's music, Bob asked him if all those songs were about me.

Stenmark said, "Yes and about thirty-five more."

Bob was so surprised and asked if I knew how lucky I was?

Yes sir, I sure did!

CHAPTER 35
Meeting of Hearts

Mark Sissel, Kenny's closest friend and lead guitarist on all his songs, now lived in Nashville. Kenny traveled to Nashville about once a year and they wrote songs together. Mark was such a talent on the guitar, it was no wonder that he caught the eye of country music artist, Chris LeDoux, in 1989, and was his right-hand man up until Chris' death in 2005.

Honestly there was nobody like Chris LeDoux.

Garth Brooks knew it when he introduced the Hall of Fame rodeo champion and singer/songwriter with a nod in his 1989 song, *Much Too Young (to Feel This Damn Old)*. Chris' son, Ned, was one of two very talented drummers in Chris' band, Western Underground. They carried on Chris' music for several years as a tip-of-the-hat farewell to their friend, and recorded the album, UNBRIDLED in 2007, as a creative outlet. During this time Ned started learning his dad's songs on guitar and picked up solo acoustic shows that dug deep into his dad's incredible catalog of music.

In 2016 Ned stepped out from behind the drums, started writing and recording his own music while still honoring his legendary father covering some of the fan favorites in his shows. I'm sure Chris was smiling down on his talented and loving son because Ned honored him in such a beautiful way.

It was a meeting of hearts through song.

Stenmark and I attended a Ned LeDoux concert in April of 2018 in Salt Lake City. Ned and his band were opening for the

American country music icon, Toby Keith, who unfortunately passed away this year. In the words of Mark Sissel, "We lost another good one too young, Carly." As I've said many times through this journey with my husband, life certainly isn't fair.

But Chris LeDoux and now Toby Keith...*what a difference one single life can make.*

Mark Sissel always made sure we had the best seats in the house or very close to it and premier parking with the bands gigantic tour buses and we were both very grateful to him.

The show was amazing, of course. But afterwards as we were in the VIP parking area, Ned came over to say goodbye, but then as he was shaking Kenny's hand, Ned asked, "Hey we have a break for a couple of months and I was wondering if you could write some songs for me."

I think my heart literally skipped a beat, but my husband didn't answer Ned and seemed to have a curious blank stare. For a brief second, I thought maybe he was speechless, because he was touched that Ned had asked him.

So, I quickly piped up and said, "Absolutely he can do that, right honey?"

All the sudden, Kenny came to life saying, "Sure, no problem, buddy."

Ned flashed that gorgeous smile, complete with dimples, as they shook hands and agreed on it.

I was so excited and thrilled for Kenny. I spoke about it all the way home. He was so talented and there was no doubt in my mind he could and would do it. Music was his passion and to have Ned believe in his ability to write a couple of songs for him made me so happy.

Kenny was his usual unpretentious self-saying, "Now hold on, Bennett. First let's see if I can come up with something Ned likes."

HEART GET READY

I agreed but I knew he was honored and excited, and of course perhaps a bit nervous. Kenny was also very humble especially when it came to his song writing and his music. He wasn't one to boast about his many accomplishments or successes.

The next morning, he woke early, had his breakfast of a smooth, creamy peanut butter sandwich, two slices of Grandma Sycamore bread open faced with his Rockstar energy drink. Kenny despised the usual put together sandwich, unless it was peanut butter.

When I got out of the shower, I found him in his music room working on a song for Ned. I was ecstatic.

Later, Kenny asked me to sit down with my cup of coffee and listen.

I pulled up a stool and listened with my eyes closed. I really liked it. Kenny finished the song and looked at me with his usual, "Hmm?"

"Babe that is so good," I said excitedly and I wasn't lying, it was very good.

Then Kenny in his fun way asked me his usual questions, "Does it have a good beat and can you dance to it."

I would always laugh because I knew where it was coming from. That line was from the dance show when we were teenagers called *American Bandstand*. I loved that show and watched it faithfully Monday through Friday with my mom and first three younger siblings. Those words became a running joke decades after the demise of the famous rate-a record feature when the ageless host, Dick Clark would ask a boy and girl to listen to and then rate up-and-coming hits on a scale of thirty-five to ninety-eight. If the rating was high, the standard answer became, "It's got a good beat and you can dance to it."

Stenmark told me he still needed to tighten up the chorus some, but I thought it was perfect. I know I am biased. After all, he is the amazingly talented *auteur compositeur*, and I guess I am the *color'de raconteur*.

Yes, I still love my French!

So, Kenny continued to write songs for Ned and play them for me. I felt like this was just what he needed. He hadn't had a hit since the early eighties. I would come home from work and he would be busy in his recording studio.

We were well into Spring when I asked him how the songs were coming along. Kenny's answer was, "Oh, I finished those last week." Oh, wow. I was a little taken aback because he hadn't called me downstairs for a while. But no matter, they were now finished and I was happy for Kenny.

"Oh, okay. Well, do you have them ready to send to Ned?" I asked.

"I do. They are all recorded. I just need to type up the lyrics. I don't think Ned would want to try and read my handwritten copies," Kenny said with a grin.

I understood that completely. He had made me a notebook with all the songs he had written for me in his own handwriting. It was an awesome gift because it really showed me the creative process of songwriting.

However, there were things crossed out, rewritten, and the key for each verse and line. They were scribbled everywhere on those first attempts, but I loved them all because those songs represented our own meeting of hearts.

The days went by and before I knew it, close to a month had passed. I questioned Kenny again asking if the lyrics were ready yet. "Babe, I don't mean to be a *"nagatha"* (my own made-up word for nagging) but Ned is probably waiting for the songs. He seemed very excited when he asked you,"

I reminded him.

Kenny answered, "Yes dear, I'll go get them," and he hurried downstairs.

I thought to myself…*Whew-this is great-yay!*

After a few minutes, he surfaced with a blue folder and handed it to me. I opened it only to find the handwritten songs. I thumbed through about twenty pages and they were all first attempts. I even recognized most of them, they were from the "Chardonnay Sessions," which were the songs that he and Mark did in Nashville. I looked at him, and before I could say anything Kenny asked me if I could please type them up for him saying he couldn't do it. He said he tried but could only type up one. I looked at it and it was the first song, *Those Prairie Winds*, a song I hoped Ned would like. It was right there in Ned's genre of Western music, because there is a difference from straight up-country music.

I thought it was odd because when I wrote my first book in 2015, Kenny came in as I was writing from my own handwritten pages using the 'hunt and peck' method. "Bennett what are you doing," he asked. I answered, "I'm transferring my written pages to typed pages for my book."

"No, no, no Bennett. I am going to teach you to type. This will take you forever," He was so right. He pulled up a chair next to me telling me it was important to always use the correct finger position.

"Good job Bennett," Kenny said as I smiled. Then he had me type the letter F with my pointer finger four times in a row with my left hand. He then instructed me to type the space bar once with my right thumb. Kenny watched closely, "Now type D four times, then S and then the A." He had me practice this repeatedly, spelling out FDSA, adding a space with my right thumb until I finished the first line. Kenny told me to repeat this exercise over and over until I filled an entire page, then delete it all which I did.

I picked my handwritten book and placed my hand in the correct position. I made several attempts, but I was failing miserably.

Kenny told me it would come with practice.

But I was frustrated and didn't want to practice.

"Scoot over," he said, and then typed while looking at me. Impressive. And then I read what he had typed, which was "You're lucky you are beautiful, Bennett. Now practice you little *shite*."

I laughed and said, "Okay."

But now suddenly he couldn't type? What was this all about?

CHAPTER 36
Keep Me in Your Heart

I chuckled and wondered if he was just being lazy? If that's the case, he is in big trouble! Regardless, I agreed to type up his lyrics for him, even though I had worked all day and my back was killing me. But if it will help him get these to Ned LeDoux quicker, why not?

Kenny stood over me while I typed, telling me how proud he was of my typing skills.

"Well, it's all because of you, Babe, you taught me."

He kissed the top of my head as I pounded away on the keys at rapid speed, at least for me.

I felt proud of myself, too, and thought all that typing practice I'd done helped.

I was confused, though.

These were still the songs from The Chardonnay Sessions, so I asked Stenmark about it.

His answer was puzzling. "Bennett, these are songs that haven't been produced yet and they will work for Ned. I think I know more about the music business than you do."

Well yes, he did so I helped him put the pages of typed songs along with two CDs in a manilla envelope addressed to Mark Sissel at TK Productions as instructed. At the last minute, he put another piece of paper in with the others saying he'd forgotten one. I mailed them on my way to work the next morning. Then I sent a text to Mark telling him they were on the way.

Mark texted back saying he was excited to see what we came up with.

That was the end of May in 2018.

Kenny was now in full swing at the golf course and he was busy as ever that summer. Mark texted him and said he was going to be in town and asked if there was room at the inn. We always had room for Mark and he was the perfect house guest. I was so impressed that he stripped his bed, washed the sheets, neatly folded them, and left them on the dryer the day he left. Best house guest ever. Ned and the other band members wanted to play golf so Kenny arranged that with Vaughn at Park City Golf Course.

That evening Kenny grilled steaks and we had a nice bottle of our favorite Cabernet Sauvignon wine, Parallel, a very generous birthday gift for me from Mac and Ann Macquoid. Mark was a red wine drinker so the timing was perfect. We all agreed it was the best red wine we had ever tasted. A huge thank you to Ann and Mac.

During dinner I asked Mark if Ned liked any of the songs we sent. Kenny chimed in with, "Oh yeah, what did he say?"

Mark said to Kenny, "Have you listened to Ned's music? You sent him the old Chardonnay Session songs we did a couple of years ago in Nashville."

Kenny didn't answer and I stayed silent and listened.

Mark went on to say, "Kenny, you have to realize that LeDoux is a brand and Ned wouldn't be interested in all those love songs you wrote about Carly."

GULP! I knew that was true.

But I couldn't help but wonder about the song, *These Prairie Winds*, because it was original, and not part of the Chardonnay Sessions. So I asked Mark about it.

"What song?" he asked. He had no idea what I was asking about. My mind spun. I asked Kenny if it was in the manilla envelope.

"Sure, Bennett," he answered.

I thought back on filling that envelope. But I knew I couldn't say if that song was in there for sure. I asked Kenny to play it for Mark when they went downstairs as I cleaned up after dinner. I had work early in the morning so I went to bed. It was common for them to be in the music room for hours into the night.

Mark was with us for a couple of days so I just decided to let it be. It was up to Kenny to pitch his songs and I didn't want to interfere with that, so I didn't ask Mark about it again. We both enjoyed Mark being with us. He has personality plus, and Kenny has known him for over forty years.

After Mark left, Kenny told me a funny story. They were downstairs playing guitar, listening to Kenny's music from back in the day of The Stenmark Mueller Band, when they played together on the road with the exceptionally talented singer, LynnDee Mueller. Kenny was playing one of his very best songs, in my opinion called *Cain*, which he wrote about his father who struggled with alcoholism. "You know the lead guitar in that song right Bennett?" he asked.

I answered, "Yes."

"Well, last night Mark and I were listening to that song and Mark asked me who was playing lead guitar. I looked at him, and he was waiting for an answer."

I laughed and said, "He was joking, right?"

Kenny answered, "No I thought he was goofing around, too, but he was dead serious!"

I asked, "What did you say?"

"I asked him, are you shitting me? That's you, Mark!" by now, Kenny was laughing so hard, he had to wipe tears from his eyes.

I asked him if Mark laughed and he told me he did. I hoped Mark realized how incredible his guitar playing was. He probably was struck at just how good that guitar playing really was and thought it couldn't possibly be him! But yet it was, Mark Sissel was truly up there with the best.

The irony here was that Kenny had remembered something important that happened a long time ago. Yet Kenny couldn't remember to transcribe handwritten lyrics using a keyboard.

But now as I look back, I know my husband wasn't being lazy at all, he didn't remember how to type and it began years ago just like Dr. Skuster had told us when she examined his MRI the first time.

Here is my take on our new reality; things will never return to the way they were, nor will they get better. Like it or not Kenny's memory issue is our new normal. Alzheimer's disease is the fifth leading cause of death in seniors and it's the only cause of death in the top ten that can't be prevented, slowed down or cured; at least for now, there are simply no survivors.

My husband had been given a death sentence.

As of 2022, over 6.5 million Americans aged sixty-five and older live with this condition, and this number is expected to surge to 13.8 million by 2060. These staggering statistics lead to a safe assumption that every family is or will be touched by this brutal disease in some way.

Even if I would have understood that these behaviors were not part of the normal aging process, it really would have, sadly, made no difference. By the time I actually knew he was *off*, Alzheimer's had taken almost total control of Kenny, and I simply had to accept this difficult truth and deal with it as best I could by taking care of him until I no longer could. As I've said before, caregiving isn't for the faint of heart. But can you even imagine what the person with this disease goes through? At least in the beginning. I shudder to think.

What's hard to deal with is, unlike Kenny, *I know that I am getting more forgetful as I age.* Alzheimer's only takes little bits from the person in the beginning—a few short-term memories here and there.

But then slowly, but surely, it robs you of all of them. Then in time it begins to steal your long-term memories as well until eventually they are all gone. I can't even imagine how that felt for Kenny. All along you know this is happening, but there isn't a single thing you can do about it. We were in the thick of it and were living it day in and day out. When will it get better? Honestly, the answer is it won't. I read the only time peace comes for Alzheimer's patients is when they pass away. Isn't it strange that for Kenny to finally find peace, everyone around us, me included must then grieve our enormous loss?

Oh, my precious husband…please keep him in your heart.

CHAPTER 37
TIL'

Stenmark had always been a bit "Peter Pan-ish" and he was the first to admit it. He did in fact when I had my first golf lesson. He crossed his arms across his chest and happily exclaimed, "I'll never grow up!"

I believe that's part of the reason he was able to unknowingly hide his Alzheimer's disease for all those years. Perhaps he did know, but didn't want to accept the fact he was losing his memory. I can only imagine how tough that was. I bet he battled between what he knew and what he felt deep down in his soul. I could second guess *whats*, *whys* and *hows* all day long, but the unimaginable truth was Alzheimer's was here to stay.

One day I ran across a gratitude list that Kenny and I had put together when we were celebrating our tenth anniversary. It was written on stationary from the Hotel Park City, which was adjacent to the pro shop at the golf course. I teared up as I read his list:

1. My Whiney Wife (there's his humor again)
2. My son and family
3. My health
4. My wife's health
5. How hot my wife is (lol)
6. My music
7. Our beautiful home

8. My intellect
9. My wife's hot bod (lol)
10. That my wife is *fun* (I couldn't write the last word he *really* wrote)

My list was as follows:
1. My awesome hubby
2. My family
3. My health
4. My hubby's health
5. My eyesight
6. The beautiful place we live
7. Newbie and Lola (our cats)
8. Our friends
9. My job and clients
10. Life = Happiness

Our lists weren't that far apart along the gratitude path and were written on September 30, 2016.

Kenny was big on lists. Three months before we got married, he handed me a notebook and a pen. I noticed as he sat down, he had his own tablet and pen.

"What's this for," I asked.

"Before we get married, I want each of us to write a list of what we can or can't live with or without," he answered.

Oh, wow that's interesting and kind of cool.

I was excited. Kenny was busy writing as I thought of my own list of *cans* and *can'ts*. "Bennett, I am being brutally honest and I hope you will be too," he said.

I smiled thinking that was the psychologist in him. "Okay, you asked for it, Stenmark," I retorted in my smart-ass way.

After about twenty minutes we exchanged lists.

The beginning of his list was beyond beautiful as he wrote: "Bennett-I will believe in you til'. I will need you til'. Til' the sun drops from the sky and the morning don't kiss the moon goodbye. Til' the mountains turn to dust and a dollar don't read In God we Trust. I will love you til'."

I learned at our wedding these were partial lyrics he wrote for the song we walked down the aisle to. I was so touched and I knew how much I was loved.

Kenny's List:
1. Learn Shit! If I fall off the face of the planet, you need to know how to do some of these things like the computer, the lawnmower, the snowblower, etc.
2. Get used to a Bossy Companion. I don't want to hear the words "You're not the boss of me, Stenmark because I am." (Lol. He softened it up at the end but again, we all know there's always some truth in humor.)
3. Don't interrupt all the time. *(OUCH!)*
4. Glasses On! With a chain. Kenny always wore his glasses on top of his head or on his face, which is why he tripped often. His readers brought things closer.
5. Admit when you fart! Why this was important to him, I have no idea why. (Girls don't fart!)
6. Don't be defensive! (Oopsie)
7. Stand up! Kenny had perfect posture and mine...not so much. Forty years of doing nails had taken its toll.
8. Shorter Stories—Sometimes!

I am a detail-oriented person and often I would be telling a story and he would listen patiently for a while. But when he'd had enough, he would bring his arms out to the side and say, "Land the plane, Bennett."

Heart Get Ready

EAT MORE! I don't want to invest time with a wife who hardly eats and I will lose her one day. (Okay, that's valid. I am very bad at remembering to eat.)

I changed my ways after reading his list. It was like a slap in the face, but Kenny was spot on. My list was almost twice as long as his with longer explanations.

You're not surprised, are you?

Carly's List:
1. More guitar playing please. Less watching television and more music.
2. I don't want to be talked into or tricked into skiing Jupiter Bowl, McConkie's Bowl, Ski Team runs, or Daley Bowl. I will probably ski them at some point (or maybe not) but please let me do it at my own pace.
3. Never stop being each other's boyfriend or girlfriend. Let's always keep it fun.
4. Please try not to be cranky when I go out of town with Zena to golf.
5. We must make time for the two of us to go on a little get a way. Let's try for every six to eight weeks.
6. Throughout our marriage that will last our lifetime and then some… I think it's important to keep it "datey" and fun.
7. I love taking pictures. Those will be our memories later in life so let's take lots more! *Little did I know…*
8. Please don't lecture me or get upset with me about my eating habits. I promise I will eat healthier and not starve myself, but I don't require as much as my six-foot-three, 205 lb. man. Your woman is five-foot-nine and 138 lbs. Please keep that in mind.

9. We need to consume less wine. A bottle of wine (or two) every night is not good for our bodies or our looks. Too much sugar.
10. Please keep your sense of humor and the teasing. I am getting used to it and I like it.
11. We need to go out for dinner or lunch at least once a week. We can change it up and even go to Costco for your polish hot dogs.
12. No pecking. As you know, I love to French kiss!
13. Please continue to sleep naked and hold each other all night long.
14. Please don't ever stop kissing my bare shoulder during the night.
15. Let's not ever let *Life* get in the way of *Love*. I love my man!

After Kenny went into the care facility and could no longer use his electronics, I was clearing his computers by transferring his data to an external hard drive, *(I did learn shit, as requested)* and I ran across yet *another* list he had made. This time it wasn't a gratitude list or what he expected after getting married. It was a list of all the women he had slept with during his lifetime. I kid you not. There were names, descriptions, occupations, cities, towns and states. But only Patti, his first love, had a last name attached to her number one status: Patti Brown. Kenny never talked about her, only saying he used to play the guitar and sing the Herman's Hermits song, *Mrs. Brown You've Got a Lovely Daughter* to her.

It wasn't until Kenny was noticeably affected by his disease that he began to talk about Patti, and it was constant. I heard every story from their junior high school romance until they moved from Minnesota to Utah together so he could teach skiing when Kenny was in law school at The U of U. But it wasn't just me he told these "Patti" stories to; it was also to all our friends and believe me all the details were included.

Remember, before meeting me he was a musician on the road and a self-described alley cat. Years ago, Kenny wrote a song about me and the first part of the song was, *"Lonely is the way I used to be, only a man in misery. Looking for a love like yours, I must have tried a hundred different doors."*

Well, the *over-achiever* did. He tried one hundred *plus five doors,* according to his list. I stared at the list and they were all numbered so I recounted just to make sure… yep! There were 105.

Thankfully, I was the last name written down. *Lucky me, number 105.*

I wondered when he had time to play music!

CHAPTER 38
WALLS OF MY OWN INVENTION

Before my husband had the clear diagnosis, I kept going back and forth with Kenny thinking he was okay one day and not the next, sometimes even weeks of this back and forth. Of course, this was before the serious things began to take place and then there was no denying it. I began to put up an imaginary wall around him when we would socialize. I was trying to protect and help him.

In November of 2020, after he had received his "death sentence" Alzheimer's diagnosis, we were at a social gathering and I had my wall constructed. It was tall and wide, metaphorically speaking, and I just kept building it higher and higher to protect him.

Finally Kenny turned to me and quietly said, "Bennett stop. You're acting like a wife."

I did stop, dead in my tracks. Kenny was undeniably right. I'd just broken one of my own cardinal rules and I didn't even realize it. *Never stop being your husband's girlfriend.*

I apologized sincerely and he kissed me. I went over that in my head and thought about his intellect and high IQ. Maybe he didn't need protection in these social situations with friends. Maybe I had invented that in my own fragile mind. I knew one thing for certain, I had to stop and simply let it be, watch, wait and see what happens without my gigantic wall. This was hard, but I know it was necessary. Kenny never asked much of

Heart Get Ready

me and this was one thing that I knew was significant to him. I saw the emotion in his lovely blue eyes. It was one of sadness with a touch of disappointment thrown in. How many times can a heart break?

One morning, I heard on our local radio station, KPCW Park City, that Adolph's Restaurant was closing its doors permanently. It would be open until the end of April 2022, after forty-seven years of the Switzerland-native owner Adolph Imboden bringing the cuisine of his home country to Park City. I shared the news with Kenny and we were both saddened by it. Adolph was a very close friend of my husband's and Adolph's was our favorite place to dine, or just stop in for a drink at the end of the day.

But that's not the only reason, not by a long shot. It was the place we first met. I saw this beautiful, blonde, tall man stroll in dressed in golf attire. I've always been attracted to tall men due to my own height. I passed up a few short ones in my day, because they made me feel too big. It's me, not them. I am a big girl.

Our eyes met and he asked Mary, our friend and bartender extraordinaire, who I was. Apparently, Mary told him I had a boyfriend, but Kenny told her that's not what he asked her. Mary told him who I was, but not before calling him a "horny little devil," as she handed him a glass of chardonnay. I found all this out much later, and I just rolled my eyes, shook my head and smiled.

Kenny walked over to the side of the bar where I was sitting with my friend, Karen. I had my back to him as I spoke to Karen and her perspective date, Dennis. But I did notice when he sat down that he skipped two bar stools. I thought that was good because I did have a boyfriend at the time, but he lived in North Carolina. We were doing the long-distance thing and we'd only seen each other three times in the last six months. There was no talk of being exclusive this early in the dating game. (Fun fact, Bartender Mary introduced my long-distance boyfriend and me.)

Kenny was polite and didn't bother us while we were deep in conversation, drinking our red wine. Finally, I turned to Mary as she was refilling my glass. Kenny looked at the huge glass as Mary poured the wine. "Are you going to drink that hot tub full of wine by yourself," he asked.

I just laughed and turned back to Karen and Dennis.

A little while after that, I turned to back him and noticed his legs were up on the two stools between us, and his feet were right next to me. I leaned over and pinched his toe through his shoes and said, "Hi."

Stenmark looked amused and smiled back, and said, "I'm Stenmark."

I stuck out my hand and said, "I'm Bennett." We talked for a good hour, mostly about music. Then he asked me if I golfed. I told him the story about buying lessons, with Karen, at the city course last year. "But then I broke my ankle playing softball. I didn't really care for my instructor. He offered us tequila from a flask and he smoked. "Yuck," I said.

By that point, I noticed Karen and Dennis were ready to leave, so I said my goodbyes to Mary and Stenmark. Dennis paid the bill and said something about going dancing uptown on Main Street. Just then Stenmark asked me, "What if I can get those lessons back for you with me? I work at the golf course."

Oh man this is embarrassing; he probably knows my previous golf instructor.

"You've already paid," he continued, "you might as well use them."

Stenmark had a point. "Okay," I answered.

Heart Get Ready

"How can I get in touch with you? he asked.

I reached in my purse and pulled out one of my business cards.

"I'll be in touch," he said, as he flashed me that awesome smile.

I thanked him and ran out to catch up with my friends. I wasn't into being the third wheel any longer, so I passed on going uptown as much as I love to dance. As I drove home, I wasn't thinking of my dentist in North Carolina. I was thinking of this cool, handsome man that I'd just met, who was into music as much as I was, and he lived a hell of a lot closer than the boyfriend in North Carolina. *And no wedding ring…bonus!*

Stenmark called me the next morning and set up my remaining six lessons every Monday at three. After my first two-hour lesson, he asked me if I wanted to go to Adolph's and have a drink. I said yes and we met there. I've always preferred meeting a guy where we were going, *just in case* I had to look at my phone, pretend there was a small emergency and make a quick exit. But I knew that wasn't going to happen. I felt it in my heart.

We were there about an hour when suddenly I had to ask Stenmark, "you're not married are you?" What made me ask, I have no idea. It just came out.

To his credit he didn't lie. "Yes, I am."

I turned my head away from him and said, *"fuck."*

I asked him why he wasn't wearing a wedding ring.

He told me it bothered him in the golf glove.

Okay, I get that but there's just no way. And I told him so as I finished my wine.

Stenmark finished his wine as well and that was that. We left and he walked me to my car. But before I got in my car, he said, "You should still do those lessons, Bennett. That's a lot of money."

I nodded my head and said, "Yes, but just the lessons; no wine afterwards."

Stenmark agreed as he opened my door for me and said goodbye.

The rest, as they say, is history.

No more walls of my own invention.

CHAPTER 39
Lovin' Mood

I woke up very early on this cold winter morning and decided to pop into Alta Ridge. I left the house at seven-thirty in order to arrive by eight o'clock, right when the doors opened. That way, I could help get Stenny up and dressed for the day. When I walked into his room, the heat wave when I opened the door almost floored me. I walked over to the electric wall heater and it was like a furnace blast. I quietly turned it in between cool and heat as the thermostat read eighty-seven degrees. I walked back to the door and propped it open. Stenny's room really needed some fresh air so I opened the window as far as the window allowed, about six inches. Another safety precaution, I'm sure.

I made my way to his treat box and filled it with the chocolate chip cookies I made when I woke at four that morning, mini-Hershey bars and Hershey kisses. Those were my precious man's favorite treats, but of course Alzheimer's had taken over his palette now and he would eat anything with sugar. (His neighbor, Sweet Alice, could attest to that.)

*** *** *** *** ***

Rosemary told us in our caregivers support group how the taste buds change with Alzheimer's and they only taste sugar. It all made sense now.

Lovin' Mood

I was frustrating myself trying to find something Kenny would eat. One day I suggested we go to the store and he could pick out some food he liked. Of course, he chose Walmart and I went along. I'm learning, no arguing.

Kenny picked up the small blue carry cart and wandered off, saying he would pick out his food. I told him I would be in the fruit and vegetable section as I pushed my large cart in that direction. I looked over the organic bananas, strawberries and the granny smith apples, knowing those were favorites of his.

As I strolled up and down the grocery isles gathering our food for the week, Kenny walked up to me with his food. The entire handheld cart was filled to the brim with packages of strawberry Twizzlers. I just stared at the basket.

"Just those, I asked in disbelief, don't you want anything else?" I knew he loved strawberry Twizzlers, but seriously?

"This is what I want to eat, Bennett," he said sharply.

I could tell he was irritated with me so I let it go and got in line to pay.

Kenny sat the basket down as the cashier asked if he liked Twizzlers. "Only the strawberry ones." Then he picked up one of the scanned bags and proceeded to open it asking the cashier, "Have you ever tasted them," and he tried to hand her a couple.

She declined saying that was okay, but Kenny insisted. "They are really good." The cashier looked at me and smiled as I nodded yes. She said thanks and I mouthed a silent thank you. I handed her one of my Alzheimer's cards and we walked to the car.

When we arrived home, I pulled in the garage and watched as Kenny walked into the house and closed the door. Gone were the days of me expecting help unloading the car. But it was okay. I reached into one of the three Walmart bags filled with the strawberry Twizzlers…all forty-two packages of them.

I took four out to take into the house with the rest of our groceries. Guess it's back to Walmart in the morning.

❦ ❦ ❦ ❦ ❦

I quietly walked over to Stenny's bed. He was sleeping so soundly. He looked so sweet and had such a serenity about his angelic face, I truly hated to wake him. I leaned over and kissed his face as I said good morning to my love. Stenny opened his eyes and patted the side of his bed next to the wall. "Lay with me," he said ever so softly and I felt a little touch of heaven.

I climbed over him as he opened his now frail, thin arms and reached for me. I laid my head on his sunken chest, and a tear fell from my eye. I knew it no longer mattered to him, but my heart was full in this moment of his *lovin' mood*. I had so much love for this wonderful man, I wondered if my broken heart could hold it all. But it did. That's when I realized that grief was just love disguised in a heavy coat. Without deep love, there would be no grief.

The nurse came in to get Stenny up and I looked at my watch. We both had fallen fast asleep and it was now close to ten o'clock. Once again, I climbed over my husband. When I went in to use his restroom, I stopped dead in my tracks. There on one side of his toilet seat, was one of his long ski socks. I knew what had happened. Stenny had slipped it on because the seat was probably cold. Every place we lived in, he immediately replaced all the toilets with heated seats that went down without slamming, except this last place. Another thing Alzheimer's had stolen from him, but I couldn't help but chuckle and take a picture. Humor once again saved me.

Honestly, there are so many instances where I just had to laugh. But I always followed my laughter with, "You're so cute Babe," and that always made him smile. I would never make him feel as if I was laughing at him. Not in a million years.

I was happy knowing he was happy there and I never ever saw a mean or angry side of him the entire time. I know some people afflicted with this cruel disease show a mean side, even if it wasn't present or noticeable before. I am sad and sorry for you if your loved one has taken that turn on their journey. I imagine that's very challenging for everyone. My heart goes out to you and I pray for your continuing strength during your own journey.

I have to also say that prayer has helped me with my journey. I have prayed to God, and I've also prayed to Jesus. I've prayed to the Universe, my angels, my spirit guides, my loved ones in heaven and even my spirit animal. I have prayed to anyone else who will listen to me, and it has brought me comfort, given me patience, and helped me deal with my own brokenness, sadness, regret, anger, and yes, even my grief. I have been grieving since this first began because I knew I was losing my husband to this *new* life partner, Alzheimer's disease.

Remember, Carly, we lose them twice.

I often questioned how I would feel when the second loss came around. Would I be relieved on some level? I couldn't imagine, but who knows? Would I feel more anger towards this new partner whole stole his health and our beautiful life together. *Is that even possible?* Or would I be happy for my wonderful man, knowing he had his bright brain back? That is a given, for sure, as I think about him having his beautiful spirit right there with him, now healthy and strong, once again in perfect form with no flaws. I know he will be so happy that

Heart Get Ready

he is no longer bald and has a full head of hair again. That alone would make him grin from ear to ear.

My thoughts of Stenmark consumed me each and every day, in a constant replay over and over in my brain. Memories of the past flood in and out as if I had my brain on repeat. This particular day, as we were nearing Christmas of 2022, I thought back to our first Christmas together.

Back then, we celebrated before Christmas with McLane at our home, having dinner and opening gifts. It was always a fun evening of music, laughter and stories of Swedish celebrations. Of course, I had all the Swedish decorations and certain foods (mostly pastries) for Stenmark and McLane. They both were overjoyed and so was I.

Then on Christmas Eve Stenmark and I celebrated in our loving way. I made a beautiful steak dinner, baked potatoes, and of course a huge salad. We drank our favorite Parallel Cabernet red wine with our meal, as it paired so beautifully.

After dinner, it was time to open our gifts to each other and we both got very spoiled by *Santa*.

As the end of the evening, we opened a bottle of our favorite French champagne, Veuve Clicquot, and had a variety of Swedish pastries. I purchased sexy new Christmas outfits from The Blue Boutique and we changed into them before we had champagne and dessert. I'll leave the rest up to you and your imagination.

Life was so wonderful back then.

♥ ♥ ♥ ♥ ♥

By December 2020 everything was so different. I bought our Apple watches with GPS and internet and cried as I wrapped them up and put them under our tiny tree that I decorated alone. Stenmark wanted hamburgers from Five Guys so I placed an order and we walked over together holding hands to pick them up. I didn't dare leave him alone and it was only a four-minute walk, hardly worth starting up the car. The night air was refreshing and we sang our favorite Christmas song, *Baby, It's Cold Outside,* as we walked.

After we finished our dinner, we opened our gifts from *Santa*. Stenmark couldn't figure out how to set up his watch (another sad fact), so I did mine and helped him with his. Then it was off to bed as the watches charged. That was a sad, unexpected ending to what used to be a loving, tender, intimate evening. Those days were long gone and *his "Lovin' Mood"* had become a thing of the past and I had become his caretaker.

And the hits just keep coming as time continues to march on.

CHAPTER 40
Love Looks Like You

At this point, we were approaching Christmas December 2022. Stenmark had been in his new home now for fourteen lonely months. I think back on it and some days it felt like forever while other days seemed to pass in the blink of an eye. This disease is tough in so many ways. On one hand, I wanted time to stand still so I could have Stenmark with me longer. But then the guilt would set in, as I knew deep in my soul that he would absolutely hate being here like this, if he knew. Alzheimer's disease is so humiliating for the unsuspecting recipient. I was just being selfish, longing to keep him with me for as long as I could. I knew it, but I couldn't help it. I was (and still am) so in love with Stenmark, I really couldn't imagine life without him. The tears started to flow as I envisioned my empty world crumbling.

I changed my thinking, as it was another brand-new day, still hoping for a reversal of this unfair life sentence. Tonight was not only the Alta Ridge Christmas party, but it was also the day that Rick was to be released from the hospital and brought back to the facility, now medicated. He had been gone for a couple of weeks. So, I had two things to look forward to as I drove to Alta Ridge. One with joy and excitement, the other with fear and hope. I knew the dinner and party would be lovely, so I prayed the meds had kicked in and Rick would be docile and kindhearted.

I met McLane and Retta there and we walked in. After a few minutes of pleasant conversation, Stenny turned to me and asked me who Retta was. I quietly answered him and he looked at me furrowing his brow, "What's *she* doing here?"

I told him she came with McLane, his son. His surprising reply was, "I don't like her, she's mean!"

I kissed him on the cheek and told him softly to be nice because it was Christmastime. "Yes dear," was his response.

During our entire time together as a couple, Stenmark never uttered a bad word about Retta. He always spoke highly of her saying he simply fell out of love with her and they grew apart. There was no name calling or complaining about Retta… ever. Stenmark always said she was a great lady and he was so grateful that she was a wonderful mother to McLane. He even said he felt if things had happened differently between us, Retta and I would have been good friends and hoped that would come to fruition one of these days.

♡♡♡♡♡

In fact, one day when I was picking him up from Retta and McLane's house, she came out with his guitar and other heavy musical equipment. She helped me get it into the back of my car telling me to be careful not to hurt my back. I thought to myself, *wow…she has come a long way from not even wanting my car in her driveway!*

But I was touched as I drove up Parleys Canyon to Park City. After we arrived home, I got Stenmark settled in and I picked up my phone and texted her. I wrote something I should have written all those years ago.

"*Dear Retta,*

Thank you for your help today with Kenny's musical equipment and for your kindness towards me.

I know I owe you a huge apology for my behavior years ago and have for a very long time.

I realize I hurt you and it was very hard on you and McLane, and for that I am deeply sorry.

I know I don't deserve your forgiveness and rightly so, but I feel compelled to express to you my feelings of remorse. I was completely in the wrong and my actions were inexcusable.

Thank you again for your kindness towards me since this all began.

Carly"

Later that same evening Retta replied.

"Carly thank you for this message…I have honestly waited a very long time for this closure. So thank you for that.

But it's all water under the bridge and all we can do now is press forward. God bless you and Ken,

Retta Good night."

♥♥♥♥♥

From that time on, Retta and I had several conversations, some very in depth as she told me she couldn't admit it up until now, but felt she always knew, that I was Kenny's one true love and he was mine. Retta's remark touched me deeply and I couldn't help but tear up. Mostly for the realization of what a tough step that had to be for her. To admit such a hard truth directly face to face with me. God bless her.

I was also very grateful to Retta for being such a huge help to me during this journey with Kenny. She truly was there every step of the way. She had so much knowledge in her medical field that it was invaluable to me. Retta knew everything about geriatric care and I was so appreciative. She knew the "tricks" to get Kenny to do the things I had no idea about. Everything from collecting his urine specimen to using that little grey sponge on the popsicle stick when he was thirsty and couldn't manage to sip water. Retta and I would text about Kenny and her words were always so soothing during that time. They made me wish I hadn't waited so long to offer up my long overdue apology. I now consider Retta a friend and I believe she feels the same about me, at least I hope so. Stenmark was right all those years ago. I know this would have made him smile.

♡♡♡♡♡

Stenny was used to sitting at the first table in the lunchroom, so he went to his seat, even though the rest of the residents were at large tables with their own families. The facility had decorated the social room and added extra tables. They also hired a three-piece band that was playing beautiful Christmas music. It was lovely.

Stenny sat at the table while we went through the buffet line. It was a prime rib dinner with all that goes with it. They even had salad which made me happy. I did Stenny's plate with extra prime rib. As I neared the end of the line, I glanced over at him. He flashed me a smile and winked at me. I was in heaven. Stenny still had the blank stare in those once mesmerizing blue eyes, but it was wonderful to see his sweet smile and the wink that always made me melt.

The dinner was delicious and Stenny ate every bite. McLane offered to get him dessert, which was chocolate chip cookies, Stenny's favorite. He ate two and asked me to get him another one, and I happily did.

As we sat there, Stenny got up without saying a word and walked across the social room to the table where Rick and Kate sat with their family.

Oh no! My heart skipped a beat as I watched Stenny closely. But my husband simply extended his hand to Rick and they shook hands like pals.

Heart Get Ready

I breathed a sigh of relief as Stenny turned to come back to the table. Rick and Kate smiled and waved to us. The meds had either kicked in big time, or they were jolly and in the Christmas spirit. Maybe a little of both. Stenny sat down next to his son, as he reached his hand across the table wiggling his fingers. This was just his cute way when he wanted to hold hands, so I reciprocated putting my hand in his.

Then as clear as can be while looking me in the eye he said, "Isn't my wife beautiful, she is so sweet and nice to me. I love my wife so much."

♡♡♡♡♡

There was no word salad, no jumbled words at all. Stenny was totally making sense and I was beyond surprised and definitely elated. I must admit it was a bit awkward sitting there with Retta while he spoke about how much he loved me. The last thing I wanted to do was make her feel uncomfortable.

So, I said happily, "Well, your wife loves you, actually we all love you." No response from Stenny, but that was okay. His clarity was so unexpected that I decided to tempt fate.

"Honey, I have a great idea," I continued. "Why don't I kidnap you tonight and bring you to our house up in Park City. We could wait for Santa together." Even though it was six days before Christmas, fortunately he no longer remembered what day it was.

Stenny looked at me as if I was crazy and said, "Bennett, I can't do that. These people still need me. I'm not finished with my work here."

It was so adorable and it made my heart swell with pride. This man was always concerned about the well-being of others, even now. These things just made me love him more and more. Stenny *was* my one and only true love and I knew I was his. He looked at me lovingly as if to say, *love looks like you.*

254

The evening was ending and after many hugs and kisses, we said our goodbyes. It was a cold dark December night, but I had the warmest feeling in my soul as I drove the short three minutes to Janice's house, my best friend of almost sixty years. I couldn't wait to tell her about my evening. Janice was, and always had been, such a sweet soul and her kindness was sincere, genuine and heartfelt. I called to tell her I was on my way. When she answered the door, she greeted me with a glass of red wine. Janice knew.

I had to be at the salon by ten o'clock the next morning so we didn't have our usual two-or-three-hour chats. It's so hectic in the salon, especially the last two weeks of the year.

I slept well that night, as I was happy about Stenny's new way of communicating. I couldn't stop thinking about it with such delight. He was (somewhat) the way he used to be. Even after all this time, I still secretly wished, hoped and prayed that he was getting better. I still held out hope he was becoming normal Stenmark. I thought about how happy we would be once again.

Before I drove back up to Park City that morning, I decided to stop and check in on Stenmark, since Alta Ridge is on my way to the freeway.

As I walked in the door, Emily stood up from her desk to face me and said, "Carly, I want to let you know that Stenny didn't want to walk this morning, so he is in a wheelchair now. He didn't want breakfast either. I don't want you to be alarmed when you walk in and see him. He has been pretty tired this morning, but that happens often with this disease. They get over stimulated when there is a lot of people and commotion happening, and last night's Christmas celebration was a lot to take in."

I nodded in agreement. I'd read all about that in one of my Alzheimer's books, so I understood. I thanked her as I entered the in the safety code.

When I entered Stenny's room, he was asleep in the wheelchair. I knelt down beside him, lightly rubbed his now thread-like arm, and said softly, "Hi, Babe. Emily told me you were tired this morning."

My husband opened his eyes and nodded his head in agreement.

Then I added, "Did you have too much fun last night, and now you're all tuckered out?"

Stenny offered a slight smile and said, "Yes."

I hugged him and gave him a kiss, saying "I have to go to work, but I'll be back." I also reminded him to eat his lunch since he had no breakfast.

His answer was a short "Okay."

I drove to Park City with not as much optimism as I'd had the night before.

The day flew by as it does when you are busy. I received no calls from Emily, so I chalked that up as a good thing. My three o'clock appointment called and cancelled her two-hour appointment. I understood. This was a busy time of year for everyone.

Tis the season and all that jazz.

CHAPTER 41
I'll Never Find Another You

I was busy cleaning up my room and getting ready for the next day when my cell phone rang. As I picked it up the caller ID read, Alta Ridge Memory Care. I answered. It was Emily. "Hi Carly, Stenny has not been doing well today and we think you should come down. He has been in bed all day and hasn't eaten."

My heart sank.

"Okay, I am leaving work now and I will be there soon." I hung up and my hands were shaking as I thought about last April. My eyes filled with tears and I quickly turned to my appointment book and with my cell phone, I snapped a picture of the week's page and the following week, which was to be my last day before I sailed into retirement.

As I drove out of Park City proper and approached the stop light into my neighborhood, I made the right-hand turn remembering the last time I was going on vacation and had everything I needed in my car, and my cats were boarded. Now this time, I knew I must take a few quick minutes to feed my cats and pack an overnight bag, just in case.

I had been wrapping Christmas gifts and wrapping paper, ribbons and bows were everywhere. It looked like the sugar plum fairy had exploded in my condo, but I was in a hurry and left it all as it was. The kitties didn't care.

With my bag packed, I got in my car and began my drive down to Alta Ridge. I called my close friend, Dagmar and told her what was happening. "Do you mind checking in on my cats and feeding them if I can't get back up?"

Dagmar had the code to my door and a spare key. "Not a problem, let us know when you can."

I told her I would and she added, "Let Jeff and I know if we can do anything for you." That was Dagmar, always willing to help. I thought about how much she had helped me when this first began. Dagmar was the first person I shared my suspicions with and she was there for me every step of the way.

As I continued down the canyon to Salt Lake City, I called Janice and of course she offered her extra room for me...just in case.

As I pulled into the parking lot of the facility, I parked and turned off my car. I thought about my choice to retire so I could spend more time here with Stenny. I felt like the owner's decision to sell the salon and retire herself was my cue and I looked forward to being with Stenmark.

I bowed my head and said a quick prayer. I walked into Alta Ridge. Emily and Lindsay, the hospice nurse, met me as soon as I entered. Lindsay spoke first saying, "Stenny has been sleeping all day. I have been checking his vitals every hour and they are good. He doesn't have a fever, but he isn't speaking and his eyes are closed." Lindsay went on to say she gave him a covid test and it was negative.

I fought back tears, as we walked to his room. Stenmark was in his twin bed and he was just as she described, but he was pale. I sat down next to him on his bed and said, "Hi honey, how is my man."

There was no response and I began to cry as I laid my head on his chest. Lindsay came over to me and rubbed my shoulder in her kind sympathetic way as I sobbed. Again nothing from my sweet husband as I thought about pulling myself together. I needed to call McLane.

I reached for the tissue box holder on the nightstand that used to sit next to his side of our bed all those years ago, before life had ground me down to a nub.

I dried my tears as best I could and kissed his lips. "I will be right back, Babe."

Lindsay and I walked out into the hall. I said, "I need to call Stenmark's son."

She told me she was going home and would not be back in until after Christmas but would be calling the front desk to check in daily. "You have my number, Carly, if you need to talk to me. There will be other hospice nurses coming in every day to check on Stenny."

I knew Lindsay had young children and it was only days before Christmas. I completely understood and thought how kind her offer was. Emily came around the corner and spoke to Lindsay. I knew they both had become very fond of Stenmark during these last fifteen months. I thanked Lindsay as she turned to wave and say goodbye.

Then Emily slowly walked up to me and asked if I wanted them to "send Stenny out." I knew what she meant as I'd heard those same words back in April. I thought about his week in the hospital, all the testing with the wires glued to his head, while he tried to pull them off. The doctors suggesting they tie his hands down to the bed at the hospital. I defiantly told them, "Hell no!" So they ended up putting these big white terry cloth mittens on his hands to prevent him from being able to grab the annoying wires. I paused as those thoughts entered my head. "Can I wait until his son gets here, Emily?"

Emily hugged me and said, "Of course, Carly." I wanted to talk to Retta and McLane as a courtesy, but I knew my mind was made up.

I leaned against the wall outside of my husband's room hoping it would hold me up as I looked at my phone. My knees were weak and my hands were shaking. I made the decision to call Retta instead of McLane. I knew he only texted when he was working and this warranted an actual phone call.

Retta answered and I told her what I knew in my broken voice in between my sobs. Since she was a retired nurse and nurse practitioner, she knew all the right things to say and ask. Retta first asked about his breathing. Was it labored and short? Was it raspy sounding?

I said no to all questions.

She then told me that McLane would be off work in about an hour, then they would be over. "He should finish his shift, since it isn't dire," Retta said.

And I agreed.

I used my key and went back into Stenny's room. I sat down next to the mere shell of my husband. I laid my head on his sunken in chest. My mind flashed back to the time when he was normal Stenmark. I pictured him in his blue golf shirt and tears filled my eyes. The shirt he was wearing the night I met him.

Stenmark was so big and strong with broad shoulders and a smile that made me weak in the knees. I sat up and pulled myself together long enough to create a text to this week's clients.

I knew I wasn't going anywhere anytime soon.

Stenmark had not spoken or opened his eyes since I arrived. The nurses were in and out every hour checking his vitals and taking his temperature. The entire staff came in on and off, checking on him throughout the day. I knew how much he meant to all of them. Retta showed me how to use the gray sponge on the popsicle-like stick that was in a small dixie cup. I was amazed as I watched Stenmark put his lips around the sponge taking in the small amount of water it provided.

I learned from my mom's nurse that hearing is the last to go as we all sat by her bedside thirteen years ago. So I knew Stenmark's perfect hearing would still be going strong, and I also knew Retta was aware, given her professional training, so when they arrived it was only positive words. Retta knew exactly what to do, and look for, as she was also giving him the little gray sponge and listening closely to his breathing.

This was a very difficult time for all of us as we sat in Stenny's room. He was unresponsive, eyes closed. Retta told their son that the time was now if there was anything he wanted to talk to his father about.

McLane agreed and we left him alone, with his father, to have the time he needed.

Before Retta and McLane went home, I told them I'd made the decision not to have Stenmark sent out to the hospital, and Retta fully agreed. Why prolong this cruel and insidious disease? I wanted my wonderful husband to be set free from the grasp of Alzheimer's. I knew it would be what he wanted if he was able to understand. There was no way he would want to live like this.

I talked with Stenmark about it after they left, as I sat by his side tearfully explaining why. I told him, "As much as we all want you with us, your brain is rapidly shrinking and dying. It breaks our hearts to witness this disease take over such a beautiful man." I cried as I told him how his mother, father, and sisters were up there waiting for his arrival. An arrival that would be a big celebration and he would walk towards the light with a healthy body and his big bright brain all back intact, as I held his hand.

Then suddenly Stenmark squeezed my hand!

I sat up quickly and looked at his sweet face knowing he heard me. I said a prayer out loud asking the Lord to watch over his precious soul and deliver him back into His arms.

Stenmark held on tighter and that made me smile through my tears.

I stood up to use his bathroom to discover he had a very tight grip on my hand. "Babe, I am just going to use your toilet and I will be right back."

The hold he had on my hand did not ease up at all, so I sat back down saying, "Okay honey I will stay here," and he loosened his grip ever so slightly. I looked at his thin pale face filled with so many lines, lines that I'd never seen before fifteen months ago. Yes, Alzheimer's had taken its toll, ravaging not only his incredible mind but his physical appearance as well.

Oh how I hate this fuckin' disease.

I couldn't continue to dwell on it. I refused to give it any more energy than necessary. I had high hopes that one day there would be a cure and Alzheimer's would be a thing of the past. Although it would be too late for my wonderful husband, I found solace thinking about the millions of people in the future, who wouldn't have to be faced with this, and their loved ones who wouldn't be forced to watch it happen.

I switched my brain off the Alzheimer's loop and began telling Stenmark about Christmas in four days. "Your favorite holiday is almost here, Babe," I said, trying to sound as joyful as I could. "You love Christmas and guess what I told Santa? I told him you wanted a new pillow." Stenmark loved a good feather pillow and it had to be the real deal, no down alternatives for my guy, or me for that matter. He always bought at least two, sometimes four, pillows. I was merrily chatting away when I realized I *really* had to use the bathroom and I tried to free my hand, as he held on even tighter.

"Babe, I have to use your toilet or I am going to pee my pants. I will come right back; I promise my love." Stenmark loosened his grip and I did return as quickly as possible. But before I sat down, I walked over and turned on the television purchased those short fifteen months ago.

"Guess what, Babe? I am putting on your very favorite; Christmas music!" In our house he would turn on Christmas music as soon as he heard it playing in Costco, which drove me a bit cuckoo. Don't get me wrong, I do enjoy it, but I'd prefer to start it around December 20th, then off it goes December 26th and its back to rock and roll.

I found the perfect channel, "Songs for the Season." It was in between songs as I took the few steps to Stenmark's twin bed, took hold of his hand and his favorite Christmas song began to play, *Mary, Did You Know?* and I laid my tired head on his chest and cried. I let it play even though it was breaking my already broken heart. I knew Stenmark loved it, so I told his nurse to leave it on all day and all night. They happily agreed.

I laid there for what seemed to be an endless amount of time, trying my best to "dry up," which was my own made-up term when my kids, and particularly my grandkids, were little and cried for no apparent reason. I would put my hand on their cheek and softly say, "Okay, it's time to dry up now." But I found it harder to follow my own rule now. I cried way more than I laughed these days.

It was close to midnight when I left that first night and my sweet friend Janice picked me up. I planned to stay with her until who knew when. My car became a permanent resident at Alta Ridge after dark due to my inability to drive at night. Janice was a real sport and I thanked her every time she arrived, and every time she dropped me off early in the morning before work. I sat with Stenmark and talked to him positively. I met visitors at the door and motioned them to the hall. "Please only positive speech in the room. Hearing is the last sense to go and I want the conversation to be pleasant for him."

I knew that everyone would be in complete agreement.

Heart Get Ready

My daughter, Channy, walked in and gave him a kiss on the cheek saying, "Hi Kenny Stenny," and I thought how endearing her pet name was. All of my kids came in and out every day, as did my grandkids. They all loved their Grandpa Ken and I was proud of all of them for making the time. Three of them had children of their own and all of them had jobs and lives as well, but still they were there to support me.

I have the best family ever.

This particular night, emotions were high. As my children left, I walked outside with them. There were lots of waterworks.

The crisp night air felt good against my tear-stained face. We said our goodbyes and all of a sudden, my son, Rick, came running back to me saying he didn't get to say goodbye and hug me. My mind was not my own and I forgot as he was busy helping April, his sweet wife get their young boys in the car seats. I threw my arms around my sensitive son and he began to sob. It isn't often I see my sons cry, my daughters yes, especially Channy, my little weeping willow tree. My youngest child, Megan, as she has grown and evolved with Mario, her husband, has become a little weeping willow tree herself. My boys are both extremely sensitive, especially when they see me cry. But tonight was a different type of cry from Rick. It was almost primal, and I felt his sorrow deep down in my soul, as we both sobbed uncontrollably. "I'm so sorry, Mom. I love you," my sweet son said.

I managed to say, "I know, sweetie, I love you so much. Thank you, Ricky."

It was a tender moment that I will never forget.

The next morning my longtime friend and client, Kathy Richards called bright and early. We both have prided ourselves on being early risers knowing we can text or call one another any time after five a.m.

Kathy has been a trusted friend and client for over forty years and I love her dearly. "How about I stop by today and sit with you and Ken for a few minutes. I am coming down to Salt Lake to run a few errands."

I told her I would love that. Since everyone was at work today and also busy with last minute Christmas shopping, I was excited to see a fresh face.

Kathy is a lovely Mormon friend of mine who never once in all of these years tried to convince me I should get back into the church. She has only supported me with love and kindness. She knows I was a wild child back in the good ole days and she loves me anyway. Kathy read my first book, which is filled with stories in great detail of my sordid past. It's all in there, the good along with the bad and the embarrassing.

But she didn't care saying, "I like real, Carly."

Kathy arrived close to noon with lunch in hand. I was so grateful for the delicious grilled chicken salad. The staff was kind enough to bring me what would have been Stenny's lunch each day, but I was elated to have a salad. I don't think there was a leaf of lettuce in that place. But then again, most of the residents were toothless.

My husband, who had four implants in his mouth, was now missing three teeth due to his lack of dental hygiene, but his implants were still standing.

Kathy stayed a good hour and I even asked her to say a prayer with us. She was happy to do so, but of course she would never ask. It was a beautiful prayer filled with love and positivity about visualizing Ken in the arms of Jesus and I was so touched and appreciative.

I hugged Kathy goodbye, thanking her again and again. As I unlocked the door in the social room, I thought about how blessed I was to have so many wonderful friends who loved and cared about us. I knew for a fact there would be a special place in heaven for Kathy.

The days were rapidly running into each other and I wished I could truly turn back time.

I want more time with my husband, but yet I also want him to be free. I feel so guilty wishing for him to return to heaven as a complete spirit, healthy and happy once again. But then I feel selfish wishing for him to stay here with me. Please don't leave me, I cried to myself, silently holding my feelings inside. I knew I could never express my thoughts to him, especially these last four days. It would be too selfish, but I was so torn.

Finally, it was Christmas Eve and McLane and Retta called that evening. They wanted to stop by before going to their traditional Christmas Eve dinner. They arrived with lattes in hand, and that was just what I needed.

Stenny was still unresponsive but his vitals were going strong.

After they left, I sat with my husband deep in thought. I remember thinking how quickly these past two and a half years had gone, especially the last fifteen months.

Time is a thief.

My thoughts turned to the past twenty-four years and how we were just living, loving and enjoying our lives. We had our arms wrapped around the future and were ready to make the most of the life we'd created together.

Then Alzheimer's came through the door, an uninvited guest that you don't know what to do with. It taught me that I am no longer in control, Alzheimer's was now the pilot of our life. It consumed every minute, every hour, every day and night, weeks, months, and years. It was a tricky and unforeseen minefield. The disease left an unseen path of destruction as it rushed into our comfortable life. Alzheimer's didn't care if we were unhappy that it had arrived, or if we lacked the funds for caregiving, or even if we knew nothing about it at all. Alzheimer's was not only an uninvited guest, but it was also an *unwanted one* as well. A guest that came without warning, not even a phone call, text or email, but it could care less. It was here now and it was here to stay right up to last call.

I stopped. I laid my head on Stenny's chest, but I couldn't stop the tears as I listened to his shallow breath. His big heart was beating in my ear and it sounded strong. I began to talk to him in between teardrops. Finally I said, "Oh my sweet man, how the fuck did we get here, I love you so much."

Then I heard an extremely faint, "Luh u, Ben," as his frail voice trailed off.

I sat straight up and spoke, "Oh honey, thank you," and I kissed him tenderly. I was so elated that he had tried to say *Love you, Bennett*. I was filled with ecstasy because I knew my amazing husband just gave me the best Christmas present ever.

I arrived early Christmas morning kissing Stenny and wishing him a Merry Christmas. I told him that Janice had invited me to have Christmas breakfast with her family. I didn't want to intrude, but she assured me that it wasn't an intrusion and her daughters really wanted me to come. Janice picked me up at Alta Ridge and we drove together. I was so pleased I had received the invitation, because it not only was a lovely Christmas morning, but it was a well needed diversion for me and I was very grateful.

Janice dropped me off and Stenny was just as I'd left him earlier that morning. I stayed for a few more hours until it was time for my own family Christmas party. We usually do it up at our condo in Park City, but under the circumstances my daughter Channy suggested we do it at her home right around the corner from Alta Ridge. She and Jay, her husband had driven all the way to my condo to retrieve every present under the tree, as I'd understandably left in a huge rush. I have four

Heart Get Ready

children complete with spouses, fifteen grandchildren also some with spouses or significate others and ten great grandchildren, so it took Channy and Jay a few trips up and down the seventeen snow covered steps at my condo.

We had a delicious potluck as everyone pulled together and brought lots of tasty dishes and treats. We exchanged gifts, and as I looked around at my family, I was so touched by how they all stepped up and made this work. It was a beautiful Christmas Day, and in spite of it all, I knew I was blessed.

After that, I went back to the facility and stayed the rest of the day, singing along to the Christmas tunes playing on Stenny's television while I sat next to him.

Before it got dark, I decided to go home that night. I called Janice and told her.

She was concerned, "Are you sure?"

I told her I was. I felt deep down in my heart that Stenny would make it through another night. In fact, I was so sure he would not leave, the feeling was *that* strong. "I need to go home, sleep in my own bed and see my cats," I said to Janice, "I want to take a shower and wash my hair in my own bathroom. I just need to do this."

Of course she understood. But she made me promise to call her, no matter the time, if anything happened, so she could drive to Park City and pick me up.

I laughed, "That's the exact same thing Channy told me."

So I promised *both* of them I would do as they asked. I kissed my husband goodnight and told him I was going to feed the kitties and would be back early in the morning. That was the one thing that worked in the last two years. So I was hoping it would again. I drove up Parleys Canyon and I felt very content that everything, for now, would be okay.

My mother passed away the day after Thanksgiving thirteen years ago and Stenmark was happy she waited. He then told me, "It's so much harder when someone passes away on a holiday. That's all you think about for the rest of your life, and you dread that upcoming holiday on the anniversary of their death."

I never thought about it before, but I admit he had a valid point. I remembered that and I know that's why I felt confident enough to leave that evening.

I arrived home, ate some cheese and crackers and poured myself a large glass of Chardonnay. Then I toasted Stenny, praying for the most benevolent outcome. I didn't want my husband to leave, but I didn't want him to stay either…not like this.

I needed a diversion so I turned on the television and found our favorite Christmas movie, *It's a Wonderful Life*. I sat down with the heated blanket and two very happy kitties on my lap.

My thoughts drifted away from the show and I wondered why I was torturing myself on Christmas. *Really, Carly? You must be an eejit (which is a foolish or senseless person).* I probably should have picked some silly comedy, at least that would have been more of a diversion.

The next morning I woke up early and hopped in the shower. That felt beyond wonderful. I had wrapped a new pillow complete with a very soft new silk pillowcase for Stenmark as his Christmas present from Santa. As I said, Stenmark was funny when it came to bed pillows. It was a joke between us whenever we made a bet and if I lost, he would say, "Okay I get the good pillows on our bed and you have to sleep on the shit pillows for a week." I found that amusing since *all* our pillows were good, but apparently there were two he liked more than the rest.

I was in the Alta Ridge parking lot when they opened at eight a.m. the day after Christmas, December 26, 2022. It was not only the day after, but it was our friend Dagmar's birthday, and also Trinity's birthday, one of my beautiful granddaughters.

The staff was late getting in to unlock the front doors and a line was starting to form so I called Emily. She in turn texted one of the night shift nurses and soon it was unlocked so all could enter.

I went into Stenny's room and he was still the way he had been for five days now. I paused for a moment to observe his breathing only to find it wasn't labored at all. I walked over to the television saying, "Guess what, Babe? Christmas is over now, no more Christmas music. It's back to our rock and roll," as I changed the station to Classic Rock.

I walked over with his wrapped gift exclaiming, "Stenny, look what Santa brought you." I knew there would be no reaction, but I sat next to him as I described the Christmas wrapping paper and carefully opened it for him. "You're still tired from all the festivities and the visitors you've had, so I will open it for you. Is that alright with you?"

Of course there was no movement or answer.

I said, "Good! I will do it for you," and then I kissed him. I described the pillowcase in detail and telling him it was so soft. I removed the red and white Santa Claus hat I'd brought for him to wear during the Christmas dinner, five *very* long days ago. Stenny looked very peaceful and content, but then he was on a cocktail of morphine and an anti-anxiety medicine.

I was so happy he was out of pain and wished his doctor could do something to ease MY pain.

I told Stenny, "I love you a million, billion, trillion and then some." That was another one of our sayings to each other. I even found the dollar bills that coincided with those terms in a gift shop a few years ago and had them framed for his Christmas present, which hung in his music room, and now in his room at Alta View. I laid my head down on his chest once again. I could feel his heart beating and his chest rising ever so slightly up and down.

All of the sudden I could no longer feel the rising of his chest and it seemed like he was holding his breath.

I jumped up fast and said, "HONEY!" My own heart pounded so hard, as I looked at his face. Then Stenny took a big inhale.

I said, with relief, "Oh, Babe, you scared me!"

To my surprise, it was followed by a very long exhale and I literally saw his soul leave his body, and I knew he was gone. I sat down on his bed once again, told Stenny he was now free, and I wept at my sweet husbands bedside for the last time. My tears flowed like a whispering stream until I calmed myself enough to speak to what I hoped was Stenny's lingering spirit, telling my true love to find the staircase and bright light leading up to his new heavenly home. Through my tears, I said, "I deeply love you and will forever. I know it doesn't look like it now, but please rest assured...I will be okay. Don't worry about me. I will see you soon... when the time is right." I then reminded him to look for his mom and sisters up there in that beautiful place where he would now live, as a happy and healthy flawless soul.

Then I jokingly told him he best not be looking for Laurie, an old girlfriend that had passed a few years before he got sick. I laughed slightly, kissed him, and gave him the go ahead to finally be free. My sweet husband was gone. I kissed him softly for the very last time and whispered, "I know I'll never find another you."

CHAPTER 42
Two Hearts Coming Home

It had only been a few hours since I knelt at my husband's bedside and whispered in his ear how proud I was to be his wife and told him it was okay to let go; that he didn't need to hold on any longer. I could see the pain in his face and hear his short, labored breathing. I knew he didn't want to leave me, but I also knew just how tired he must be. Kenny always loved life and he lived it to the fullest, making the most out of every single minute, taking it all in.

Of course, he didn't want to leave but honestly, I couldn't bear to see him stay in this state with his poor ravaged body and blurred mind. As much as I loved him, I felt an incredible sense of selfishness wishing him to stay. I reassured him that I would be okay. Over and over again.

There is a grace of being at the bedside of someone you love as they transition out of this world. At that moment when they take their last breath, there is an incredible sacredness in the space, as the veil between the worlds opens. When Kenny left, I gave myself about ten minutes to just be, as I knew I would never get that time back if I didn't take it now. I felt like being present in that moment was an incredible gift to myself and a gift to Kenny. I knew he was just a slight breath away and was starting his new journey in the spirit world without his sick body. I hoped that by keeping a calmness around his body, he would launch in a more beautiful way. During this tender moment I honestly felt that my soul kind of left my own body, that it was off searching for Kenny somewhere in the ether.

I closed my eyes as my soul searched to find the one, the one I had just lost and already missed so deeply. As I followed closely searching for him, it was like our souls recognized each other but then Kenny told me to go back and live. I opened my eyes and realized when the time is right, Kenny would find me and I was so happy I took that time to pause, breathe and take it all in.

Although I understood the all-embracing sorrow of saying goodbye to a loved one, I now know the unavoidable, nearly suffocating sorrow when I had to say goodbye to my dear husband. I've always believed in life after death and in my lifetime, I've witnessed proof of just that. My faith in that belief is strong, as I know this life is only temporary. But this was my husband who left and I found myself praying to God for a sign, no matter how minor, just to let me know my belief system all these years was spot-on.

Nothing.

I suppose this is where the *faith* part comes in.

Channy, drove me home that night and her husband, Jay followed us in my car. We said our goodbyes as none of us were up to visiting. We had been with Kenny all day until the assistants from The University of Utah hospital came at six o'clock the evening of his death to pick up his body. I prayed his spirit was quietly and calmy watching over his now empty body. At his request, Kenny was enrolled in the body donor program at the University of Utah. I smiled proudly at how even after death, he longed to continue to help and be of service to others.

The next morning, I walked over to the Starbucks near my home. I stood quietly in line, waiting to order my tall nonfat latte, willing back tears. *Don't let them fall, Carly.* I searched desperately to find some shiny glimmer of happiness right in that moment. But the searching was all for naught. I was completely heartbroken. As I walked back to the condo, I realized there would never be two hearts coming home again.

I was so aware of the enormous hole in my life during this holiday season, so painfully aware. After all, the holidays should be a time filled with joy. There's always something to be thankful for. Sometimes you have to look really hard.

I woke up the next day in the fog I would undoubtedly become used to.

It was time for me to get out the notes I made before Alzheimer's had tightened its grip on my husband. That in-between place where we had clear diagnosis and Kenny was aware his disease not only existed, but there was no cure. He still had some clarity and we both took advantage of that.

♡ ♡ ♡ ♡ ♡

I remember the day well. We were driving down to the city when Kenny said, "So…Bennett since I have this going on there are some important things we need to discuss." My heart sank as my eyes stared straight ahead at the road and I said OK, trying not to lose it completely.

Kenny was calm and collected as he said, "You are going to need to sell my music equipment since I won't be around to help you financially and you are going to need some cash." I felt the lump in my throat and the tears began to well up in my eyes. I blinked them back as I was driving knowing I must keep us safe. I managed to speak, "But what about McLane," I asked. His son was following in his dad's footsteps and played guitar extremely well. He wasn't at his dads level yet but was definitely getting there.

"McLane has his own music gear and he isn't ready for this level of equipment. You need to sell it, Bennett. Please listen to me on this."

I nodded my head as he added, "You can give him the blue Washburn guitar when he turns thirty, but I want you to sell everything else. It is my way of taking care of you after I fall off the face of this planet. Promise me, Bennett." *Oh, Lord this is killing me.*

I managed a quiet, "Okay, Babe."

Then Kenny continued, "Bennett you know I've never loved the words funerals, memorials and celebrations of life." I smiled as I nodded once again.

It was at this tough time Kenny told me to refer to his as a "shindig" and make it a fun occasion. Kenny smiled and said, "when we get home, I want us both to sit down, pour a glass of Chardonnay and I will tell you how this shindig is going to go." Then he squeezed my leg and told me he loved me.

Upon arriving at home, we had a pleasant dinner and moved to the loveseat as I turned on the television. This was another well-loved ritual we both looked forward to at the end of the day.

I would curl up next to him and put my head on his shoulder. Kenny would kiss me as we watched and enjoyed *our shows*.

Gotta love those British detective shows!

Things were different tonight. Kenny needed to plan his *shindig* with me. As he sat down, he handed me one of his yellow legal tablets and a pen. His voice was soft and lower than usual as he began, "At my shindig, I don't want any of my songs played."

"But honey, they are so good," I exclaimed in surprise. "Bennett, listen to me please. I know how good my songs are. You don't need to tell me."

I giggled slightly and told him I would honor his wishes.

I gulped down the last of my wine and poured another glass for both of us. I sat back down, this time facing him with the yellow tablet on my lap and pen in hand. Kenny reiterated, "so none of my songs, Babe."

I answered, "Got it, love of my life." To which he quipped, "So you say."

I jotted down my instructions complete with the songs I could play beginning with Sixteen Tons. This song was no surprise. I knew this was at the top of his favorite songs as it reminded him of playing football all through high school and college in Minnesota. Plus he sang it all the time snapping his fingers to the beat.

I wrote down the list of songs as he named them off and which versions he wanted. After Sixteen Tons by Tennessee Ernie Ford came My Back Pages written by Bob Dylan but sang by The Byrd's, Drift Away by Dobie Gray, Lean on Me by Bill Withers, and Shower the People you Love with Love, by James Taylor. Kenny said, "that's it, just make the rest of it fun."

❦ ❦ ❦ ❦ ❦

I opened up the bedside drawer and took out my purple folder that contained all the important papers concerning my husband. I picked up the only yellow one inside and opened it slowly. I stared at the paper and at very top was written, PLAY NONE OF HIS SONGS and I sobbed remembering the day clearly. The day we planned his *shindig.*

I laid on the bed trying to shake the memories from my brain. I had things to do and so I began the arduous task of organizing Kenny's farewell. First off, I needed to find a place. He wanted it held at Park City Mountain Resort but since it was now January in Park City that would prove to be challenging. Let alone with the ski tourists, the Sundance Film Festival was also fast approaching. Zena to the rescue.

As well connected as Zena was, I think she called on the majority of the Park City residents, spaces and abodes to no avail. They were generally rented to Sundance or not large enough to accommodate those who loved us and were beyond curious what a *shindig* would entail.

Silver Shears, the salon I had been working in since 2002 had been sold and I'd made the hard decision to retire. I learned from my experience last April when Kenny *died the first time to be prepared...Ugh!*

Anyway, I'd taken a picture of my last two weeks in my appointment book. I reached out to everyone by text, who were in my book for that last week, to let them know I would be back at work beginning Tuesday. Nearly all of my clients / friends asked if I was sure I wanted to come back to work so soon after Kenny's passing. *I have the best friends and clientele.* I was certain.

Besides, what else was I going to do? Just sit home and reflect on the last week incessantly? I didn't really know what I needed to do for myself right now but working was definitely in the plan I didn't know I had. Honestly, it was important for me to finish what I started over forty-five years ago, so on December 31, 2022, I laid down my nail file for the last time at Silver Shears Salon.

CHAPTER 43
Love Knows the Difference

Zena had run out of options for Kenny's *shindig* but that didn't stop her from trying. I had another client, close friend and confidant, Christina. She and her husband were close with Kenny as well. He met them giving them golf lessons and couldn't wait to introduce them to me. Not only were they interesting people but they were both extremely intelligent and hilarious!

Enter a great sense of humor once again to make me fall in love, and Christina was so easy to talk to I would turn into Chatty Cathy at every appointment. She was usually my last appointment every other Wednesday and that made it easy for me to tell her anything and everything.

Have you ever had a three-hour pedicure? Christina has.

This particular Wednesday evening we were discussing the obvious when she offered her beautiful home for Kenny's *shindig*. I was so touched by her offer but I declined saying I couldn't impose on her and her family. I knew her home could easily accommodate the many friends and family we had. It was built for exactly that, Christina reminded me. But still when I resisted, she insisted so I thanked her and gratefully accepted. To be honest, it was a relief and it really was the perfect place. The fact that they were very close friends of ours was a bonus. We set the date for Tuesday January 10, 2023.

The day I went over to discuss all the particulars with my dear friends, Genevieve and Donna (also very close with

Christina) we walked in and I understood just how perfect it truly was. *The sugarplum fairy had exploded.*

I thought about how much Kenny loved Christmas and I smiled.

All of the lovely Christmas decorations were still up, including a larger-than-life Christmas tree. It was stunningly beautiful, decorated perfectly and shining brightly against the gigantic floor to ceiling windows that overlooked the beauty of Park City, including Park City Mountain Resort. I walked over to the Christmas tree and looked out at the falling snow.

I was crying but knew in my heart and soul that Kenny was smiling.

Genevieve and Donna dropped me off at home and as I walked up the seventeen steps to my door, I thought about how blessed I really am to have the wonderful friends I have. Then I sat down at my computer to write the first draft of Kenny's obituary.

My friend Nancy was going to help me get it formatted correctly so it could be published in the Park Record newspaper. I found the perfect picture of Kenny to add to my carefully crafted words and sent it off to Nancy. I had a list of must do's and right now nothing else mattered. Not my sorrow, the shock, the guilt, my lack of sleep, the numbness I felt, or any of the other strong emotions swirling around me.

The next morning I decided to attend church. I really needed some spiritual healing and wanted to see close friends. My dear friend Bonnie plays the organ every week. Her talent is colossal, as she adds in her own little touches to the music. Then I always get an index finger wave accompanied by her sweet smile.

Then there is Bishop Wade Peers and his lovely wife Lesa. Their visits, phone calls, texts and kindness during those last fifteen months meant the world to me. I asked Bishop Peers to

HEART GET READY

preside over Kenny's *shindig*. I also love and enjoy sitting with Lesa during the meetings. They are both gems.

Another close friend, Connie, was my client over thirty years ago. She is one special lady who lost her husband Phil six months before I lost Kenny, so we have a lot in common. They had an extremely close, unbreakable bond as husband and wife...just like we had.

So when I sit in church on Sundays, I am surrounded by those close and dear friends. Truth be told, I believe it doesn't really matter where I sit on Sundays, it could be any faith or I could be on a golf course, a ski hill or a grassy mountain top as long as I have Jesus in my heart, which I do. But it's the people who draw me to the Mormon church, and familiarity of course.

As I sat at my desktop putting together Kenny's slideshow, looking at the thousands of pictures that captured our wonderful life together, I can't help but wonder why. Why us? We were so happy, so in love, we had fun, we travelled, we teased and joked with one another, there was never a dull moment when Kenny was around.

Now here I sit alone with my kitties writing an obituary, I never dreamed I would be writing, making a photo slideshow coupled with the songs my late husband chose before Alzheimer's disease put him in a choke hold. A slideshow that will be played at his *shindig* as family and friends watch and reminisce.

And I will smile. But remember just because I am smiling doesn't mean I am not grieving. Grief has robbed me of the life I once knew. It has unraveled everything I am and everything I once knew. I honestly believe my heart is learning how to beat again after it has been completely broken in countless pieces.

Not a day goes by that I don't stare at Kenny's picture and cry, or smile or both. I try to be strong but I am exhausted trying to be stronger than I feel. I feel like I exist in two places, here and where Kenny is. I miss my old life… the life where Kenny was still in it. But life is different now. I still love Kenny and love knows the difference.

Yet, I had to soldier on, I had a *shindig* to put together. I began adding more and more pictures until my eyes glazed over from hours of staring at the computer. I sent a text message to Retta and McLane asking if they had pictures to include. McLane sent a few and I included them before I was off to bed hoping sleep would come.

I had a familiar dream last night. The one where Alta Ridge called and told me Stenny was all better and I could come and pick him up anytime. In my dream I screamed it was a Christmas miracle as I jumped up and down crying tears of joy. Then I woke up and cried for real but thought about how I had to pull myself together. Genevieve and Donna were picking me up for a much-needed girls lunch.

They picked me up right on time and we had a delicious lunch with pleasant conversation. There's truly nothing like good friends!

They drove me home and I asked them in for a glass of wine. As we walked up the steps there sat a package I prayed for. We went inside and I opened it up to find Kenny's wooden cremation urn. Just in the nick of time.

Although Kenny's cremains wouldn't be released for a couple of months, I wanted to make a nice display on the table Christina set up in the entry way.

The day was finally here and it was a major blizzard. Mark, Genevieve, their son Michael and Donna picked me up at three o'clock as the shindig was scheduled for four o'clock.

When we pulled into the circular driveway, I saw Nancy's new white Tesla. *Wow she is an early bird.* The boys dropped us off at the front door as they parked. Mark and Michael always the consummate gentlemen. I walked in to find Nancy sitting with her laptop in the perfect spot for the Zoom of the shindig. She had been collecting tons of addresses all week. Like I say, smartest woman in Park City.

Bishop Peers and his wife arrived shortly after to get the lay of the land. I was once again moved by his kindness, as he asked how I would prefer he introduce himself - Bishop Wade Peers, Dr. Wade Peers (he is a retired oral surgeon) or just Wade Peers. I chose Bishop Wade Peers but was so touched by his consideration.

There were one hundred eighty-one people who signed the guest book and that doesn't count the ones who didn't see it. There were also close to one hundred fifty people on the Zoom and several others who later told me they couldn't get on and the ones who couldn't come due to the blizzard that evening. Yes, my husband was well loved and admired.

I know he was happy at how well attended it was and that his loving wife followed the rules. Except right before the closing prayer by Zena, I stood up to the microphone and told the story of his songs. Then I added, "So I know how to mind. All the songs played tonight in the slideshow were chosen by Stenny.

But there is a song I'd like to play for you. He didn't write it, but he is singing it, so I'm not really breaking the rules as it isn't one of *his* songs.

In fact he always said he wished he wrote it." Then I played the famous song, Hallelujah, written by Leonard Cohen and sang by him and so many others, but I played my favorite version, sang by Stenny. There wasn't a dry eye in the place.

CHAPTER 44
Don't Apologize

Now, as I approach the one-year mark since my husband took his final breath, I am in the throes of what they call deep grief. The deepest of griefs is classified as the loss of a child. The loss of a spouse is next. As losses go, and as hard as it is to say goodbye to a parent, it doesn't even come close to the pain of losing a child or in my case, a loving husband. I've experienced the loss of both my parents and it was very painful, but losing Stenmark was, and at times still is, outright devastating. I am still trying to navigate my way through the seemingly never-ending sea of grief. Well-meaning friends told me how it was time to be happy, time to get over it, and time to move on. My entire world revolved around my husband and now I am walking around in a fog.

"It's time for you to be happy, Kenny wouldn't want you to be sad, especially during the holidays." Of course, I know that. Kenny loved the holiday season and we always celebrated in style with lots of love thrown in.

But when you are grieving nothing is lonelier than the holiday season. For me it is now the season of long emotional, physical pain and social obligations that I don't want to engage in. But every day, I push down the pain and try to carry on, pretending to be whole, when in actuality I am in pieces, hurt and broken.

The feelings of grief are described in so many different ways but this particular poem truly spoke to me and it spoke volumes:

" I held a party last week and grief came. She wasn't invited but she came anyway-she barged through the door and settled in like she was here to stay. And then she introduced me to the friends she'd brought with her-Anger. Fear. Frustration. Guilt. Hopelessness. And they sang in the loudest voices, took up space in every corner and spoke over anyone else that tried to talk. They made it messy, loud and uncomfortable. But they finally left. And long afterwards, when I was all alone, I realized there was someone still there, quietly clearing up after the rest. I asked who she was and she told me, "Love."

And I assumed that's why she looked familiar-because I had met her before.

"Or perhaps," she said, "It's because I've been here the whole time."

And I was confused then because I hadn't seen her all evening. But when I looked more closely, when I looked in her eyes, I realized that she had been here. All the time… She'd just been dressed as grief."

Becky Hemsley 2023

A long time afterwards as I sat alone with my broken heart, this poem resonated with me. It *was* love. I didn't recognize it at first because it had been a very long time since I'd felt or seen it. But I do need to remember that underneath my grief, there was love simply disguised as grief and it was there all along.

I still have the ever-present tinge of sadness and it shows in my eyes. People who have recently lost someone have a certain look. I have noticed it on my own face and I notice it now on others. The look is one of vulnerability, accompanied by extreme pain. It is nakedness. I read somewhere that people who have lost someone look naked because they see themselves as invisible and I felt that to my core. Even being around family and friends, the feeling was there. As much as I tried to force down these feelings, I was only pretending to be whole and I wondered if I ever would be again.

There are days when I feel good but then reality will sweep in and I remember that I am completely alone in this process. Sure, I have a wonderful family (who have been amazing) and a surplus of friends (who try and keep me busy) checking in with me regularly. But nobody can fix this for me, it's all up to me.

Now in the last eighteen months, I have experienced an overabundance of love, support, suggestions, ideas, comments and advice from not just people close to me, but even slight acquaintances, including unknown friends of Kenny's, as well as complete strangers who find out I lost my husband. It is truly touching.

However, I do not like being referred to as a widow. *The widow Stenmark.* I have an image in my mind of an old hunched over woman dressed head to toe in black. She is a woman who never made her way through the unchartered waters of grief and is forever broken. I correct anyone who refers to me as a widow by politely telling them, "I am a surviving spouse. I don't like that word, *widow*."

So far, it works.

I miss my sweet husband so much. I miss his smile, his laugh and his cute ways. I miss the partnership we had coupled with a complete banner of trust and deep love. I miss the way he looked at me from across a room, his cute wink, his incredible sense of humor and the way he just *got* me. I also miss the way he made me feel, so safe, secure and protected. I always felt so unbelievably loved by him and I miss the deep connection we had. There are so many things I miss about Kenny. I really could go on and on.

The first year was truly a blur, it all felt surreal. Some people would say it couldn't be *too bad*, since he didn't live with me the last fifteen months of his life, and his death wasn't a surprise.

Seriously?!

Others were so uncomfortable around me they just didn't say anything. I found both reactions very strange but decided my love and my grief (which I now know are the same thing) won't be shaped by anyone's feelings of obliviousness or discomfort. It is mine and mine alone to navigate.

And for God's sake, don't ever tell me to look on the bright side, because there isn't one right now. Don't point out that Kenny is in a better place. My head knows that, but my heart is at a standstill. When you've lost the foundation of your life, when the pain is so blinding that you can't tell which way is up, those words mean very little to me. The words, "at least" are also completely off limits. Please don't *"at least"* a griever, ever!

I also had others telling me how strong I was. Funny, I don't feel strong. Greif makes words like "strength" feel completely empty. I never feel strong, I only feel like I am just barely surviving. Sometimes I want to scream out in pain, while other times I sit with my grief trying my best to understand it, because grief is so difficult. There are days when I can't stop crying.

At that point, I reached out by email to a counselor I'd met through Jewish Family Service. Her name is Katie and she is literally saving my life right now.

Katie is always upbeat and positive, one of the many things I love about her. I couldn't bear to golf at the Park City Golf Course and looked upon going with dread. I would end up in tears when I tried. If I forced myself, I couldn't focus to save my life and I played terribly and that upset me even more.

Don't Apologize

Katie taught me to look at going to the golf course differently and to ask myself, "what would Kenny want me to do?" Of course, I knew he would want me to play golf at *his* golf course! She also taught me to think of it as a way to honor Kenny, so that's what I did. I played nearly every Tuesday on ladies' day, and with the help of Katie, I made it through that emotional hurdle. One down, hundreds more to go.

There are so many memories that flood over me on any given day. Music is a huge trigger for me, as it was a huge part of our wonderful life together. So much so that I began listening to completely different genres that we never listened to before. I began with rap, then moved to K POP, some songs were okay, but some were not. I don't mean to *dis* any artists out there, but most rap and K POP music simply doesn't speak to me. I'm old, okay?

Now, I am just trying to figure out who I am without Kenny. What does life look like as a singular couple of one? I know we are all vulnerable when it comes to love. It's almost certain that in life our hearts will be wrung out and probably broken. Kenny used to say that everyone needs to experience a broken heart at least once in their lifetime to fully understand deep love.

I am here to tell you; I have learned that time does not heal a broken heart. We just learn how to cope and live with it. Where I am now is where I expect to live forever. I have really surprised myself at what I have been able to accomplish in this forever changing life of mine.

I have grown and I shock myself sometimes at what I'm still capable of doing. After the initial shock of losing Kenny began to dissipate, friends and family would ask me how I was doing? My standard reply was, "Well, I'm still alive, dammit." Because that was exactly how I felt, disappointed when I woke up in the morning. In all honesty, I would never in a million years commit suicide. But if I died tomorrow, simply because my time was up here on earth, that would be just fine with me.

Kenny isn't my past. He is my every day, all day. That will never change. He still exists with me and my broken heart. Grief for me is not linear. People keep telling me that once this or that happened or that passes, everything would be better. Some gave me one year to grieve because they looked at grief as a straight line, with a beginning, a middle, and then an end. But truly there is no closure to grief, just a beginning, a middle, and the rest of your life. Grief is not about moving on but carrying them with you.

This is how I look at it now because this is how it feels right here, right now in this moment and I won't ever apologize for how I am feeling or for how I chose to survive. I love how I don't care as much anymore about what other people think. It's not in a hurtful way, but in a peaceful way and that feels good.

But grief is disjointed. One day I would act like a normal person, even managing to shower, put on makeup and blow out my hair. I'd even sometimes get out of my "soft clothes," as Kenny used to call them (a.k.a. sweatpants and sweatshirts). I'd gaze outside at the autumn leaves looking so beautiful and I know soon the snow would be crunching under my feet. And in that moment, I seem upright. Please understand that my loss has brought me to my knees.

Then a song, a smell, or maybe even nothing sends me back into the arms of grief. It isn't one step forward, two steps back. It's more like my own personal slippery slope. It is hours that are OK, followed by days then weeks that are not even close to being OK.

But I know we are not meant to stay wounded. I am supposed to move through my challenges and tragedies. I feel

Don't Apologize

like I am moving, but it feels like I am moving through a bad dream I can't wake up from. Oh yeah, and I am in quicksand.

Grief is me constantly asking, *"why?"* It is feeling lost in the places I've been a hundred times before and finding myself completely homesick for the past. Grief feels like a deep ache that I can't pinpoint where it hurts, but it's definitely there.

Most of the time, it feels like a part of me left when Kenny left. I used to want to save everybody. Now I just want to save what is left of myself as I slip deep into the clutches of grief. It is so hard and I miss so much of my past life. I miss knowing there was someone out there who couldn't wait to get home to see me. I miss my sweet husband the most when I see a spider, when I struggle to open things, when I have to make decisions alone, when I have to do both the boy *and* the girl jobs, and even when this bored Gemini wants to rearrange the furniture every other week. *Thanks, Mom.*

Grief is also people saying a lot of unhelpful things to me, because they want me to feel better. I want to feel better, but right now, grief has other plans. It is a constant tug of war, a war of holding on tightly to what was, and letting go of what could have been, if Alzheimer's hadn't stepped in.

For me, I am just going through the motions of the day in a steady haze, walking around in a thick brain fog with my loss always on my mind. I learned it is called "widows brain," and it can last anywhere from eighteen months to five years. It is defined as your mind feeling foggy or blurry. *Check.* Your concentration and memory is affected. *Oh, joy.* Your mind is so overwhelmed with processing this deep loss that it cuts down some functioning.

Since Kenny's passing in December 2022, my brain has been so foggy. In fact, most of the time it either seems to be filled with nothing but song lyrics and thoughts of my sweet music man. My brain is never idle as thoughts of Kenny swirl

Heart Get Ready

around endlessly. He consumes my every thought. So much so that I often return to Kenny's favorite places, as my heart continues to search for him. *Thank you, widows brain.*

I console myself by saying it is better than having what they call, "widows fire," a term as denoting the strong sexual desire following the death of a partner. Recent research has found that sixty-three percent of widows and widowers experience this phenomenon, with fifty-eight percent beginning to feel these urges within six months of their partners passing and more than half acting on it.

I'll keep the spaciness and forgetfulness, and the inability to focus as described in widows brain, thank you very much.

Also, please don't think you need to remind me of someone I could never forget. But you can always remind me that you remember Kenny. Talking about him is something I can truly appreciate. I want others to remember my love, my soulmate, my life partner, my protector, and the man in the songs.

Please talk to me about Kenny, tell me funny stories, serious conversations, post memories and pictures of him on social media, and honestly any remembrance of my sweet man will truly touch my soul and make me smile.

I want this wonderful man of mine to be remembered, so please... say his name!

I now know that time is not a complete healer and I am continually doubting if it ever will be. Was this being really God's will? Because if He knew how much I've l lost, my husband would still be here. But he isn't. Kenny wasn't my first love, but I will say with conviction he *will* be my last. He is now an unfinished life, made finished long before its time. That's the thing about life, it's fragile, precious and unpredictable. Every day is a gift, not a God given right. I often have to remind myself to be thankful for each and every day in spite of my sorrow.

Don't Apologize

These days grief has a way of leading me instead of tagging along behind me. I now know that grief is a testament of love. I was blessed with a husband I deeply loved and he deeply loved me...and that's the great part of grief. Love is a very mystical and wondrous creature. The deeper the love, the stronger the grief and that hit me hard on the grief chart.

It may have paralyzed me emotionally, but I've been doing the work it takes to pull myself out of grief's firm clutches and it is exhausting. My physical and emotional energy levels are drained. I feel empty most of the time, with no sense of purpose. I've been sick more times in this last twenty months than I have ever been in my entire life. Kenny used to marvel at how I never was sick, but that has not been the case since he left.

♡♡♡♡♡

My counselor told me it's normal and common for the stress and therefore, grief, to manifest itself in changes to our physical well-being. My primary care physician agreed, saying Katie is absolutely right. Grief is a bit like a pinball game, where you're the ball and get whacked by a metaphorical flipper every now and again, bouncing and bumping all over the place. One constant remains... grieving is stressful and that lowers our immune systems, leaving us more vulnerable to contagious diseases.

We may experience aches and pains, trouble sleeping, headaches, dizziness or shaking. Let's not forget exhaustion, chest pains, heart racing, muscle tension, jaw clenching, high blood pressure, stomach issues, and digestive problems. I was told it doesn't matter if I stay away from people, I will fall sick while I am in deep grief. Of course, I would never purposely be around anyone I knew was sick, but I did nix becoming more of a hermit than I already am.

I mentioned the salon I worked at for the last twenty-plus years sold so I had the idea to retire. My retirement lasted about six months or so until with the help of Katie, my brilliant counselor, I went back to work. Being alone day and night was extremely difficult for this social butterfly. These days I try to practice self-love and self-care. I also do at Katie's suggestion, a method known as scheduled grieving.

Every night at nine o'clock, my set alarm goes off and I light a candle in the darkness of my room and I grieve the loss I so deeply feel. I talk to my sweet husband and tell him anything and everything that comes to mind. I close by telling him how much he is loved and missed, then I kiss his picture.

Losing the person I thought I couldn't live without, the one my soul was connected to, the one my whole life was intertwined with, is mind blowing. There really aren't the words to sufficiently describe it. The loss is excruciating, terrifying and completely overwhelming. Everything about my world has now shifted and that scares the hell out of me.

CHAPTER 45
How Do We Carry On?

I was unaware of the triggers. Sure, I knew music would be a huge one, but there were unsuspecting triggers hidden in the aisles of the grocery store. The soup cans may as well be grenades as far as I was concerned, while the potatoes seemed like landmines. I was not prepared emotionally for the river of tears these ordinary things brought to the forefront. In the bakery, I felt like I was being ambushed by a dozen wheat dinner rolls tightly sealed in a plastic bag, while the frozen prepared entrees seemed to scream at me to free them from their ice-cold prison. Everywhere I turned I was unprepared for the emotional onslaught of my friendly grocery store and I left emotionally wounded. Oh, the many faces and emotions of grief, so vast and so deep.

The day finally came that I could take Kenny's cremation urn out of the Amazon cardboard box home it has lived since I picked it up from the University of Utah. I took the urn out, sitting with the heavy wooden box on my lap. I stared at the picture in the heart shaped frame as I ran my fingers across the words I had inscribed; Kenneth Joel Stenmark "Stenny", May 12, 1951 – December 26, 2022, My one and only True Love.

Logic tells me that it should be bursting at the seams, that something this size can't possibly hold someone so big. And yet, it does.

It holds seventy-one years of a happy and rewarding life, full of treasured memories. Memories I hold safely in my own broken heart.

It holds twenty-four years of my undying love and devotion.

It holds a magnificent six-foot-three-inch man as I remember him. A man who was nothing short of pure love, humility and a caring, humorous and loving soul.

It holds a man full of sensitivity, intelligence, kindness, thoughtfulness and the pure generosity of my savior and protector.

It holds caring blue eyes, a beautiful smile and a handsome man who always made me feel loved, treasured and admired.

It holds arms that were both strong yet gentle and always there when needed. Those strong arms gave the best hugs.

It holds hands that were there to help anyone at any time. Strong hands always there to help me and hold my hands, even if we were just watching television. Just holding his hands made everything seem right.

It holds a father overflowing with love and pride for his son. It holds a father willing and wanting to spend as much time as possible with his son.

It holds a grandfather happy to spend time with his many bonus children and bonus grandchildren. It holds a man who went with it and loved it.

It holds a loving husband, brother, uncle, cousin and friend to so many.

It holds enormous respect for and from his co-workers in the golf, ski, and music industry.

It holds a man so bright he could build or fix anything. A man who knew the answers to just about everything, a man who was willing to learn if he didn't have the answer.

How Do We Carry On?

It holds a heart that completely loved me for reasons I will never be able to fully understand or explain but will be forever grateful for. It holds a man who showered me with that love in every possible way and on every precious day we were together.

I will always love Kenny, there will never be another person who compares to him. Kenny isn't only my past; he is my future. He is my hope. Hope that he is waiting high in the heavens for me.

I long for the day when I will see him again. I wait patiently for the day when these feelings of grief will ease as time goes on, and for the day when I will smile after a memory crosses my mind instead of fall apart. When that day comes, I know I will be proud of myself for how hard I worked to move through my grief and for just how far I have come carrying it with me.

I didn't just lose Kenny twice; I lose him every time I open my eyes. It's a shuddering bolt of lightning that rips into my heart reminding me that my one true love is still gone. Again. For me, losing Kenny is a continuing journey, not just a one-time event. There is no end to my loss as I learn to float there in the deep end as the waters wash over me.

When I was going through my husband's belongings from the care facility, I found a song that he wrote sometime in 2021, but never finished. As I stared at the handwritten piece, his writing almost scribbled on the lined page, my eyes filled with tears. My sweet music man's words were there, but it just didn't have the old Stenmark spirit or the clever lyrics I've become accustomed to.

"How do we carry on-too young gone-
You know we still gotta carry on-
For one day too soon we will be meeting with the Lord
For one reunion with the Lord

For one day together
How can we break it to our heart-
When a heart is on the mend you can't pretend
How do we break it to our hearts-
Our angel is waiting at heaven's door
There is pain no more
How do we break it to our hearts "

I transcribed this exactly how he composed it and I wondered just how much his brain understood about his illness and I wept. Once again grief brought to the surface that memory of overwhelming loss and love. It tried its hardest to pull me down into that deep, dark hole that I'd climbed out of many times before, when it all felt so hopeless.

Because when we first fall in love, it is intense. That's why they call it *falling* in love. It is overwhelming and all consuming. It's all we can think of and we constantly ache for the one we love.

As our love continues to grow, it becomes less intense and we grow more comfortable as it deepens and settles in for the long haul. It's as if it now knows it is not fleeting or superficial and it settles deep in our heart where it knows it will stay.

I have found that grief does the same.

I know that loss is an inevitable part of life and with that comes grief, like love, intense and all-consuming sitting deep in my heart as I long for Kenny.

It takes courage to live and grieve. I try my best to face the day with a smile when I am crying inside. It is so hard for me to look toward the future. I wish my mom was alive, I need to talk to her.

I sit and dream that I could just return to the night we met. I would do it all over again. Every. Single. Day.

How Do We Carry On?

I used to pray for forgiveness, then I prayed for strength, now I pray for hope. I search for it endlessly. I hope for my own inner serenity, desperately clutching to even the slightest sliver of it. I grasp at every tiny beacon of hope. Kenny is more than a memory for me. He is part of my soul and he is in my heart. Even though he crossed over to the other side our hearts are still connected. I pray that I will indeed see Kenny again and I know that we will both be whole.

Whether you believe in God or not, this *hurts*. We all come from different walks of life with our faith, or lack of thereof. I hope, *I pray*, that these memories will one day allow me to smile instead of cause me to break down. I hope that I will become stronger.

I know that grief must be witnessed to be healed. Grief is fragile and I didn't realize that until I tried to hold onto it.

But now I am doing the work it takes to move through this deep loss of mine and once again become whole. I have so much to live for and I'm not talking about dating. Becoming whole after loss does not require I find another person. It requires I find myself. I am talking about being present with my beautiful family and wonderful friends.

I'm talking about showing up for my life, building the bridges I need to cross, all the while knowing I *am* getting better. I get up in the morning, I shower, brush my teeth, put on makeup and get ready for another day. No matter how dark the days seem, I know hope, love and joy are possible as I take a deep breath and whisper to my soul, "I got this!"

Grief may have robbed me of the life I knew, but never of the love that lives on and the happiness that is well within my reach. Death ends a life, not a relationship. All the love we created is still there along with all the memories. Losing my husband broke me but I refuse to let it defeat me. That's not what he wanted for me.

You now know this woman you've never met, as I've shared with you some of my most vulnerable and intimate moments of love, loss and pain. I feel I hold so much more understanding, and empathy towards the pain of others, after I finally started staring my own grief in the face. I am willing to stand and stare at the emptiness with you. We all have a story. I believe that telling mine can be healing. Maybe when you read my words, you will feel less alone. I hope we all find peace along our journey, each of us on our own unique paths, different yet so very much alike. Grief *is* grief, but I think it's important to remember that grief truly is just love in a very heavy coat.

THE END

Ken Stenmark, five days before he passed away, December, 2022.

ACKNOWLEDGMENTS

I am blessed to have a multitude of people in my life who have shown love, care and compassion towards Ken and me. Although it would require another book to express my gratitude to each of you individually, I am confident that you know who you are.

First and foremost, I want to acknowledge the incredible support of my children. I've experienced first-hand the difficulty of watching a parent suffer and I am deeply moved by the love and support you showed me through your phone calls, text messages, and visits. Your presence in my life is a reminder that I am not alone and I love you all so much.

My sincere thanks to my clients and friends for their love and support, particularly during these past four years. The emotional distress that crept in following Ken's diagnosis was almost unbearable at times. Thank you for your loyalty and support during this trying time.

I am deeply grateful to the staff at Alta Ridge Memory Care for providing my husband with the care he required. Thank you for possessing the skill to care for Ken with empathy, humility and compassion. Thank you for your genuine kindness and thoughtful understanding of this devastating disease.

I would like to express heartfelt thanks to Dr. Gary F. Holland, MD for your exceptional kindness, awareness and medical expertise while caring for my husband, demonstrating a deep understanding of compassionate care. You brought a tremendous comfort to me during an extremely trying time.

Thank you to Jewish Family Service for providing me with a wealth of resources to manage Ken's disease effectively.

I would like to personally thank Ellen Silver, former Executive Director, who was instrumental in connecting me with Rosemary Quatrale, Older Adult Manager and facilitator for the caregiver support group, which has been a constant source of comfort. I still feel the love and support from Rosemary and the group. Thank you from the bottom of my broken, (but healing) heart.

I'm deeply grateful to Katie Young, CSW-Older Adult Service Coordinator for Jewish Family Service, for her selfless dedication. Every Monday, Katie helps me find the strength to face my grief and daily challenges after losing my husband. Her weekly guidance and commitment to my well-being has been invaluable as I find my way onto a path toward healing. I credit her with helping to mend my broken heart. She's truly an angel!

I want to express heartfelt gratitude to my friend and editor, Stacy Dymalski for generously sharing her time and expertise, skillfully guiding me through the emotional depths of my journey. Thank you for your understanding and patience when writing the final chapter proved difficult, and for knowing the perfect moment to suggest a much-needed epilogue.

Thank you to my pal, Dagmar Marshall for proof-reading this book. Having her additional set of eyes was extremely helpful and I so appreciate the time she spent, as well as her candid and honest feedback, which I consider a true blessing.

Alix Railton, my friend and additional proofreader deserves my sincere appreciation for kindly offering her services and temporarily putting her personal grief aside while reviewing my writing. Her additional perspective was extremely valu-

ACKNOWLEDGMENTS

able and her willingness to help during that time truly touched my soul.

Thank you to Katie Mullaly at Surrogate Press for her incredible talent and capability in formatting this book, showcasing her outstanding publishing skills. Thank you for trusting your instincts to choose the perfect font and adding your special finishing touches. Absolutely spot on!

Warmest thanks to Michelle Rayner, at Cosmic Design for crafting the cover. This book was a labor of love and you captured its essence perfectly. Thank you for trusting your intuition and spiritual wisdom to guide your design. I'm deeply grateful for your expertise and insight.

It would be an oversight on my part not to recognize my husband Ken, the true star of this story, for his remarkable talent in songwriting. I struggled finding an appropriate title for this book, making several changes along the way.

However while browsing through Kens list of songs, I came across the perfect title: Heart Get Ready, a standout hit by Ken. Subsequently I started using his other songs to name the chapters. Incorporating his clever song titles is another tribute to my love for him.

About the Author

Carly Bennett Stenmark is an extraordinary individual, a retired salon owner, nail technician, and published author. As a loving mother of four, grandmother of fourteen, and a great-grandmother of ten, Carly's life is a shining example of love and resilience.

While enjoying her family, golfing, skiing, writing her first book, working full time, and singing backup vocals with her singer/songwriter husband, Carly attended night school three nights a week. Driven to obtain her high school diploma, which she successfully earned in 2017 after a three-year effort, making her a Park City high school graduate…just like her children.

Living in Park City, Utah, Carly enjoys a variety of activities including running, snow shoeing, hiking, listening to music, reading, golfing, skiing and watching British detective television shows. But life took an unexpected turn in the fall of 2019 when she began noticing significant changes in her

About the Author

husband's memory. And then the devastating diagnosis: Stage five Alzheimer's disease.

With courage, humor and determination, Carly transformed a life-changing experience into a powerful story and felt compelled to share her experience of living with her husband before and after his diagnosis all the while acknowledging the harsh and painful realization that it can happen to anyone at any time.